I0199637

I Spy

How Not to Collude With a Russian

A True Story of Cold War Espionage

John Pansini

RtS Publishing
Colorado Springs, Colorado

TITLE: I SPY: How Not to Collude With a Russian

This book is a work of non-fiction. Certain names of FBI agents have been changed for their protection.

For more information about this title or to order other books by John Pansini see website: *JohnPansini.com*

LCCN: 2023900548
ISBN: 978-1-7351873-9-6 (Hardback)

Printed in the United States of America.

Cover & interior design: John Pansini
Cover photo: Eric Aiden/unsplash.com

First Edition: February 2023

U.S. Department of Justice

Federal Bureau of Investigation

Office of the Director

Washington, D.C. 20535

May 8, 1998

PERSONAL

Mr. John Pansini
Apartment 2
1313 East San Miguel
Colorado Springs, CO 80909

Dear Mr. Pansini:

On behalf of the FBI, I am pleased to recognize your help in connection with a sensitive investigation during a period of time in the 1980s. Your commitment to the task at hand was commendable, and we appreciate your cooperation and strong support of our investigative efforts.

Although belatedly, I hope you will accept our sincere thanks and congratulations.

Sincerely yours,

Louis J. Freeh
Director

HOW TO ACCESS AUDIO

This book contains 63 minutes of audio in 32 mp3 files.

Audio begins with Chapter 18.

Use a cellphone to take picture of QR code. Listen to example below.

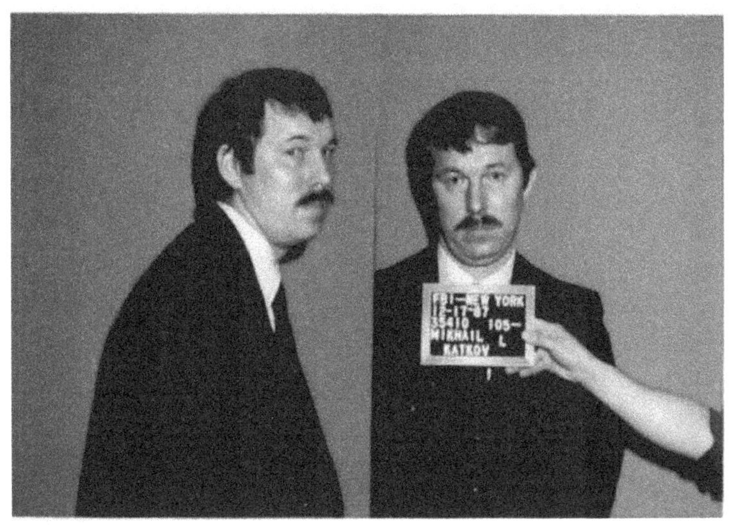

GRU officer Mikhail L. Katkov at the time of his arrest 12/17/87.

John Pansini: good guy or bad guy?
Let the reader decide

[Photo Taken by joan Fanuele, a.k.a Mom,
Colorado Springs 1993]

Praise for I SPY

[Former title: ROOFMAN: A True Story of Cold War Espionage]

"I SPY is an intriguing, behind the scenes read about being trapped in a spider web of espionage during the height of the Cold War." — Fred Burton, former counter-terrorism agent and VP of Intelligence at StratFor.com

"If you've ever imagined what it would be like to step into James Bond's shoes, then you need to read John Pansini's book. John has a literary style that equals any of today's leading writers; his book is eloquently written but also astounding to read simply because it is all true. Add in the audio files, you have a true multi-media experience." — Paul Jones, author & journalist

"The true story of John Pansini, a roofer and professional librarian with a Masters Degree in Library Science. The language comes across very readily as that of a native New Yorker." — Terry McCallister, author, blogger about books

"This book is just as interesting and exciting as if it were fiction , which is why I understand Mr. Pansini's insistence on the audio. It is difficult to believe that someone can get in neck deep in counter intelligence in real life." — Haresh Daswani, a reviewer for GoodReads.com

"I SPY is a spy story with a healthy dose of humor. Looking closer, many of the themes have been seen in countless works of fiction — except Pansini's tale is true! His use of embedded audio files takes advantage of new technology and makes this book unique. Pansini's writing is solid, poetic at times, but a rough edge reminds the reader that the narrator is a roofer." — emilysb, reviewer for GoodReads.com

"Regards for all your attempts that you've set on this really interesting info." — Andrey Gorbatskiy, former professor at Uniwersytet w Białymstoku, lives in Brest, Belarus

Chapter 1
Fortune Favors Risk?

Got this guy on the phone; he sounds like Boris Badenov with a head cold. I figure him for a Russian.

He tells me, "Mr. Pansini, I would like to discuss with you a business arrangement of mutual benefit, yah?"

So he's either a telemarketer, a scam artist, or an enemy of the state. What to do? Hang up? Hear his proposition?

TBD.

***

Tuesday, December 6, 1983

An ice storm had whacked our four-man roofing crew pretty hard this morning: wind, freezing rain, ice and cold. Plus, the house was a two-story horror that was not only high, it was steep; made for a shit fucking day.

A thin layer of crystals coated my black knitted cap and outer layer of clothing. Driving headwinds spit thousands of tiny needles into my face. Beads of ice clung to my mustache and beard. The glove I wore on my left hand was cutoff at the tips — to better grip the nails — so I felt like a combination Frosty the Snowman and Michael Jackson. I had to flex and roll my fingers to keep them from going numb. As for being two-stories up on a glacier without grappling hooks — fuck that shit.

Around noontime I told Dom, the foreman, "I'm outta here."

When I got back to my apartment in upper Manhattan, I threw

my cap on the floor, tore off my jacket and layers of sweatshirts, and walked out of my pants and long johns one leg at a time. I headed for the bathroom to fill the tub. I dared not turn around because of the parade that might be coming up behind me: goose-stepping pants and long johns, crawling jacket and sweatshirts, and a black cap that bounced after the rest of us like a ball. Me and the march of the zombie rags, we all needed a hot bath.

After a long soak, I laid me down to rest; i.e. a nap on the sofa while Bennett and Sinatra crooned softly on the radio. Ballads from the 40s and 50s always soothed me. I sure needed that after the morning I just had.

At exactly 3:57 p.m., the phone rang. It was Mitzi, the girl from the answering service who handled my calls. She said she had a guy named Ketco on hold. After shaking some awake into my head, I asked her to patch him through.

"Good afternoon, Mr. Ketco. This is John Pansini of Computerized Information Retrieval. How may I help you?"

Mr. Ketco used a lot of words to say a lot of nothing. After pitching "our mutual benefit," he added that he worked at the United Nations for U.N.E.S.C.O. "I am technical expert." Sounding a bit full of himself, he added, "I have negotiated many contracts. Is it possible to meet for lunch on Friday?"

I told him I had a full-time job in addition to my business. It would be difficult for me to take off on such short notice. That was true but not the real reason. This *mutual benefit* stuff from a mystery man seemed too damn weird, like something out of a movie. I needed time to think, so I asked if we could meet next week.

"I know that you are a very busy man, Mr. Pansini,—"

That ain't it, pal.

"At your convenience. Please choose a day."

I said Monday, December 12th, worked best for me. It would give me a whole weekend to figure this out. He chose the time, 1 p.m., and the place, a Chinese restaurant on E. 35th and Madison Avenue. I asked for a number where he could be reached in case I had to cancel.

"Not to worry. If you are not there, I am sure it will be for good reason."

If he got stood up, like no big deal? Was this how he negotiated? And what kind of contracts was this guy talking about? Had they been parleyed in good faith out in the open where the sun shined? Or had they been nefarious dealings finagled under a tree, and then squirreled away beneath a rock? Nothing about Mr. Ketco or his proposition sounded right to me. Rather than do the easy thing and hang up, I asked, "Mr. Ketco, can you please tell me more about yourself?" I wanted to know more about his job at the U.N.

"Of course, how can we meet if I do not describe myself?" He gave me his height in meters which meant nothing because my mind worked in inches, feet, and miles. Then he added that he was thirty-five years-old and had light hair. Not much help there either.

"That's not what I meant, Mr. Ketco. Can you please tell me about your job at the U.N.?" I had doubts this guy was for real.

"We will have plenty of time to discuss that at lunch, ya? And how will I know you, Mr. Pansini?"

I described myself to him: 5'8", brown hair, glasses, and a youthful looking thirty. In reality, a youthful looking thirty-five. Back then I shaved a few points off my age; now I do decades. "I'll be wearing a gray suit."

Right away I'd figured his accent for Russian. Still, it's always good to check: "One more thing, Mr. Ketco: you have a very pronounced accent. Are you Russian?"

"Yes. I am Russian," he said flatly; then a pause on his end of the line.

From that primitive part of my mind wherein the sum of all fears lay, a small voice whispered a caution: *A U.N. big shot, a Soviet, wants to take you to lunch? He says he's a technical expert, but what if he's a whacko?*

And then came a different voice from a more developed part of my mind wherein all woe was stored. It loudly reminded me, *You're nowhere, going nowhere. What's to lose?*

"OK, Mr. Ketco." Then I gave him one of my home phone numbers. I had two, one for business and one for pleasure. Ketco got the business number. I asked him to call me again on Friday, December 9th, after five to confirm.

***

Every time I opened up to Tuesday's Computer Services Guide in the *New York Times* and saw the ad, I thought: *Yep! That's my baby.* (See Fig. 1.1 at end of chapter.) The ad read as follows:

"DATA BASE SEARCHING w/ABSTRACTS, DOCUMENT DELIVERY

All fields researched. Business, Medicine, Patents, Sci-Tech."

I was not the only information broker to advertise in this section; I would have to bring this to the FBI's attention. If I was contacted by Ketco, then maybe these guys were too. Regardless, I was the first to advertize here, and the heading, "Accessed Electronic Library," was my creation. I chose Electronic Library because it best described the services I offered. I tacked Acccssed in front so the ad would be ideally located in the uppermost left-hand corner of a very large half-page full of rows and columns.

Like any proud parent, I had great expectations for that ad, it made me proud — too bad, though, because it wasn't making me any money. Despite a good response none of the callers knew what an information broker did. I had to draw the following analogy for them:

"Think of me as a freelance librarian. You go to the library and ask a librarian to help you find a document. You come to me for the same thing. With the aid of my computer, I can offer you quick access to, not thousands, but millions of books, journals and technical reports from all over the world."

"Oh," was the usual response, "thought you were into computers." Then came a polite thank you followed by a dial tone.

Like I said, pride is a good thing, but you can't eat it, and it doesn't pay the rent.

Although the general public knew nothing about information brokering in the Pre-http//www-Age, Mr. Ketco sure did. And his proposition, "a business arrangement of mutual benefit", sounded vaguely familiar. And then I remembered that an unknown person or persons had placed an ad in the April '83 issue of the *Bulletin of the Special Libraries Association.* The ad mentioned, "mutual benefit."

I answered the ad, but no one ever replied. Until today? Ketco?

***

Since I studied engineering and computer science for three of my seven years as an undergrad — which meant I took a lot of higher mathematics — I had no difficulty coming up with a simple equation: Soviet + U.N. = KGB. I called a friend of mine, Mike, and ran it by him. He said if I was so worried, I should call the FBI.

"It's after nine, think they're still open?"

Mike, a real smart ass sometimes, snickered at my naïveté and assured me the Bureau was always on guard. I dialed 553-2700, the FBI's general number in New York City. The Night Desk gave me the name of an agent, Joe Hengemuhl[1], who was "concerned with matters in this area." They told me to call back tomorrow. Before hanging up, I reminded the Night Desk that I would be meeting Ketco for lunch on Monday.

I Googled Agent Hengemuhl on 5/24/2022. Turns out the man had quite a notable career.

In 1962, KGB officer Aleksei Kulak (then 39) walked into the FBI office in Midtown Manhattan. Kulak was assigned to the Soviet Mission to the U.N. He told the Bureau there was a mole inside the FBI. One of the lead investigators assigned to find the mole was a young Agent Hengemuhl. The mole hunt went on for decades but no mole was ever found.[2]

Kulak was given the codename FEDORA[3] by the FBI. The mole was given the codename "UNSUB Dick." UNSUB was a term used by the Bureau that meant "Unknown subject."

The next morning, before running out the door for work, I called the FBI. I got the Day Desk this time. I had to explain the whole thing all over again. The Day Desk told me Hengemuhl was unavailable. On the job, I drove to a pay phone at lunchtime to call the FBI. Again the Day Desk said that Hengemuhl was unavailable. When I got home from work, I called my service. No messages from the Bureau, so I

1 Sadly, FBI Special Agent Joe Hengemuhl died during open-heard surgery on 8/17/89. He was only fifty-seven.

2 Wise, David *Smithsonian Magazine*, November 2015.

3 A lot has been written about FEDORA and the FBI mole hunt.

called them. Hengemuhl was still unavailable.

Maybe I had the whole thing figured wrong:

Soviet + U.N. = No Big Deal.

I did not have access to classified information, so why was the KGB interested in a guy like me? Despite a Master's Degree in library science, and a failing business on the side, I banged nails for a living. I drove a ten year-old Dodge Dart and lived in a rat trap apartment in a rundown neighborhood on the tip of northern Manhattan called Washington Heights.

In the Reagan Era, those who sat with their fat asses on top of the pile — an image of that *Monopoly* guy logo popped into my head — figured people were poor because they were too damn lazy to be rich; true in my case. The trickle-downers in the top hats told people back in those days that they should wait patiently for a rising tide to lift their boats, too. And it looked like mainstream America had bought it. Not me. My boat was still stuck in the sand, and I wouldn't be floating anywhere until I opened the damn floodgates myself. That had been my motivation in the spring of 1983 to set up a side business, CIR (Computerized Information Retrieval). I performed database searches and document delivery for high tech clients — too bad I didn't have any. That made CIR more a hobby than a help.

The 1980s marked the dawn of the digital age. Bytes of text zipped through phone lines that connected servers and desktops at an unheard of speed of 1,200 bits (150 bytes) per second. I sure wanted a piece of that action, so I climbed down off the roof and became an information broker. Armed with a higher education, a Radio Shack TRS-80 computer, a 1,200 bit modem, and a big table, I was good to go. Then I placed an ad in the *New York Times* that had apparently caught Mr. Ketco's attention.

Not where I expected to be at this stage of my life, midway between thirty and forty. When I graduated library school in 1978, my intention had been to run off to Saudi Arabia for a couple of years. Seemed the Saudis had a pressing need for American librarians at the time. After a stint in the Middle East, where I'd make a shit load of money, I'd come back, get married, and raise 2.3 kids. And then I learned that Saudi Arabia wasn't nearly as exotic as I thought. It was heat and sand, no women, and nothing to do all day except work. Shit! I had that right here. All Riyadh would add to my life would be a whole lot of granules. So, after a couple of dead-end library jobs — two I left and one that left me (as in fired) — I eventually went back to doing what I'd always done: roof. Although a bright, young man living in the Greed-is-Good-Eighties, sometimes I felt like a garbage truck plodding along in the slow lane while everyone else my age cruised past me in their Caddies.

Guess I whine too much, but even today, so many years later, I still feel like that. Only now the garbage truck has a lot more miles on it, the body's all rusted and banged up, and the hydraulics aren't what they used to be. What a drag it is getting old.

***

Talk about anal: on Friday, December 9th, at exactly 5 p.m., the business phone in the front room rang. Ketco and the digital clock on my VCR were in synchronicity. He apologized that he would be unable to keep our appointment on Monday. Then he asked if I would clarify a few things for him:

"First, I believe you said you have office in your flat?"

"That's right, Mr. Ketco, in my apartment."

Then he asked if I was incorporated and did I have any partners.

I answered no and no, adding, "I run a small operation, but you won't find my services small, Mr. Ketco. You can call me anytime, day or night, weekend or holiday. CIR is not nine to five."

"Yah is true. Big companies are often impersonal. Now, if you would be so kind, please tell me, do you subscribe to DIALOG?"

At the time, DIALOG was the world's largest database vendor, but despite its size, the general public knew nothing about them; however, in the world of library and information science, DIALOG was a big deal. And this Russian's knowledge of DIALOG in particular, and information resources in general, further fed a theory that began to formulate in my mind, one I was anxious to share with the FBI if the dumb fucks ever got back to me.

Ketco asked how much I charged.

I said $35/hr with one-hour minimum charge. "A real bargain considering—"

He was not considering. He cut me off with: "When I order documents to you, do you mail them or is it possible for me to pick them up?"

"Whatever is convenient for you, Mr. Ketco."

"OK. Mr. Pansini, is it possible for me to stop by your flat sometime for maybe ten minutes so we can chat? Where do you live?"

Again that part of me where all fear hung out warned, *He outflanked me! Giving my address to a Russian who might be KGB, that's way outside of my comfort zone. Better just tell him, "Thanks but no thanks" and hang up.*

But then I remembered: *For big payoffs, sometimes you gotta take big risks.*

I balanced my warring halves with: "I live in Manhattan, Mr. Ketco. You can come over anytime you want, just give me a call, and I'll give you my address."

He wished me a happy holiday and promised me, "A fine lunch someday."

The Marke

Attention Information Brokers—University library interested in contacts with information brokers for mutual benefit. Write to Box 5255, Special Libraries Association, 235 Park Ave. S., New York, NY 10003.

(Fig 1.1) SLA ad

Chapter 2
7th Deadly Sin

This guy kind 'a reminds me of that Chucky doll. The crazy one who kills people. Gotta admit, though; this guy has better hair.

***

Monday, December 12, 1983

A stormy, stormy Monday morning: I got off the A Train at Chambers Street. Despite the shitty weather, my spirits soared high above the black clouds that tried to dump their resentment on me and my umbrella — no way would I let foul weather foul my mood. Agent Dan Pierce, from the Day Desk or Night Desk or whatever damn desk, had called this morning to invite me down to 26 Federal Plaza.

This morning, I'd shaved the grizzly areas on my face between beard and mustache. With no intention of getting my only (100% wool) suit wet, I threw on a pair of blue jeans and a red sweatshirt. An old green parka, which looked like shit but was warm and waterproof, completed the ensemble. The subtext of the preceding statement: *I'm here on business so damn important that I don't give a rat's ass what I look like or what you think of me. It's the message not the messenger.*

I stood outside the huge glass office building and looked up, proud to be an American. The way I figured it, I was here on urgent business.

Once inside the building, scruffy me and a bunch of clean-cut young men and women all in business attire got on the elevator in the lobby. None of them looked FBI, so I figured them for governmnent bureaucrats. Suppose to them I looked like an ethnic, petty drug dealer making an office call — back in the 80s, cocaine was big with the white collar crowd. But when the doors opened at the 26th floor, a large sign announced, “Intelligence Division.” I was the only one who got off. The others I left behind to rest in peace in their Wonder Bread world.

At reception, I presented myself to the girl behind a counter shielded by thick, double-layer of bulletproof glass: “My name is John Pansini. I have an appointment with Agent Dan Pierce.”

“Have a seat, Mr. Pansini,” she replied in a New York accent that outweighed mine by several hundred pounds. Her attitude was best described as bureaucratic indifference; not how I expected to be treated. Also, I was here because of national security. I didn’t expect Agent Pierce to keep me waiting for more than a New York minute. I took a seat and looked up to watch the clock that hung on the wall behind reception.

Sitting across from me was a guy with big, black 70s hair, a bushy mustache, and bushy eyebrows. His ensemble consisted of a burgundy sports jacket and plaid, bell-bottomed slacks. The pants kind of reminded me of my sofa, only uglier. And for whatever reason, the needle on his stressed-out scale lay well inside the red zone.

Soon I spotted an FBI agent coming down a corridor, headed our way. I figured he came for me, so I stood, ready to greet Agent Pierce. Wrong! He went straight to Mr. Retro Guy. As they walked back up the corridor, the FBI agent put his arm around the guy’s shoulder to calm him. Given that this was the 80s, and given the way Retro Guy had dressed himself, I figured him for Eastern European — just some wild and crazy guy in deep shit with the Bureau. I almost felt sorry for him, with the keyword here being “almost.” I looked at the clock again. Twenty minutes gone. Now I was too pissed off the feel anything for anybody. Then I spotted another agent coming my way.

This guy better be Pierce!

***

In the reception area, Pierce had clipped a plastic badge, light green with black lettering, to my parka with a safety pin. The badge meant that I was an invited guest of the Federal Bureau of Investigation. Made for a nice souvenir; not at all concerned with how many hundreds of dollars the federal government paid for it, I decided to *accidentally-on-purpose* forget to give it back when I left.

Pierce then led me to a conference room where I would be debriefed. A big white sign with big red letters hung on the wall. It read, "All matters discussed in this room are classified SECRET."

Not quite. The way I figured it: *All matters discussed in this room will be in my memoir.*

Special Agent Dan Pierce — early 30s, tall, slim, neatly trimmed dark hair, wispy mustache, and a boyish face — sat at the head of the table. Across from me was Agent David Nelson: reddish hair, freckles, he looked even younger than Pierce. His grim stare scrutinized me like I was a turd on the sole of his gumshoe. He kind of reminded me of Chucky the horror doll, but more intense.

I read from notes that described my phone conversations with Ketco. Every so often I'd look up and catch two unimpressed faces staring back at me. Perhaps a shirt and tie would've added more credibility to my substance. Anyway, since Ketco had specifically asked about DIALOG, I'd brought along one of their catalogs. It described their services and listed all the databases they offered.

"I think it's significant that Ketco had mentioned DIALOG,

full-text, sources, etc." I slid the catalog across the table to Pierce. "It indicates that he's quite knowledgeable in the field of information science."

Notepads and pens lay on the table, but neither Pierce nor Nelson made a grab for them. Looked like the only way I'd get a reaction from these guys was to pass gas.

When I finished reading aloud, Pierce finally showed mild interest in the DIALOG book. He flipped through the pages before sliding it over to Nelson who showed no interest at all. They were noncommittal when I asked if I should meet Ketco in my apartment.

"What if this guy's not a spy but some kind of — you know — nut job?"

"What makes you think he's a spy?" Chucky the crazy puppet said. He shot Pierce a, *This Guy's a Piece 'a Work, Isn't He?* grin.

"Uh? I dunno. Thought the U.N. was full of spies. What if he's a nut job?" I repeated.

Pierce shrugged. "That's a possibility."

Not what I needed to know.

Chucky leaned forward. "It's also possible that his interests are legitimate."

"Whadda ya" — a pause to clear a dry throat and get my diction back in good order — "What does he want from me? I don't have access to classified information."

"That's hard to say," Pierce replied.

These guys were the real pieces of work, monuments to suffering public servants who had to suffer the rest of us.

They say Pride is the 7th Deadly Sin. That's what they say. Not me. I say, Fuck that shit. I came down here in the rain with the Star Spangled Banner playing in my heart. Where did these mooks get off! I'd been ready, willing, and able to do my duty and stand tall against the Evil Empire. But these fucking guys made me feel like one of those assholes who come to them claiming visitations by little green men. (If this had been the 90s instead of the 80s, a certain TV show would've come to mind.)

"There's something that isn't quite clear to me," Pierce began. "A man calls you with a business proposal. He wants to take you to lunch. Nothing wrong with that, right?"

I nodded and folded my arms across my chest, my body's way of saying, *And fuck you too, pal.*

"He says he's Russian, works at the U.N. You call us. Why?"

A deep breath before letting loose my theory: "For many reasons, beginning with computer networks.[1] It's true that all the information I have access to is unclassified and publicly available, but—"

"You mean there's nothing to stop him from sitting down at a computer terminal and doing it himself?" Nelson asked.

"I'm not sure. Some databases may not be open to Soviets." I pointed at the catalog still sitting unmolested under his Pokka dot nose. "Maybe the answer to your question is in there. Have a look." Back to Pierce, "Regardless, unclassified technical information can still be of interest to the Soviets. My services as an information specialist can save them a great deal of time and effort tracking down documents. And even if Ketco's not a spy, the information he requests is obviously on behalf of his government. Knowing what

---

1 Stoll, Clifford, The Cuckoo's Egg (c1989). That's exactly what the Soviets did in Stoll's case.

he is requesting gives us clues to the Soviet State of the Art, so in a sense, we'll be spying on them." I paused to let that filter through the shit-for-brains that floated around in their porcelain skulls. "Finally, I suspect that this may be part of a much larger effort: to use Americans like me to infiltrate our nation's computer networks. You guys probably know better than me" — a bit of diplomacy on my part because I didn't think these guys knew shit — "that there are plenty of classified databases out there. Wouldn't the Russians just love to have someone who could plug into them?"

In my mind, these were the only plausible explanations for KGB Ketco's interest in a guy like me. Then I showed them a photocopy of the *New York Times* Computer Services section, adding, "Maybe you guys should take a look at these other information brokers. Maybe the Soviets contacted them too."

After a brief pause, while their faces remained inscrutable, Pierce said, "While we're not about to tell you what to do, John, the Bureau would be grateful if you went ahead and met with Ketco."

From deep space came the first signs of intelligent life from whatever planet these two mooks orbited.

He continued, "We'd like to get his picture. If you're uncomfortable about meeting him in your apartment, why not suggest an outside location? Like a restaurant. After all, he suggested it in the first place."

"Should you decide to go ahead and meet him," Nelson added, "try and get as much details about his personal life as you can without being too obvious."

Finally Pierce picked up a pen. He asked for the spelling of my name, date and place of birth, address, telephone number, and, "Do you own a car, John?"

I grinned. "Yeah I own a car. You guys gonna check me out now or what?"

"Just routine," Pierce assured me.

After leading me back down to the reception area, Pierce thanked me for coming down on such a lousy day. We shook hands at the elevator; then he removed the badge from my parka.

Shit!

Outside, a gust of wind caught my umbrella and collapsed it. That meant a long, wet walk back to the subway station. As for the pride I'd felt this morning, that rolled off me and my parka onto the street and into the gutter, a swirling mix of environmental impurity.

Fuck! Fuck! Fuck!

Chapter 3
Sunshine Superman

"Governments are bullshit. My government and yours too."

***

Thursday, December 29, 1983

Today I would meet the guy. What was his proposition? Steal the plans to the B-1 bomber? Didn't think so, that was way above my access and skill set. Another thing, I got to slip out of my Roofman personae and hide it in my toolbox for awhile.

I am *an educated man. I have to look like one and speak like one.*

***

I was not at the front room window to admire the lay of the land. This particular window offered a good view of 183rd Street where it crossed Audubon Avenue. Good referred only to its vantage point. These were two mean streets. Seven p.m. in winter meant darkness, shadows and cold. Except for an occasional car that passed by on Audubon, the blocks were, for all intents and purposes, dead zones. Washington Heights was, and still is, one of the most dangerous neighborhoods in the City of New York. Every other year the Three-Four, the local precinct, led all other city precincts in homicides. I think '83 was one of those off years when we either placed or showed. If Ketco made a wrong turn in the Heights, he could end up in a really bad situation.

Even in neighborhoods as dangerous as this one, there were certain blocks that should be cordoned off with yellow tape and marked: "To Be Avoided." One such pocket was the block just west of me on 183rd between Audubon and St. Nicholas Avenues. Gloom and despair, it was hard to imagine that the sun ever shined there. Abandoned and semi-abandoned tenements, these foreboding shells loomed like phantoms on either side of the street.

Buildings where crack was made, sold and smoked, and heroin dealt. Those hulks were also homes to unfortunate families with nowhere else to live. Rotting, stinking garbage overflowed trash cans and crept up from sunken stairwells. Like a foul tide it crossed the sidewalk and seeped into the gutter. Stripped-down and burnt-out cars up on blocks with their tires and anything else of value long gone outnumbered the trees on this street. Brooding and dangerous, the block was home to too many bad tempers, bad deals, and stray bullets. Glad my tenement, as run-down as it was, squatted on the east side of Audubon.

From the front room window, six stories above street level, I waited and watched. Although I didn't know what Ketco looked like in real life, I figured he'd be easy enough to spot. Here in the Heights, English was a second language. If I spotted a gringo who looks like a spy getting into trouble, I'd grab a hammer and run to the rescue. For CIR, every potential customer was precious, especially when he was the only one.

I'd spent a long time at the bathroom mirror, prepping. Gone was all the facial hair that kept me warm in winter: a major undertaking that involved cutting away large tuffs with a scissors, then scraping away gristle and fuzz with a razor. A pressed white shirt, black slacks straight from the cleaners, yellow silk power tie, and horn-rimmed glasses made me look more like a librarian, less like a roofer.

Wish I could've put a positive shine on the dumpy apartment

I lived in. Thc squalor inside was only a marginal upgrade from the squalor outside. The apartment was shaped like an inverted L. Entering the foyer, to the left a small eat-in kitchen and straight ahead the living room. A narrow hallway with a closet on the right and a bathroom on the left joined the living room and a large room that faced the street (hence the "front room") that served as my office. Back to the living room: an old sleeping couch, light gray and with blue pinstripes, was pushed up against a cream colored wall. The couch sagged in the middle. On the other side of the room, near the windows, was a blue chair made of such abrasive polyester fiber that I rarely sat on it — hence a lesser sag.

Behind the blue chair were two double hung windows on rotted frames. To the left of the windows a nineteen inch color TV (with bent rabbit ears) rested on a white end table my sister had given me. A lint- speckled, burnt orange rug lay beneath it all. For panache, a few scenic paintings hung on the walls. They were my visual escapes to a prettier world. And finally, water stains and peeling plaster marked a corner of the ceiling. The Roofman's roof leaked.

Fred Flintstone would feel right at home here. Ketco had to think that anyone living in a place like this would do anything for money.

On watch at the window, suddenly I heard the doorbell *thunk!* Fitting that in a rat trap like this even the doorbell sounded depressed. That had to be Ketco; then it occurred to me, I never saw him enter the building.

On the far side of the peephole a tall, well-dressed man stood silhouetted by the dim lighting of the hallway. He looked nothing like my mental image of the short fat guy, dressed all in black including fedora, with a big round face, big smile, big teeth, mustache, and wearing a black trench coat.

Unlike Boris Badenov, Mr. Ketco was no cartoon cliché.

I opened the door and invited him in from the cold. I took his coat and laid it on top of the laundry wagon in the foyer. Then I led him into the living room. He sat down on the sofa; I planted myself across from him, at a safe distance, on the blue chair. He carried himself in an almost effeminate manner, arms and wrists limp, legs crammed tightly together. Still, Ketco's size and structure intimidated me a little. He was maybe 6'5" or 6'6" and built like a basketball player. He had light thinning hair, a fair complexion and a round, boyish face. And he sure knew how to dress. He wore a blue sports coat, white shirt, red silk tie and gray slacks. Not a fiber of polyester on this guy.

I smiled back at him through a small gap between my two front teeth. When I was a kid they called me Bucky Beaver. When people told me I had a kind face, I figured it had to be the teeth.

Ketco pulled a bottle of Stolichnaya vodka out of his briefcase. "Here is small gift, Mr. Pansini."

I thanked him and said I'd save it for New Year's Eve. Then I asked him to tell me about himself.

"I live in Bronx with my wife and thirteen year-old son and four year-old daughter."

I wondered what his wife looked like. Was she young, blonde, and beautiful or was she one of those Russian she-bears who could put a shot 50 meters? What about his son, his daughter? Were they cute or brats? Did his family speak English as well as he did?

I also wondered how much of me was a revelation to him. Clean shaven, shirt, tie, glasses, proper voice and diction, had we been sitting in a restaurant these trimmings would be his only first impressions of me. But this wasn't neutral ground, it was my home.

A lot can be learned about people by observing them in their natural habitat. Every so often Ketco's eyes would dart to a corner of the room, focus on a detail and snap like a camera. Mix and match furniture, paintings, general housekeeping, even the leftover smells of my cooking, he absorbed them all. And came to a conclusion,

"I see you are not married, Mr. Pansini."

Not only was I not married, there weren't any prospects in the farm system either. Compared to him, a man with a family who worked at the U.N. (possibly for the KGB), I felt like a loser.

An uncomfortable, "That's obvious." My smile served as an apology. "This place certainly lacks a woman's touch."

Maybe even a human touch.

"I have a sister," I felt obliged to add. "She has three boys."

Our frozen smiles threatened to turn to permafrost. Small talk didn't even put a tiny crack in it. The nervous energy that served me so effectively on the roof found other outlets: numerous nose rubs and head scratches, brief sorties off the chair and around the room, and loud chatter. But this Russian, even with all his training, he felt the pressure too. Every so often he'd blink in a very pronounced manner. Maybe the guy wasn't the Soviet Superman I imagined him to be. I asked Ketco to tell me something about his work.

"Before coming to New York, I worked in London for petrochemical firm. Now I am working at United Nations on special U.N.E.S.O. projects. The nature of my work is such that I am constantly doing research, but I am unable to spend my limited time in libraries." Then he asked me about my roofing job.

I babbled about how the job sucked, especially in summer, all the while hoping he wouldn't look up at the ceiling. As talk gradually shifted to the business at hand, I began to relax. Guess he did, too, because I noticed Ketco began to blink less and less.

“I prefer to conduct business on personal level,” he said. “I hope that we can become friends as well as associates. Please call me Michael.”

That was smooth.

“OK, Michael. Call me John.” Then I loosened my tie. “Since we’re such good friends now, this is the last time you’ll ever see me in one of these things.” I leaned over and hung the tie on one of the bent rabbit ears.

I could be smooth, too.

Ketco gave me my first order, a handwritten list on white tracing paper. He said he needed it for his records, so would I please make a copy for myself. Since I needed a table to write on, I invited him into the kitchen. I sat at the head and he sat on the yellow chair to my left, with his back to the stove and sink. That seat was where I usually took my lonely meals.

The first five items on the list were statistical data books published by various automotive trade associations. Item #6 was a technical paper. The title as he’d written it: “New direction(s) in organic electrone materials based in tetrathia (ending on one line and continuing on the next) fulvalene.”

Pointing at “tetrathia-fulvalene” and turning the paper towards him, “Michael, is this one word or two?”

“Yes. That is it,” he said, pointing at the word.

“What is what?”

“That.”

"You mean like it appears on the paper?"

He smiled. "Precisely."

Item #7 listed four Texas Instruments reports all beginning with the prefix ALEX. I'd never seen that prefix before. But the last two items looked like they would be the hardest to track down. Ketco had provided the following sketchy information: "8) Fustbus specification. Oct '82 US Nim Committee available from L Dept. of Commerce; 9) Trends and perspectives in signal processing. 1981-83 Quarterly journal."

When I finished copying everything, he pulled two fifties out of his wallet. Without a word, he carefully placed the bills side by side on the table in front of me. He grinned, a grin that said, *Yes, asshole, I've got your number.*

Damn right! The money gathered no dust. My hand swooped in, grabbed the cash, and shoved it into my pants pocket.

"Who knows," he said with a big smile, "maybe John Pansini will be big corporation someday. Of course I will not be giving you twenty-thousand dollar orders yet."

Twenty grand! That sure put some pop in my eyeballs.

"For the moment they will only be for $500," he continued, "because I worry for you, that you cannot handle such a large order at this time."

I assured him I could handle anything anytime.

"Yes, John, we shall see." He stood up, getting ready to leave. "You know, John, relations between our governments is rather strained at this time. People will not understand our business arrangement or our friendship. We must be careful. You must never tell anyone you are dealing with a Russian."

"Of course not, but that's governments not us. Governments are bullshit. My government and yours too," I said, shaking an emphatic finger at him. "I truly believe that the best way to promote peace is through strong economic ties. Both of our countries would be less likely to blow each other away if it's in their economic interest not to do so. Let's you and I continue to do business and wait for our stupid governments to wise up."

I truly believed what I'd just said.

He started to blink again like a *Bowmar Brain* (a primitive calculator used in the 70s) processing the raw data he'd just been fed. The end result of those pixels lighting his face? His screen offered no clue.

(Fig 3.1) My tenement at 515 W. 183rd Street

(Fig 3.2) My living room

Top: Itchy chair & crummy TV

Bottom: Sagging sofa

Chapter 4
Two Grilled Roofers

One guy looks Mafia, the other one like he pulls teeth.

***

Friday, December 30, 1983

Today was the eve of New Year's Eve. I expected 1984 to be the year I turned my life around. There was a smile on my face that kept re-appearing no matter how much I tried to hide a spirit that wanted to explode like a star burst of red, white, blue, and gold. I would do whatever I had to do to help the FBI win the Cold War.

While that in itself was plenty motivating, there was also the excitement that I would be living a movie-of-the-week: *Roofman the Spy.*

***

I'd already met with Mr. KGB Ketco yesterday and soon FBI agents, hopefully not Pierce or Nelson, would come to the job to debrief me.

I climbed the thirty-two foot ladder with a seventy-five pound bundle of shingles digging into my right shoulder. No burden at all. At the top of the ladder I heaved the shingles onto the deck — *thud!* The house was a two-story walker (a low pitched roof) on 199th Street and 67th Avenue in Fresh Meadows, Queens. The sun shined bright, and the temperature hovered somewhere in the forties: a great day to be young, alive and a roofer. I was about to head back down to grab another load, when Dom called to me. I looked up and saw his face sticking above the peak. He worked the back while I shingled the front.

"Pan-Zini," he said, nodding at something behind me, "ya friends are here."

I turned around. Two guys in suits and top coats — one tall, the other short — stood across the street next to a weathered, light green four-door sedan. They stared up at me. The short guy shaded his eyes with his right hand; he wore glasses. The tall guy had his hands on his hips. Both aimed smiles in my direction. I nodded and waved.

To Dom: "Excuse me while I go save the Free World." I was kidding, of course, but just a little.

"You're crazy for getting involved with them guys."

Grinning, "I know, but crazy in a good way."

Dom's disapproving face dipped back below the ridge line. I climbed down the ladder and laid my tools — hammer, knife and an apron full of nails — on the hood of the truck. I reached into the cab, grabbed an attaché case and put on my horn-rimmed glasses. I walked across the street and introduced myself to FBI agents Charlie Roman and Bob Haberstam. Charlie, a big guy with a bit of a paunch, about 6'2", dark, mid-30s, looked more Mafioso than FBI. Bob, about my height and build, had light hair, glasses and younger than his partner. He looked like a dentist. Unlike Pierce and Nelson these guys' smiles showed enthusiasm.

"Let's sit in the car so we can talk," Charlie said, holding the door for me.

I thanked him and sat in the front seat. Charlie crossed in front of the car and got in on the driver's side. Bob opened the back door and hopped in. I'd made detailed notes immediately following last night's meeting with Ketco. I read aloud while Charlie did some serious note taking of his own. Bob leaned forward from the back seat, his head between us.

When I finished reading, Charlie turned to Bob and said, "Wish this was our case."

Alarmed that I might get handed back to the Mook Brothers, "What? You mean you guys won't be handling my case?"

"No," Charlie replied. "We're just filling in while Pierce is on vacation. He's skiing in Vermont. No one's been assigned to you yet."

"What if I ask for you guys? I like you guys."

Charlie paused, then, "No, that wouldn't be a good idea."

Bob said that only if there was a clash of personalities between me and the agent assigned could I ask for a new one. To Charlie, "Think I know who'll get this one." To both of us, "I don't foresee any problems."

Charlie showed me a photo. "You said our friend looks like a basketball player. Is this him?"

I shook my head no. The man looked more boxy than tall. But he did look like the kind of guy who'd rip your heart out and eat it raw. When Charlie showed me the next picture, I bounced up and down in my seat like a little kid: "That's him, that's him!"

In the photo Ketco walked along a path near a brick building. He wore a well-tailored, dark three-piece suit. His right hand reached into the inside, left breast pocket of his jacket, and he looked over his left shoulder towards the camera. Ketco carried himself like a shaken-not-stirred kind of guy, nothing at all like Mr. Limp Wrist I'd met yesterday. I noted the smirk on Ketco's face.

"Looks like he knows you guys are taking his picture."

I never figured Ketco for a real name, although it sounded vaguely familiar. After checking through a log of phone calls to CIR, I found an entry dated September 15, 1983, two months ago. It listed a call from a Mr. Katkov. Katkov left no message and no phone number. Ketco — Katkov? Because of his accent did Mitzi misspell the name? I asked Charlie and Bob what they thought. Charlie smiled and turned the picture over. On the back the Bureau had written: "Katkov, Mikhail L."

New to the spy business, and I'm already James Bond and Sherlock Holmes rolled into one. Wow, wow, double wow!

I told them about the ad I'd seen in the SLA bulletin. Charlie said they'd check it out. I also gave them a photocopy of the latest list of material Katkov had ordered. Charlie asked me if I thought Katkov might be testing my competency.

"Yeah, some of those things do seem deliberately vague. And he wasn't much help when I tried questioning him, either."

"Did he ask to see a copy of your résumé?" Bob said.

"You mean like checking my credentials? No he didn't."

"That's strange," Bob said to Charlie. "They usually do."

"He didn't ask to see my computer either; even stranger, huh?" Then, borrowing jargon Charlie had used to describe certain Soviets: "Is Katkov a bad guy?"

"At this point, he's a diplomat. Whether he's legitimate or not, we can't say." Charlie must have sensed my disappointment, because he added, "This is standard operating procedure for them. They could very well be cultivating you. Let's wait and see what happens."

I was being *cultivated.* I felt like a bumper crop, important to both sides.

Bob grinned. "Just sit back and enjoy it. Think of it as a game of chess. It'll be fun. You even get a code name."

A code name! That sure lit my console. Only secret agents get secret code names.

Bob added that whenever I call the FBI on the special phone number I'd been given by Pierce, and even though it was a secure line, I should not use my real name. Since I got to choose my own code name, and given my sense of irony, later I picked Julius as in Rosenberg. Rosenberg was a CCNY alum like me. He and his wife were executed in the early 1950s for selling atomic secrets to the Soviet Union.

Charlie mentioned that sometimes these cases went on for years; as far as I was concerned, the longer the better. I sensed this business with Mr. *Katkov* would be a once in a lifetime event, one I intended to grab hold of. Bob added that if it ever got to be more than I could handle I could back out anytime with no hard feelings from the Bureau. I assured them I was in for the duration. I said that I didn't serve in Vietnam and this was my chance to do the right thing by America.

"I can assure you, this is very important to us," Charlie said. "A copy of our report will be on the desk of a senior member of the cabinet tomorrow morning." He had to be speaking about William J. Casey, at the time the boss over at CIA.

"Simply the fact that you've been able to identify Katkov is extremely important to us," Bob said.

"Yeah," Charlie added, "we can throw a net around him, watch him more closely. Totally neutralize the guy. This might be an important piece of a puzzle. Have a direct bearing on other cases and operations."

Bob went on to praise my powers of observation and attention to detail. He said he was particularly impressed with the way I fielded Katkov's remark about the current strain in superpower relations. "If you had taken the attitude, 'I hate America, I love communism,' he'd see through you in a second."

No strain on me because what I told Katkov was what I truly believed; peace through mutual economic interest.

"Next time you meet him," Bob added," try to get as many personal details about him as you can, especially about his wife. Is he happy at home? Things like that."

"You should see some of their wives," Charlie snickered. "Surprised they don't all defect."

Thus had my mental image of Mrs. Katkov been cast for all time: she-bear.

I showed them the two fifties Katkov had given me. The bills were numbered consecutively, so I thought I should bring that to the Bureau's attention. Charlie winced. Something about the bills spooked him. "Hold on to them a little longer," he said.

I mentioned that I couldn't hold those fifties too long because it was winter, our slow time.

Bob noticed my partner, Dom, waiting for me in the truck. That ended the debriefing. I got out of the sedan and waved as they roared off, heading away from Union Turnpike, a main drag. Judging from the direction they'd just taken, I guessed these guys hadn't spent much time in Queens. (No GPS in those days.)

I got into the truck. "You ain't gonna believe what they told me, Dom."

A squinty eyed, "Maybe you shouldn't be telling me this, Pan-Zini."

"Yeah, maybe, but I'm gonna anyway." I saw no reason to play the closed mouth spy with Dom. I'd come of age in the sixties and seventies, so I'd be an idiot to totally trust the FBI. Dom I did trust; so if things ever went wrong between me and the Bureau, then the more close friends who knew about what was going on the better.

"They asked me something strange, Dom. They want me to find out as much personal details about Katkov's home life as I can. Those two mooks I told you about, Pierce and Neahle, said the same thing."

Dom shrugged. "Fuck 'em all where they breathe."

As Dom started to pull out — "Oh shit!" — he jammed on the brakes.

I bounced forward — no belts in that truck — and then back again. "What the fuck!"

Dom had spotted Charlie and Bob bearing down on us at high speed. After realizing that they were headed in the wrong direction, they must have made a U-turn. At the last second Charlie swerved to avoid barreling into the truck broadside. As they zoomed by, Bob waved out the window at us as if it was no big deal they almost had me and Dom sticking out of their fucking grill.

"Ya almost killed us!" Dom yelled out the window.

"Doubt they heard. Even at the speed of sound it'll take at least three red lights for your words to catch that car. Geez!" I shook my head. "Nice guys, but they drive like assholes."

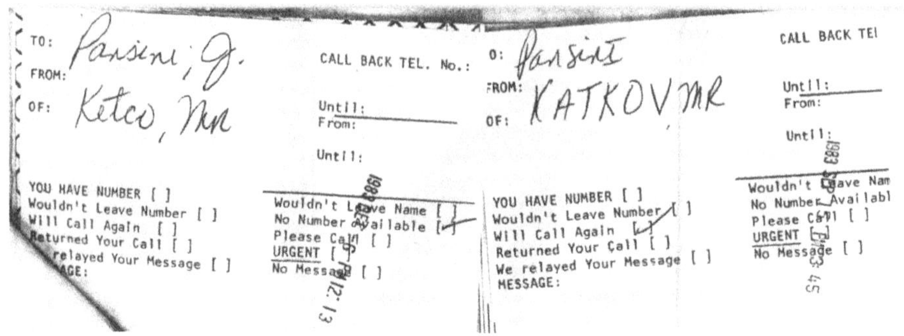

TO: Parsini, J.
FROM:
OF: Ketco, Mr

CALL BACK TEL. No.:
Until:
From:
Until:

YOU HAVE NUMBER [ ]
Wouldn't Leave Number [ ]
Will Call Again [ ]
Returned Your Call [ ]
relayed Your Message [ ]
…AGE:

Wouldn't Leave Name [ ]
No Number Available [✓]
Please Call [ ]
URGENT [ ]
No Message [ ]

1983 … PM 12:13

TO: Parsini
FROM: KATKOV MR
OF:

YOU HAVE NUMBER [ ]
Wouldn't Leave Number [✓]
Will Call Again [✓]
Returned Your Call [ ]
We relayed Your Message [ ]
MESSAGE:

CALL BACK TEL
Until:
From:
Until:

Wouldn't Leave Nam…
No Number Availabl…
Please Call [ ]
URGENT [ ]
No Message [ ]

1983 … 3:45

(Fig. 4.1) Right: message from Katkov (9/15/83)

Left: message from Ketco (12/6/83)

Chapter 5
Spy Fact Looks in the Mirror

The root of all evil in the spy game is money, lots and lots and lots of it.

Money + Fame = American Pie-a-la-Mode.

***

According to FBI Agents Roman and Haberstam, the Director of Central Intelligence, William J. Casey, would be sitting down to breakfast to read a debriefing of roofer John Daniel Pansini in regards to Soviet Katkov, Mikhail L.

Almost forty years ago I'd photocopied certain chapters from *Intelligence Requirements for the 1980's: Counterintelligence.*[1] In the margin on page 17, I'd written: "It's all coming together." A seminal moment? Roofers might not have many of those, but librarians sure do. As I write this now, in April 2022, I am grateful I'd read that book so early in the Katkov Affair. The author, Arthur A. Zuehlke, Jr., drew a clear picture of the subtle difference between CI (counterintelligence) and CE (counterespionage). He defined CI as information derived from CE. Further, he stated that while CI is passive, CE is aggressive. It uses the hostile service's own operation to obtain information about that service: fancy academic language for kicking a guy in the ass wearing his own boot.

While I was mighty proud of myself for figuring out the Ketco-Katkov thing, in the spy game, I was still a rookie. The Library-Man

---

1 Consortium for the Study of Intelligence, Intelligence Requirements for the 1980s, edited by Roy Godson, Transaction books.

part of me knew he had to do some heavy-duty research in order to catch up and catch on. It wasn't until I began reading that particular book (part of a multi-volume series) that I finally figured out why the feds were so hot for personal details about Katkov. And why FBI agents Roman's and Haberstam's report would be morning reading for DCI Bill Casey. Also, from reading books and journal articles, I soon discovered that very little in Spy Fact matched Spy Fiction. If Spy Fact ever looked for any recognizable semblance of itself in the world of mirrors, it would recognize only its outer garments: i.e. shirt and tie, but nothing of substance. Therefore, I decided to confine my reading to memoirs of intelligence officers, broad overviews of intelligence services, and case histories. Back in the 1980s, library shelves were packed with that stuff.

For Mikhail Katkov the name of the game was industrial espionage. For the FBI it was counterespionage (CE). That was why the Bureau was so interested in personal details about target Katkov. All counterespionage operations have three main objectives: identify, neutralize, and penetrate. Because of the nature of his contact with me, Katkov had been identified with high probability as being a Soviet intelligence officer. He would be neutralized because his continuing efforts to recruit me, a controlled asset being directed by U.S. counterintelligence, meant the less time he had for recruiting other Americans. In addition, our side learned his areas of interest and recruiting methodology. That left only one thing, the ultimate. This is where CE gets aggressive: to penetrate a hostile intelligence. DCI William Casey's top priority during the Cold War was to recruit assets within the Soviet hierarchy, to have eyes and ears inside the Kremlin.[2]

That made the Katkov Affair a very big deal.

2 Woodward, Bob *Veil: The Secret Wars of the CIA 1981-1987*, Simon & Shuster, c1987, p 304.

The object of Casey's program, a joint effort by CIA and the FBI, was to find Soviets based in the U.S. who might be turned, either willingly or unwillingly. The program, which began in 1980, was code named COURTSHIP. Information the FBI gathered on a Soviet intelligence officer, diplomat, or private citizen stationed anywhere inside the continental United States went straight to COURTSHIP. The program worked like this:

A Soviet lands in the U.S.

A determination is made whether or not the man is an intelligence officer.

FBI agents open a window on the target looking for personal weaknesses or professional shortcomings that can be exploited.

CIA psychologists do a profile of the target to make an educated guess whether or not he is traitor material.

The target is then courted with flirtations and enticements, or blackmailed if necessary.[3]

Why did some Soviet and Eastern European intelligence officers defect? In his memoirs, former CIA officer Harry Rositzke writes: "In the black-and-white days of the Cold War it was easy to see such men opting with their feet for 'freedom.' They were allegedly men who changed sides out of principle, who saw in our side the good guys."[4]

Rositzke airbrushes some reality onto this cartoon-like view:

"(We deceive) ourselves to see them as heroic fighters for freedom, recurrent testimonials to the rightness of our cause."[5]

When CIA set up boards and committees to look for patterns

3 Weiner, Tim, et al *Betrayal: The Story of Aldrich Ames, an American Spy*, Random House, c1995, p. 26-27

4 Rositzke, Harry *The KGB: the Eyes of Russia*, Doubleday, c1981, p. 250-251

5 Rositzke, p. 250

of personality and background in those men who had already come over, they found none. The Agency concluded that there had been no strictly ideological defectors, only individual intelligence officers who defected for personal reasons. What personal reasons could be so pressing as to cause a man to give up his family, career and country to flee to the West? The most common cause of defections in the early 1950s was a shake-up in intelligence headquarters that threatened the life and security of many Soviet field officers. After Lavrentiy Beria's execution in 1953[6], many KGB officers in Tokyo and Vienna came over. Thus, if a shake-up in headquarters was enough to cause many Soviets to defect in the 1950s, what effect would the impending doom of the "Evil Empire" have on Soviets in the late 1980s and early 1990s?

On a more personal level, Rositzke cites cases from the 1950s when defectors deserted from the Soviet Zone of Occupation because they fell in love with German girls and were refused permission to marry foreigners. Rositzke sums up by writing: "I am not suggesting that defectors are ignoble. They are simply human, and they act for human reasons. Men caught in unpleasant circumstances, they seek a way out."[7]

The motives that would cause an intelligence officer, either American or Russian, to betray his country are too numerous and too complex for simple answers. However, many experts who have written on the subject say there is but one root cause: MONEY. Lots and lots and lots of $,$$$,$$$.

Speaking of which, back in the winter of 1983/84, money was something I did not have lots and lots of.

---

6 Chief of secret police who attempted to succeed Stalin.

7 Rositzke, p. 251

Chapter 6
Espionage as Theater

"And for this you are charging me thirty-five bucks!"

"It's called capitalism, Michael. You're not in the Soviet Union anymore."

***

January 18, 1984

My new FBI case officer, Patrick M. McKinney, tall, slim, light eyes, mid-forties, looked like he just stepped off the cover of *GQ*: neat and clean, not a follicle of his light brown hair dared stand out of place.

Wednesday afternoon; not much of a lunch crowd in this pub on W. 75th Street — that was why I chose it to meet with agents McKinney and Dan Pierce. We sat isolated, flanked by empty tables. Then, like a mug suddenly filling with that muddy crap called stout, the table to Pat's immediate right topped off with an old guy in his fifties. He had gray, wiry hair and bushy black eyebrows. A black tangle that grew out of his nose and ears looked like pubic hair. Gross! After the guy ordered he took *On Stage* out of a black shoulder bag and pretended to read. *On Stage* was a newspaper that everyone involved in the New York theater scene read.

Pat and Dan ignored him. Not me. I knew a bad actor when I saw one.

Flashback to my childhood, to the mid-1950s, and my father, sister and I are in the automat on 14th Street.

"See those guys," my father says, "they're all communists."

Old men in black suits and fedoras, with angry faces buried in newspapers all over the place sipping black coffees; scary stuff for two duck and cover kids in the 1950s.

My dad saw commies in the automat. Thirty years later I saw one in a pub. While Pat spoke about "our (Soviet) friend," with my eyes, I directed his attention to his right. His eyes returned the message:

Don't worry about him, John.

Oh, well. Guess somewhere on my long string of chromosomes there's a gene marked, "Paranoia." Think I know where it came from, too.

I handed Pat an envelope containing the two fifties Katkov had given me. "They're numbered consecutively. Mean anything?"

"Not really. He just went to the bank that day and received these two bills. If he'd given you a whole string of consecutively marked bills — that would've been significant."

Those fifties were meant for show not keep. I expected the envelope and its contents back. When Pat put it inside the breast pocket of his jacket, I blurted out: "Why are you taking my money?"

"Technically, when you accepted money from him, you broke the law."

The expression on my face said, *Get the fuck outta here!*

Pat held up a hand and said, "I know it sounds screwy, but it's just a technicality. From now on you'll have to turn over to us all the money he gives you. We'll reimburse you later."

Damn! Didn't these guys know that in winter the longer those two fifties stayed out of my checking account the more tuna I'd be eating for dinner? "OK, Pat, but please try and make it soon. I really need the money. A guy's gotta eat."

We spoke about Katkov's latest want list. I asked, "Are they testing me?"

"Could very well be, that's why we're not going to give you any help. They know what is and what is not available to someone with your access. Keep in mind that if there's ever an item on one of his lists that wouldn't normally be accessible to someone like yourself, and we helped you get it, then they'd know you were controlled. They'd drop you immediately."

Made sense.

As I stood to leave — Pat told me to go first — Pierce, the junior G-man, nonchalantly asked, "Do you own a car, John?"

"Yes I do, Dan." Let him go figure.

I turned and headed out the door, my wallet one hundred dollars lighter.

***

The next morning me and Dom sat in the truck drinking coffee before banging out another roof. I told him that the world's premier police force still couldn't find my car registration. "Geez, Dom, if these guys are the best and the brightest, America's fucked. That damn Dart sits parked right outside the shop all day. All they gotta do is drive past the shop and look at the plates. They gotta know Jersey is just across the GW from me."

"Do they know where you work?"

"Yeah! They asked me, I told 'em."

"Did 'ya tell 'em what kind'a car you drive?"

"No, but that's beside the point. It's got Jersey plates. Kind' a stands out, know what I mean?"

"Dumb fucks," Dom replied.

I rolled down the window and dumped what was left of my coffee, light & sweet, into the street. When we got out of the truck, I spotted a beat up, light green sedan with a long whip antenna. It looked a hell of a lot like FBI Agent Charlie Roman's car. It was parked directly behind us two car lengths away; it faced the wrong direction on a one way street. Before I could see who was inside, the driver suddenly gunned the engine and made a sharp left around the corner.

"Still think this is fun, Pan-Zini?" He'd noticed the sedan, too.

"The FBI is following me, Dom, which means they don't trust me." Through my teeth, I ground out the words: "I…don't… appreciate…that shit."

***

On February 1st, at 2 p.m., the day before my birthday, Katkov sat at my kitchen table listening to me whine about, "No work today, not enough money in my bank account, and forty is creeping up on me. I'll be thirty-six tomorrow."

"Happy birthday."

"And I still don't know what I want to be when I grow up. Sad, huh?"

A disinterested: "Yah."

I'd deliberately slipped the greed and desperation cards out of the deck and laid them in front of Katkov. This was part of my plan. All the books I'd read said that greed was the primary character flaw KGB looked to exploit in their perspective assets (agents). But would

Katkov, who was so relaxed that he hardly blinked at all, pick them up?

Instead, he segued: "Why do you do this for?" By "this" he meant: Why be a roofer despite a higher education? "It seems to me it would be better for you to work in library, no?" By the look on his face, he may as well have asked: *Why do you enjoy rolling in shit, John?*

Clearly Comrade Katkov from the Worker's Paradise had no respect for manual labor. Even though I'd dealt the hand, and thereby invited commentary, nonetheless, I took offense. "It's a sideline, Michael. It enables me to devote more time to my business. And I happen to enjoy the physical work, being outdoors. (True, except in summer.) Besides, surely you of all people can appreciate the satisfaction one derives from being a member of the working class. *No?*"

His eyes fluttered. "But of course, is merely suggestion. What you've got for me?"

"Michael, that fustbus you asked for — there is no such thing."

Tracking down the fustbus specification had been a real pain-in-the-ass. I'd looked in all the technical dictionaries but couldn't find a definition. Thinking that maybe the Soviets had deliberately misspelled the word, I keyboarded in "F?STBUS." (The "?" was a wild card character that took on any value.) Then I found hundreds of citations describing a device called a fastbus, a high-speed data bus used to connect computer peripherals involved in signal processing applications.

"It's called a fastbus, Michael."

He grinned. "You must please forgive my English."

I gave him a computer printout that cited the specification and told him I could get the actual document at the Engineering Societies Library.

A glance at the printout, then, with his hand, he swatted away all my hard work as if it was an annoying horde of flies. “Is OK.”

“What about that signal processing journal?” I said, referring to an obscure journal published by a professor at MIT. “Should I order it?”

“I will let you know at another time. What about those reports?” He asked, referring to the Texas Instruments documents.

I couldn’t find them under the prefix “ALEX” online, so I called Texas Instruments. TI said these papers were *unclassified*, government sponsored research. The prefix ALEX was an old designation that hadn’t been used in years.

Proudly: “Got ‘em right here, Michael.” I handed him the reports.

“So, John, how much do I owe you?”

“Subtracting the $100 you already gave me, $80.23.”

He grinned. “Is that all? I was prepared to pay much more.”

I felt like an asshole. I was supposed to be a greedy spy, right? So why be timid? Live and learn.

He removed a fat white envelope from his breast pocket. Deliberately, he counted out eight ten dollar bills, laying one on top of the other. Then he reached into his pants pocket, took out a quarter, and held it up for my inspection. He placed it on top of the stack and pushed the stack and its topping across the table to me. I went to my penny bank, shook two out, came back, and held out the coins in an open palm. Then I slapped my palm down on the table, and with a penny under each finger, I slid two cents to him.

On Stage: Espionage as theater.

Business concluded, we moved back into the living room. He sat down on the sofa while I deposited myself, once again at a safe distance across from him on the blue chair. He asked about my education. I told him I had a Master's Degree in library science from St. John's University and a bachelor's in economics and computer science from the City College of New York. Then he asked about my parents.

"My mother lives in Queens. My father lives on Staten Island. They're divorced."

He asked why I wasn't married.

Why? Because no woman I ever wanted to marry wanted to marry me. Shit… If I was a woman, I wouldn't marry me either. Rather than bare my soul to an enemy of the state, I simplified: "Too irresponsible and too poor."

He told me about his schooling in Russia, where he trained as a chemical engineer. He mentioned a sister two years younger and that she had four boys. Then he said that his father had died of a heart attack. I mentioned that my father had a heart attack in 1976, but he survived. Then he told me that he had a brother who died young. I said I was sorry and meant it.

Finally he asked to see my Radio Shack TRS-80 computer. I led him into the back room. I asked if they had "microcomputers" in the Soviet Union.

"But of course. How else are we able to compete with the U.S.? You know, John, we Russians are not as backwards as you Americans think."

Mr. Katkov had a strong sense of national pride — another tidbit for the Bureau.

***

"Can I have these?" asked FBI agent Pat McKinney. "We'd like to check them out."

Like he expected me to just fork over my copy of Katkov's latest want list and a new, unclassified Texas Instrument report as if they were nothing more than side dishes to go along with his hamburger (rare with a raw onion) and cup of coffee?

A firm, "No you may not."

Obviously, that caught him off guard. Guess it wasn't often that guys like me said no to guys like him. It was Sunday, February 5, 1984, and we were having lunch at the same pub on W. 75th.

"The report came sealed," I reminded him, "how am I going to explain an opened package to our friend?"

"There's no reason to give him a sealed package."

"Yes there is. It looks better, less suspicious." The role I'd been playing, successfully so far, with Katkov was a greedy lowlife who only cared about money, not what was in his packages.

Again, I couldn't believe how dense these FBI guys could be sometimes.

"As for the list, you can't have that either. I need it to work from. Besides, what am I going to say if our friend stops by unexpectedly and asks to see it? 'Sorry, Michael, the FBI has it.' " Then I informed Agent McKinney that I'd photocopy the list and mail it to him.

"OK, but from now on, every document you give our friend, get a copy for us, too, so we can judge whether it's all right to pass it along."

I shot him a smirk. "You know, all this stuff is publicly available. He can get it himself if he wants."

"We know that, but while you're working with us, you'll be under certain guidelines. And don't worry about any extra costs involved. We'll compensate you for your time and effort."

"Speaking of money, do you have some for me?" I referred to the two fifty dollar bills the government had misappropriated from me nearly three weeks ago, on January 18th.

"I'm afraid not. There's still some confusion in that regards. It hasn't been decided yet, but we might put you on a stipend. When I find out, I'll let you know. You said he paid you $80."

"And twenty-three cents."

"Did you bring it with you?" Pat had just presented himself like a loose nail sticking up from a shingle. Guess he expected me to just hand the money over like I did last time. But this time was not last time. I decided he needed to be banged back in place.

"No. I deposited it into my checking account." Again a lowly roofer had challenged authority. How would he, Pat, and by extension they, the Bureau, react?

Instead of *On Stage* dramatics, Pat shook his head. He looked more disappointed than pissed off. "You shouldn't have done that. Technically, when you deposited that money you broke the law. The Foreign Agents Registration Act (FARA)."

Shrugging, "Never heard of it;" followed by a more conciliatory, "I know what you're saying, Pat, but you guys have to understand something. I had to lay out my own money for that stuff. Why do I have to wait so long to be paid? It's not fair."

“Now that’s exactly the attitude we want you to take with our friend.” Pat sounded like I’d just stepped into the bright spotlight of salvation. “Show him that need. Tell him how difficult things are for you right now. Ask him for an advance.”

As much as I hated to admit it, what he said made sense — from their POV. The FBI knew these were hard times for me financially, so the more pressure they put on me, the more I’d pressure Katkov. Made sense, but I still didn’t like it.

I asked why Katkov was so interested in me, a guy with no access to classified information. Pat said there were certain quotas Soviet intelligence officers had to fill to look good to their superiors. “You’re a plus on his report card.”

I knew from my ongoing research that recruiting assets (agents) was a top KGB priority. The Soviets recruited them by the hundreds in the hopes that one or two might end up with access to classified information. A low level pawn in a multi-leveled chess game, I didn’t have that kind of access. Not yet anyway. It would be interesting to see how both sides tried to maneuver me, a pawn who wanted to be a knight.

***

“Michael, Michael… Comrade… Let… me…’splain somethin’.” I slurred as slowly and clearly as a brain floating in 90 proof alcohol would allow. “Thirty-five dollar an hour is my minimum charge. I told you that in the beginning. This “commission” you complain about… is less than…adequate…given the information you supplied me.” Pointing a thumb at my chest, “I spent a great deal of my professional time…finding out what NBER stood for…their address, telephone number…etcetera. Considering all the trouble I went through to get these,” I made vague waving motions at the reports, “uh, these, uh…”

— *Fucking little pieces of shit!* — "things, how dare you complain to me about a" — fucking! — "stinking thirty-eight 'bucks.' By the way, when am I gonna start getting those big orders you've been promising?"

Three weeks had past, and on Tuesday, February 28th, the bottle of Stolichnaya vodka he'd given me on 12/29/83 was finally opened. It sat on the kitchen table, two-thirds gone.

Me and alcohol, we never did mix well. A glass of wine with dinner and an occasional beer were my limits. So why was I sitting at my kitchen table swigging brown, plastic coffee cups of vodka with Mr. KGB Katkov? As soon as the first cup of Stoly went down my hatch — it tasted like shit, btw — I knew this was a bad idea. I didn't need any loose nails in my head tonight. If I screwed up, who knew what this big, bad Russian bear would do to me?

I suppose I was acting all macho, or some shit like that. If this commie could down one cup after another, then a true red, white and blue American like me could too.

The end result? It didn't take long for me to be pretty fucked up.

As for his promises of a big order, he replied, "Very soon. I will order the journal to you," he said, speaking of the signal processing journal.[1] Then he gave me my next order, a list of several graduate level engineering textbooks.

More whining from me: "Michael, this *is not a big order.*"

"John, I am concerned for you. You must be careful. I do not wish for you to get in trouble with your government."

"Fuck the fucking government." (I was *not* a fan of the guy at the

1 Trends and Perspectives in Signal Processing, 1984.

top.)

"John, what do suppose will happen if I give you a $3,000 order and—"

"You kidding? Gonna spend it." I raised another mug-full to my mouth: gulp!

"— you put it in the bank? You—"

With my brain afloat inside its bony home, I assured him, "Not going in no bank, Michael."

"— will draw the attention of the IRS."

"No. I'll buy Nanette something nice. Ha, ha, ha…"

"You will get into trouble because the bank will tell them. Ya, is true. I read it in *New York Times*."

"Michael, Michael." I gave him a warm smile. "Comrade… Don'worry'boudit. I know what I'm doing. There are ways—"

"Who is Nanette?"

"Someone I like. Besides, $3,000 is not a lot of money. There are ways of—"

He leered. "She is your girlfriend, ya?"

"I wish… I have a job, Michael. I could—"

"And what if Nanette asks you where you got money to buy her nice present?"

"She wouldn't — I wouldn't. Was only kidding. I'd spend it all on me." I leaned closer and let my face slide into mock-seriousness (more *On Stage*). "You can't buy love, Michael."

"Do not be so sure, John."

My Russian friend grinned, a grin that was about to fall off his face and drop into his lap. I passed him two reports published by the National Bureau of Economic Research, a private think-tank. They cost me $1.50 apiece. To this I added a modest finder's fee of $35. Guess what I considered a "fair" markup was more than his socialist mind could cope with. Katkov complained, "And for this you are charging me thirty-five bucks!"

"It's called capitalism, Michael. You're not in the Soviet Union anymore."

The Russians have a word, *vranyo*, which means roughly this: *You know I'm lying, and I know you know, and you know I know you know, but I go ahead with a straight face and you nod seriously and take notes.*[2]

Katkov threw some *vranyo* at me: "John, I wonder if you could please clarify something? I made a small wager with a colleague. He claims that in America students keep their diplomas in folders. I say that they are on boards hanging on the walls. Could you help settle this matter? If it is no trouble, may I please see your diploma?"

I nodded seriously, stood up, steadied myself, amazing considering my condition, and wobbled a few steps to where the diploma hung on the wall right outside the kitchen.

"Here ya go, Michael, looks like you win."

He smiled. "Thank you, John. You have increased my wealth by fifty bucks."

"That makes me very happy, Michael. How 'bout splittin'?"

Grinning, "Not at this time."

Tonight he paid me the one-hundred fifty dollars — the big

---

2 Shipler, David K., *Russia: Broken Idols, Solemn Dreams*, c1983, p. 21

money? *Vranyo.*

He motioned for more vodka. I obliged him. The bottle was almost gone. I got up for a drink of water. I turned to face him and leaned against the sink, arms folded, feet crossed, and with a stupid grin on my face. Quite unintentionally, my relaxed pose somehow breached Mr. KGB Katkov's sense and sensibility.

"Why are you standing for? Sit please." He motioned for me to lower myself to his level, back on the chair. "Someone who stands while someone else speaks wishes to feel superior."

And then I remembered something I'd read: in the Soviet Union etiquette demanded that passengers in taxis or limousines ride up front so not to offend the driver.[3]

Fucked up.

At first I thought he was joking. When I realized he wasn't, *I took offense*: "No. Maybe their fucking asses hurt from sitting on a fucking roof all fucking day."

He smiled. "It seems to me that you did quite a lot of fucking today. With Nanette, no? You must be quite tired. Sit, please. You must rest."

"That was a good one, Michael. Ha, ha, ha…" I dropped my ass into the fucking chair.

Next Michael wanted to do some male bonding. "Did you watch any of the exciting hockey matches at Olympics?"

1984 was a Winter Olympic year. I didn't know, or care, who had won. I assumed it was the Russians.

(I'm not a fan of the Olympics.)

---

3 Shipler, p. 201

"Here's to you guys," I said, raising a cup of water in toast. "Especially Tradiak."

Viktor Tradiak was the great Soviet goaltender who had almost single handedly defeated the NHL All-Stars in 1972.

He raised his cup and said, "Tradiak," only clearer. His enunciation was perfect.

I remembered that Katkov once mentioned that he also played hockey, so, "What position did you play, Michael?"

An innocent question but Katkov looked like a man who'd just had his switch flicked off. All the lights in his face went out. When he started blinking like a Chernobyl control panel gone nuts, it hit me like a puck in the head: *This guy doesn't know what I'm talking about! Only ice he's ever seen is in his vodka.*

"Sorry, Michael, guess I misunderstood. Thought you said you used to play hockey."

"No, motor cross," he replied.

I made a mental note never to discuss hockey or motor cross with him again. I also wanted to work his real name, Katkov, into the conversation, but I was too far under-the-influence to even attempt it. At eight p.m. Katkov decided to leave. I followed him into the foyer. He reached down for his coat and hat, which lay on top of the laundry wagon, a wagon loaded with two bags of clothes I needed to wash.

"You're lucky, Michael. You gotta wife to do your laundry," I said, flapping an arm at the wagon.

"It's not what you think, John." He sighed. "When it comes to certain things, Russian women differ little from their American counterparts."

“It’s a woman’s world, Michael.”

“Yah, is true.”

Another tidbit for the FBI about Mrs. Katkov: she did not do laundry.

Chapter 7
Jenga

Let the Bureau be mad at me. Better them than the phone company. Those guys could shut me off!

***

Wednesday, February 29, 1984

The Roofman's checking account had developed a leak: buy documents for Katkov, pay with a credit card, and then pay my credit card bill. Then turn over the money to the FBI. And then wait to get paid by the Bureau. Wait and wait and wait to get paid — and still waiting! My good credit rating was in grave danger.

Today, the day after my meeting with Mr. KGB Katkov, new money flowed into my account. Pat had mailed me a six-hundred dollar check. I was not expecting this. One hundred dollars of which was the money the government had misappropriated from me way back on January 18th. The other five hundred, according to Pat, "Is a little something extra for your troubles."

Maybe the Bureau was not so bad. Maybe I had them figured all wrong. Since my mind always worked on the assumption that the glass was half-full, that little something extra I figured for my stipend. That made me one happy little fishy. I'd get to swim around in a bowl the Bureau would fill with $500 every month, enough to cover the rent on my apartment and most of the rent for the garage where the Dodge Dart slept.

On March 9th, Katkov phoned. "You will please order the (signal processing) journal. I would like it a week from today. I promise you extra compensation for your efforts."

On March 12th, I called Pat. "I ordered two sets of the journal, one for you and one for our friend. I had to lay out a lotta cash on this one ($900 on my American Express card), so I'd like to get paid ASAP. The last five-hundred you paid me was for February, right? When will I be getting March's stipend?"

"That's not a problem, Julius. We know that things are a little tight for you right now. That's why we gave you the extra $500 last month. We foresaw that something like this might happen."

"Thought that was my stipend?"

"Don't worry, Julius, you'll get paid. But don't expect this to be a monthly thing. We're not in a position to offer you a stipend. We want to project the image that this is entirely a business operation. We don't want the Soviets to get the idea that someone is subsidizing you. We want you to show them that need. Understand what I'm saying?"

That made sense. CIR had to be real world, and in the real world CIR had more money going out than coming in.

***

On Friday, March 16th, at two p.m., six neat little piles of twenty dollar bills were all lined up in a row on the kitchen table; each pile totaled $100. The cash represented a previously agreed upon figure for the signal processing journal. What followed constituted a little something extra that Michael had promised me for my troubles.

One, two, three more twenties hit the table; a new sixty-dollar stack was created.

"Why'd ya stop? Keep going." I tapped the last stack. "How about topping it off? Two more. An even seven hundred. I like symmetry."

From Michael a wry grin, "It seems to me it is quite sufficient for now, John. I do not wish to spoil you."

The next day, Saturday, St. Patrick's Day, found me mad at the world in general, and one Irishman in particular. I was about to part with a large chunk of green. Pat had called this morning. He said today's debriefing would have to be short, so we met by the Riverside Church at 120th and Riverside Drive. He pulled up in a late model blue sedan, dressed in his Saturday casuals: pressed jeans, a New York Yankee warm-up jacket, and gleaming white sneakers. This guy would look patrician even in a burlap pullover.

I got in the car.

"How much did he pay you?" Pat asked, taking out a notepad.

"Six hundred." I handed him a sealed envelope filled with all twenties.

He wasn't so quick to put it into his pocket this time. Still holding the envelope, he put on his cop's face. Guess he figured he could intimidate me; he guessed wrong. His body language said: *Kaktov is following the standard KGB procedure, so we know he paid you a bonus.*

"Is this all of it?" Pat finally asked.

"Yes, that's all of it." Those were my words, but I let a grin tell the rest of the story: *Yes, he paid me a bonus, and I know you know, and I don't give a rat's ass. It's called vranyo, pal.*

"OK," he said, writing something in his pad. My guess: This guy's skimming.

Ok, I'd taken action, but pocketing sixty-dollars was timid not bold. Guess the FBI still scared me. But I did have some news guaranteed to piss them off.

"Michael asked me if I wanted an advance."

The smug expression on his face told me this was what these guys wanted to hear. The way they figured it, this was the next block to go on top of the pile regarding my relationship with Mr. KGB Katkov. And that was why, after a dramatic pause, I crashed their Jenga.

"I told our friend no, that I trusted him. 'I know you're good for it, Michael.' "

That drew a pronounced reaction. He put down his pen, closed his eyes, and rubbed the bridge of his nose. "Why did you say that?"

"Why not? You guys are just gonna take it anyway, right?"

If the FBI wanted reality, reality had a price.

"I know that as a businessman you're not happy with the current arrangement, money going out and nothing coming in. As a matter of fact," Pat said, sounding more upbeat, "that's what I was working on this morning: the paperwork to get you paid. You should get the money sometime next week."

Yeah right. Check's in the mail. "Let me ask you something. What if I register with FARA? Can I keep the money then?"

"You could do that if you want," Pat said, nodding his head. "Just call the Department of Commerce and ask to register as an agent of a foreign government. I'll tell you what will happen, though. Sooner or later the Soviets will find out about it. And when they do, they'll drop you like a hot potato."

Made sense, still something about FARA bothered me, so on Monday, March 19th, I called the Commerce Department's library and made some discreet inquiries. The librarian there referred me to Foreign Agents Registration at the Department of Justice, the same Department of Justice Pat worked for. I spoke with a lawyer from the FARA section named Jim Katz. I told Mr. Katz that I was an information broker gathering non-classified, publicly available documents for a client who happened to be a member of the Soviet Delegation to the U.N. Mr. Katz assured me that FARA did not apply in my case.

The Bureau had given me my first taste of disinformation. It was sour, but at least I knew something that they did not know I knew.

In the car, Pat let me know exactly what the Bureau expected from me regarding our friend: “We want to know more about him.” He drew three small circles in his notepad. “He goes from his home, to his office, to the U.N.,” he said, moving the pen from circle to circle. “Three places we have no access to. You’re our window. From you we get our picture of him. What does he think of the United States? What’s his home life like? How does he feel about his wife? His job? Boss? How good is his English? How politically aware is he?”

Then I let Pat know exactly what I expected from the Bureau: “I’m not happy with the current financial arrangement. It’s gotta change.”

***

One month later, on Friday, April 20th, I leaned against the doorjamb outside my apartment, arms folded across my chest. I shot the good guy, the one who paid his bills on time, a grin. Michael came up the stairs. He reached the top landing with his tongue hanging out. Theatrics no doubt because Michael looked a lot more fit than me, and I never had any trouble with stairs.

“What’s the matter?” I said. “Why didn’t you take the lift?”

He gave me a tired smile.

I led him into the kitchen. On the table sat a bottle of Rubesco wine. My roof buddy, Dom, had recommended it.

"I know you guys don't celebrate Easter, so here's my May Day present to you, Michael."

He hesitated.

"Take it; it's good wine, imported from Italy."

"Oh, then is OK," he mumbled.

Also on the table was a stack of new books, still in their plastic wrappers. "And for all this," I said, gesturing, "you owe me seven hundred."

"Is that all?"

Every time he said that I figured I was cheating myself. Damn! One of these days I was really going to jack up the price on this guy.

He counted out the money in the same deliberate fashion as last time, twenties in piles of one hundred dollars. At seven hundred, he paused and smiled. "And this is my Easter gift for you, John." Five more twenties joined their comrades, for a grand total of eight-hundred dollars, all of which went into my checking account the very next day. I was through playing games with those fuckers. If the Bureau got pissed about it, too bad, because I had bills to pay. I'd rather have the Bureau mad at me than New York Tel. By now I had figured out that the Bureau were paper tigers, but the phone company, they could shut me off.

Back in the living room Michael noticed a picture of Jesus hanging on the wall. My aunt had given it to me for Christmas. He asked, "You are a believer?" His eyes were wide, innocent, like a child asking, *Is there a God, Daddy?*

What to say? The truth or what I thought he wanted to hear?

"Yes I am."

He changed the subject: "I would like to start giving you bigger orders, but we must be careful of IRS," he said, taking the index and middle fingers from each hand and crossing them to form a tiny rectangle. Then he peeked through his fingers as if through a peephole.

He questioned me about my current financial condition: business income, roofing income, how much rent did I pay, and did I own a car? Such information was crucial to Soviet intelligence, because this was what they based their payments on. They paid an agent just enough to keep him hooked, but not enough to radically change his lifestyle. Such a change might draw the attention of American counterintelligence.

Then he asked, "How many customers do you have?"

Other than the KGB and FBI, there were none. "A few, but you're my biggest and best customer."

"Your biggest private customer. As you yourself have said, 'Michael, I am like priest. I say nothing.' " He made that weird peephole sign again.

My *New York Times* ad was up and running, but only for the month of April. Apparently Michael had seen it. Maybe it was the ad that had prompted this new line of questioning. He asked how much it cost. When I told him, he said, "Why do you do this for? Why do you waste your money?"

"To attract more customers. How am I gonna stay in business without customers?"

He shrugged. "As you like."

Michael sat on the sofa, me the blue chair. "I want to give you your next assignment." He handed me a list to copy, not keep. "You will please forgive me for being so lazy and make you do all this writing, but Mikhail means grizzly bear in Russian. As you know, grizzly bears are quite lazy."

Katkov's usual posture when he sat was with his legs close together as if he had no balls. And sometimes when he walked his arms slung loosely at his sides while he kept his wrists limp. He could appear almost effeminate when he wanted to, but not this time. A big Russian bear sat across from me with his legs spread, arms tightly controlled, and wrists firm. His non-verbal message: *Remember, little toad, this grizzly bear can squash you.*

One of the books on his list, *A Directory of Fee-Based Information Services*, was a directory of information brokers in the U.S. and Canada.

He said, "Perhaps you can use the services of these people. You will see, soon you will be millionaire. You keep the money and let other people do the work."

Involving innocents in the Katkov Affair did not go down smooth with me. But I hid my true feelings with a sly grin and these added words: "And let them take the risks."

When I told Pat on the phone that Michael wanted me to use the services of others, he sounded happy: "This marks a significant turn of events."

Looked like the Bureau had rebuilt their Jenga.

But I didn't share the joy. "I'm not comfortable with this, Pat, using innocent Americans."

So Michael never did get that book. Not from me, anyway.

Chapter 8
Into the Cross Hairs

His nation has tens of thousands of missiles aimed at us, so however I feel about him personally has to take a seat in the back row of my conscience.

Wednesday, May 2, 1984

***

I took off from work to meet Pat for a debriefing. He chose a tonier restaurant right across the street from the pub on W. 75th. No old commie actors with hair growing out of their ears could afford to eat here.

"The last time we spoke," Pat began, "you voiced some strong objections to the current business arrangement. I have some good news. We understand that you're a businessman and the government does not wish to make it any harder for you than necessary." He leaned back and smiled, about to take a heaping helping of personal credit. "It was difficult, but I was able to convince some people that we should let you keep the money our friend pays you. Please keep in mind that yours is a special case. We don't do this for everyone."

"Thanks, Pat. I'm glad we were able to work it out."

A win-lose as far as I was concerned. I got what I wanted, but he didn't ask me anything about the eight hundred Michael had paid me on April 20th, so I couldn't gauge his reaction. Too bad, but the way I figured it, they figured it out anyway. But by reversing themselves the FBI had given me a sense of my own power. Since I was their window, if I dropped the shades, they'd be in the dark.

Up to now, I'd assumed Michael Katkov was a KGB officer — wrong! Pat said that he belonged to that "other organization," that other organization being Soviet military intelligence. He left a door cracked open, so I was happy to barge through to display some newly acquired knowledge:

"Oh! You mean the GRU. Are they as good as the KGB?"

"Every bit as good and in certain areas better." He added that the GRU and KGB employ the same recruiting techniques and much the same tradecraft. "This should make you happy: the GRU serves the military, which means they have a lot more money to spend." Pat picked up his lite beer, a self-satisfied grin on his face. He said, more to himself than to me: "We have some big plans for our friend. We're going to make him a rising star."

After he'd finished the last of his beer, I said, "You're talking about making him a defector-in-place."

Somewhere on its way down his esophagus that lite beer must have re-wadded into hops; or was it my accumulating knowledge that put a lump in his throat? Mr. GQ seemed a bit unsettled. Was that a hint of concern I saw in his eyes when he said, "Why? Writing a book?"

To the guys who live in a world of mirrors secrecy was like oxygen. They couldn't live without it. Now with me, the opposite was true. Secrecy was not in my self-interest. The more people that knew about my involvement in the Katkov Affair, the less likely I'd meet with an "accident." So, as for writing a book — my intention from Day 1 — rather than lie, I ignored the question. That was a technique

I'd picked up from Michael.

Instead I asked, "How do you guys think you're gonna turn our friend?"

Judging from the way Pat's eyes shifted in their sockets I assumed he was uncomfortable with this line of questioning. "We haven't worked it out yet. This is going to be a long, careful process."

I paused, letting him climb out of the hole he'd jumped into and dust himself off. I knew, and so did he, that he'd already *confirmed* way too much.

"We want to make things as easy as possible for him," he added. "We want to make his stay in New York a pleasant one." Pat smiled like a man assured of a specific outcome: the one he wanted. "All we ask is that he cooperates. Whatever information he's willing to provide us will be appreciated. New York is a plum assignment for these people. He wouldn't do anything to jeopardize his position here."

Ironically, Michael was doing his best to ensnare me. But I was merely the bait in a trap that had been set for him. Although I'd grown to appreciate Michael's charm, wit, and generosity, I had to hold fast to a cartoon-like, Boris Badenov view of the man. I also had to keep in mind that his nation had tens of thousands of missiles pointed our way. So whatever guilt I felt about what I was doing to a guy I had genuinely grown to like had to take a back seat in my conscience.

Pat casually mentioned that Michael owns a bright red 1984 Pontiac Firebird that, "He drives very fast." Then he added, "By the way, John, do you own a car?"

I chuckled. "Tell Pierce to look in Jersey. That's where you guys will find my car registered. I got a lotta tickets here in New York."

Pat grinned. "So, John, you're a scofflaw."

"Only the Lord is perfect, Pat." *And I ain't Him.*

***

So Mikhail Katkov was not KGB — damn! That sure put a damper on my sense of drama. The KGB had always been part of pop culture. Who the hell ever heard of the GRU?[1] I only stumbled upon this "other organization" while reading about the KGB. Thus would the Tcheka, the Sword & Shield of the Party, the Kommittee for State Security, and The Friends of the People (various names for the KGB) drop down on my reading list. Now on top was the Glavnoye Razvedyvatelnoye Upravleniye, which reads like a chemical compound but translates to The Chief Intelligence Directorate of the Soviet General Staff.

Pat told me that Michael had been born to Russian parents on a cooperative farm somewhere in the Ukraine. Michael's beginnings might be even more humble than mine. He'd obviously had to work hard to achieve success. Me? I'd simply gone skating.

It's a long way to the top from the Ukraine to a GRU officer on foreign assignment; moreover a GRU officer who had snatched the biggest, ripest apple on the tree: New York City. Only the best and the brightest KGB and GRU officers are posted to New York. My research on the GRU netted the following results: unlike the KGB, which recruited sons of the Soviet elite (Moscow Boys as the Bureau called them), the GRU's chosen few were purposely selected because of their peasant or proletariat backgrounds.

First stop for Mikhail Katkov was the Red Army where he was free to be all he could be. After graduation from a military engineering college he would be commissioned a junior officer; from

1 Except for the GRU's Fancy Bear in 2016.

there came a stint in the Red Army's Spetsnaz (Special Forces). The majority of GRU officers were former Spetsnaz. But life in the Soviet military was hard and the payoffs small; so when the GRU extended an invitation, few refused.[2] However, this same pursuit of life, liberty and happiness (Soviet style) made GRU officers susceptible to what CIA psychologists call "normal vulnerabilities."

What were Katkov's vulnerabilities that the FBI hoped to exploit? Dissatisfaction with the Soviet system? Dissatisfaction in his marriage? Money? Greed? Power? A hunger for the American way of life? It's not always the soap opera of our lives that do us harm; sometimes it's the little things. Take the case of another Soviet intelligence officer named Sergei Motorin whose normal vulnerability was a passion for high quality stereo equipment.

KGB Major Motorin was posted to Washington, D.C. In 1981, as 3rd Secretary at the Soviet Embassy, he was attached to Line PR, a KGB line tasked to gather political intelligence. It became known to the FBI that Motorin frequented a discount electronics store in downtown Washington. Sometime in 1983 he walked into the store with two cases of vodka he wanted to trade for a stereo system. From across the street, an FBI surveillance team duly recorded the Stolichnaya-Panasonic trade-off. A few days later a FBI agent approached Motorin. The agent showed Motorin pictures they had of him and threatened to send them to his embassy. Since Motorin had purchased the vodka at a diplomatic discount, and then traded them for his own personal gain, technically this constituted a firing offense that could get him recalled back to Moscow. But Motorin knew that such conduct was winked at by his KGB superiors. Most of them

2 Suvorov, Viktor *Inside Soviet Military Intelligence*, Berkeley Books, c1985 (paperback)

eagerly engaged in similar activities. Motorin just laughed it off and suggested where the FBI agent could shove his pictures.

A heavy-handed, clumsy attempt that ended in failure? Not exactly. Motorin had stepped into the FBI's crosshairs; for him there would be no way out. The same FBI agent kept approaching him on the street, in restaurants, at other public places, and these meetings were always surreptitiously photographed. It began to look as if Motorin was having clandestine meets with an American counterintelligence officer. Finally, when the agent showed him an entire photo gallery of them together, Motorin knew that a recall meant coming face-to-face with a string of gun barrels all pointed at him. Motorin had no choice. He became a mole inside Soviet intelligence for the FBI and CIA. He betrayed many of his KGB colleagues while at the same time feeding disinformation composed by U.S. intelligence back to Moscow. The stress Comrade Motorin was under must have been tremendous. To save his own life he had to betray his country, betray his colleagues, and betray his family.

The Motorin Affair had been a major triumph for the FBI agents and CIA officers who worked the case; they received praise and promotions. Bad for Sergei Motorin, code named GTGAUZE by CIA. He had done unto him what he had done unto others: CIA officer Aldrich Ames betrayed him to the Soviets. Sometime prior to October, 1986, Sergei Motorin was executed.[3]

How low would I go just to save my own ass? I had yet to be tested.

---

3 Adams, James, Sellout: Aldrich Ames

Chapter 9
Troubled Waters

This is like playing a scene from a John Le Carrè movie: The Spy Who Came Carrying a Yellow Envelope. *The movie stars me, John Pansini.*

Can't wait until the director, also me, says, "Action!"

***

Monday, June 18, 1984

Today found me in Midtown Manhattan pacing the plaza of the J.C. Penney Building at W. 53rd & 6th. I was the guy with the attaché case. The other guy, the spy, he'd be the one carrying an envelope. So where the hell was he already! Was he one of those prima donnas sitting in his trailer waiting to make a grand entrance? Or was he off somewhere scoping me out? I also wondered if Pat McKinney and his pals were hiding somewhere watching for the both of us.

It had rained that morning. 6th Avenue, as native New Yorkers called Avenue of the Americas back in the 1980s, was a slick streak of black pavement; its cross streets were filled with grimy puddles. Despite a shielding layer of gray clouds and temperature in the low 70s, I still felt like a baked potato wrapped in a woolen sock. Stuffed inside a winter-weight, gray herringbone, three-piece suit, I might have been a little cooler had I left one of those pieces at home. But I came here to meet a new customer, so I figured I'd best make a good first-impression.

Last week's blazing sun and air you could swim in had sapped the life out of me. Residual heat radiated from my back and shoulders, and every so often I felt a bead of sweat roll down the Rift Valley that creased my spine. The elastic band that held my jockey shorts up had turned into a clammy, wet belt. I couldn't wait to finish up with this guy and get home, get naked, and jump into the tub. I put my case down and stared into one of the big picture windows at ground level. I adjusted my yellow power tie with blue Pokka dots, ran my fingers through my hair, and admired my reflection.

"Impressive," I told myself.

Then a specific worry snuck up on me and whispered in my ear, *"What if he doesn't show? What if the FBI has scared him off?"*

A definite possibility even after I'd warned the bastards not to be there.

***

Usually me and my hammer, we have our own rhythm: *Tap-tap-bang! Tap-tap-bang! Tap-tap-bang!* Not last week. Last week the harsh elements altered our syncopation to: *tap... tap... tap... tap.*

Monday… Tuesday… Wednesday, I could not get my ass in gear. The hammer felt like a mallet. I kept telling myself: *John, you gotta get a desk job.* By Thursday, June 14th I'd had enough. I stayed home. The only way to keep cool on the top floor of a six-story tenement in an apartment with no air conditioning was to spend most of the day getting in and out of the tub.

With a towel wrapped around my waist -- I'm modest even in my own home -- at 3:15 p.m. the phone rang. I drip, drip, dripped into the living room and picked up.

"John, I have someone on hold," said Mitzi, my operator. She spelled his name for me: BOLOCHINE. "He called in reference to your *Times* ad. He asked about acccssed electronic library. He's foreign, speaks with an accent. I think he's a weirdo, John."

The exact same reaction she had to Michael Katkov's first call.

"Patch him through, please, Mitzi." To the caller: "Mr. Bol-chine. This is John Pansini of *Computerized Information Retrieval.* How may I help you?"

Bolochine sounded tense and wary; not at all businesslike. He also sounded European. My guess: East German. Were all these commies running around, scanning the *Times* looking to recruit industrial spies? The way I figured it, one wrong word from me and the next thing I'd hear would be a dial tone. Not to spook him, I mostly listened and let him talk.

Bolochine finally got to the point: "Mr. Pansini, could we meet for lunch sometime?" He chose the date, time and place: "I will meet you Monday the 18th, at plaza of J.C. Penney Building at 53th and Avenue of the Americas at one o'clock."

When I asked how I would recognize him, he said he'd be carrying a yellow envelope. I told Bolochine I'd be wearing glasses, a gray suit and carrying a brown briefcase. I hung up and waited ten minutes before dialing the FBI.

"Hello, Pat, this is Julius. Think I got another one."

"Another what?"

"Another spy, that's what, I growled. This guy calls. Asks for CIR. Asks about DIALOG and what other networks I access." With my voice gaining momentum: "Knows his shit. Foreign. Speaks with an accent. Think he's East German. Wants to take me to lunch Monday. So what do you think, huh?"

"Uh… Are we talking about someone other than our friend?"

"Yeah." It annoyed me that this guy couldn't even field a slow roller. Then I spelled BOLOCHINE for him, a name that for some reason I could not pronounce. I paused long enough to let Pat scoop the letters up in his glove; then I sent a line drive right at his face: "Wouldn't leave a number. Said he was calling from a hotel, some bullshit about being outta the office all day. Said he'd call me again from a public phone, so I give him my home number, you know, the one reserved for spies." I chuckled at my own wit.

"Let's not jump to conclusions, Julius. We'll check this out. I was just about to enter a meeting concerning our friend. Call you back in an hour."

I waited and waited. No call back. Guess he got held up at the meeting. Wish I could've been there when Pat rushed in and announced: *"Julius caught another one! Call the White House!"*

When Pat called back on Monday, just as I was leaving to meet Bolochine, I gave him a warning to pass along to his Bureau buddies: "I don't think this guy's Russian, but in case he does have a connection to our other friend, don't be there when I meet him. Just in case somebody's watching."

"You mean you'll be upset if we take his picture from our van, the one stenciled 'FBI' in big letters on the sides?"

A good one; I grinned. "Just *don't be there*, OK?"

"You worry too much, Julius. I promise we won't be anywhere near you. And don't mention our other friend. See if your new friend brings him up first."

At the J.C. Penney Building on W. 53rd Street, I paced, walked, and stalked back and forth across the plaza. My mind grumbled like it had a bad case of gas: *Where the hell is Bolochine? Tomorrow will probably be another hot one. Shit! Why did he have to pick today!*

The J.C. Penney plaza was so spacious, so white, and so clean as to be a tiny oasis in the cramped black and gray landscape of Midtown Manhattan. It was also a place where a person could be easily observed from any number of vantage points. I didn't see any FBI vans, but I felt their lurking presence. Maybe the Bureau had cameras and microphones planted in one of those white concrete bowls that held scrawny trees? And who was that homeless guy on the concrete bench pretending to be asleep? My guess: Pat McKinney. Nice ensemble.

I stopped pacing and stood near the main entrance. From there I could better observe the foot traffic that passed along 6th Avenue. Suddenly, it was as if the building had reared back, flung open its doors, and hacked out people. Office workers wearing dull, blank looks — it was, after all, a Monday — spewed through the doors like projectile vomit. Glad I was *not* one of them. My life had meaning, purpose, adventure. I was a *somebody;* they were nobodies.

My personal growth had been exponential.

After the initial surge ended, I spotted them: a group of five clean-cut, All-American types in dark suits. When did the building cough up five hair balls in cheap suits? I hadn't noticed them before, they just sort of appeared. They were about fifty feet to my right nearer the avenue. A rational mind would assume they were just a few young execs enjoying the outdoors, but we paranoids are not so easily fooled.

The guys in the suits ignored me. Only when a pretty woman passed did their heads swivel. Eventually, the text message my glare was sending was received: *Hey, assholes, I told you guys not to be here!* So much for Pat's assurance, "We won't be anywhere near you." Yeah right! Fifty feet qualifies as coloring outside the lines in my book!

First one, and then another, and then another head turned in my direction. Soon they were all looking back at me, talking. Not hard to guess what they were saying either:

"Who's the asshole over there in the glasses giving us the dirty looks? Let's go kick his ass."

Then, out of the corner of my eye, I spotted a bald-headed man. He'd just separated from the herd of passersby crossing Sixth Avenue with the light. He walked right towards me pressing a manila envelope to his chest — guess in his country yellow means manila. Was it the gray suit and attaché case that he recognized? In keeping with the bucolic image of the Penney plaza, he passed the Penney boys as if they were steaming heaps of cow patties.

I smiled and moved towards him extending a hand. His grip was firm.

"Mr. Pansini is pleasure to make your acquaintance."

Bolochine was about six feet tall, had an athletic build, a mustache, and thin, dark hair on either side of a round, shiny head. He looked to be around forty. His pleasant smile and relaxed manner put me at ease. I forgot all about the "Penney" assholes.

I always prided myself in being able to recognize accents. Growing up in New York City, I heard quite a lot of them. But his I could not place.

"Do you like Chinese food, Mr. Pansini?" When I said yes, he replied, "Good. I know a place not far from here."

We headed downtown along 6th.

"What do you do at the U.N., Mr. Bol-Chine, and how may I be of service?" I still had difficulty pronouncing his name, but he made no attempt to help or correct me.

"I am a scientist trained in chemistry and physics." He pronounced "physics" the same way Michael did. "I work at United Nations. I do research on energy related topics."

"I don't recognize your accent, Mr. Bol-Chine, but your name sounds French. Are you French?" I said, pulling some *vranyo* out of my ass.

"No. I am Russian. At United Nations they give us French spellings."

More v*ranyo.*

I asked how long he'd been in New York; he said four months. He looked awed when he added, "Is very big, very busy, much like Moscow. My wife is with me. She likes New York, too. She studies languages."

Languages? I wondered if she might also be connected with Soviet intelligence.[1]

Once inside the restaurant, Bolochine's demeanor went from relaxed and friendly to nervous and paranoid. He moved quickly towards a booth near the entrance. I followed. He sat stiffly with hands in his lap. He aimed a grim face at the front door. I sat across from him, my back to the door and the rest of the restaurant. Bolochine spoke in such low murmurs that I had to say, "What?" several times. His eyes shifted constantly, like an antelope on the savannah looking out for lions. And like one of those fleet-footed creatures, he seemed ready to bolt any second. There were only a few other patrons in the dining room, an ideal setup for spotting surveillance. I admired his

1 FBI told me that KGB had only one female officer. Later, I happened to see, not meet, her at a library conference.

tradecraft.

I was also a bit unsettled but for a different reason: what if the FBI spooked Bolochine? I did not want to lose this guy. He was another plot point in the story.

The waiter approached to take our orders. Bolochine said, “Would you be so kind to order first, Mr. Pansini.”

“Sure. And please call me John.” After six months with Mr. Katkov, I was getting pretty smooth with the schmooze.

“Of course, and would you be so kind as to call me Val, John. Is short for Vladimir.”

I ordered a spicy dish, and Val said, “The same please.”

Pat once told me that if Michael ever did take me to lunch I should not be surprised if he ordered the same thing I did. He said all Soviets did that. They thought it helped hide the fact that they were foreign. During the meal, Bolochine followed the standard recruiting technique that I’d read so much about. Bored, I listened to him plod along step by step; then I decided to speed things up a little.

“Hope you won’t mind paying me cash?”

We had jumped from step 5 to step 25. Poor Val, I’d unintentionally knocked him off script. He seemed at a momentary loss, stumbling to find his place. Time for me to play dumb and get him back into the role: “Will you require any receipts, Val?”

“That will not be necessary.”

“Good, then I won’t have to report this on my income tax.”

He smiled and nodded. I asked if there was a phone number where he could be reached.

“No. I would prefer that my colleagues not know of my research.

At present is personal and not related to my work at United Nations." Then with a confident smile as if he could see his own future, "Perhaps someday supervisors in my homeland will make me a supervisor too."

I raised a cup of tea in toast: "Good. Let us prosper together." That's what I said, but not what I meant. Mr. Bolochine's future was grim. The FBI owned his ass; but I didn't stress over it, because, after all, none of this seemed real to me. Mr. Vladimir Bolochine was only a character in my movie.

He returned my toast, his round face shined even brighter, like a three-way bulb going from 60 to 100 watts. Then Bolochine mentioned that he was currently researching high voltage power lines and their biological effects.

That sounded kind of sinister to me. I wondered if the Soviets were working on some kind of bio-weapon; for example, CIA's Havana station personnel's unexplained brain injuries circa 2020.

"Is for me personally, John, and I do not yet have much money. Would you please be so kind to give me a reduction in rate?"

"I'm sorry Val, but I run a very small operation. I can't afford to give discounts. But I more than make up for it by providing good, dependable service."

He smiled. "Pansini Company sounds very good to me. What are your requirements for greater success? Good connections?"

"More customers. And good connections. Why? Think you can help me?"

Val raised an eyebrow and smiled. "Perhaps."

Guess Mr. Vladimir Bolochine truly believed he was living the dream, Soviet style. Instead, he was a little fish swimming in a tank filled with big, hungry sharks with "FBI" stenciled on their sides.

And I'd better keep in mind that I was also swimming in those troubled waters.

***

My Dodge Dart and I slowly prowled the other side of a chain-linked fence that separated St. John's University from the rest of Fresh Meadows, Queens. I always liked roofing in this neighborhood. The slate and shingle of tightly packed, upper middle class suburbia comforted me. It always seemed to me that the sun shined a little brighter out here than in the Heights. The campus, where I got my Master's Degree in 1978, was an enclave of large, rectangular, cream colored brick buildings, rolling green lawns, shade trees and winding foot paths. What a refreshing change from the grit and grime of Washington Heights.

I wanted to park as close to the side entrance at 188th Street as possible. When I finally found a good spot, I put the Dart in it. I walked over to the entrance and waited. Then I noticed a sedan parked on a side street just off 188th sitting discreetly under a tree. Two men got out. They approached me. One was Pat. The other one, the one wearing a big smiley face, extended his hand. He said, "How you doing, guy. My name is Mike Berns. I'm on Pat's squad."

Mike had soft, pencil-pushing hands but a death grip. He squeezed like he was trying to crush a can; and he pumped my arm so vigorously he almost unhinged it from my shoulder.

"Easy, Mike. This is my banging arm. Need it for work." A roof nearby was waiting for me to get back from lunch.

The new Michael was about my height but stockier. He had brown hair, long by FBI standards, and a mustache. In Hoover's day he would've been considered a damn hippie. He looked to be in his early 30s.

"Mike's one of our language and computer experts," Pat said proudly.

Mike had an *Ah, Shucks* grin on his face.

I asked, "You speak Russian, Mike?"

"Some. I'm of Ukrainian descent."

Before I could follow up with a string of questions, Pat said, "Let's go find a place to eat."

We crossed 188th and got in their car. Pat drove.

When on the government's tab, I liked to eat expensive; so did Pat. But today we had to settle for one of those fast-food King MacShit Something-or-Other Huts. Pat led the way to a secluded table in the rear. He took out his notepad and asked how my lunch date went. While I read aloud from notes describing yesterday's meeting with Bolochine, Pat flipped photos of known Soviet intelligence officers to me. The images included some of the foulest, cruelest, inhuman beings I'd ever seen.

"Who are these guys?" I said, pausing my monologue. "You sure didn't catch 'em on good hair days."

Pat began to point out, and make jokes about, certain individuals: "This one over here, he's a Senator—"

"Must be a Republican," I duly noted.

"This one's a friend of Mike's. And he's—"

"Who's this guy?" I said, flipping another picture back at him. This monster had a long, narrow face, a large nose, a crew cut, and eyes that pointed in different directions. "Looks like a pervert."

Pat picked up the photo. A deadpan: "That's our boss."

I cracked a smile.

Guess Pat was running out of Republicans, bosses, and friends of Mike's. Finally, he dealt me an ace.

"That's him!" But before I could flip the picture over to see what the FBI had written on the back, Pat snatched it out of my hand. I'd be quicker next time.

The photo, black and white and passport size, looked official. Bolochine, as un-photogenic as his pals, had a blank look on his face and big bug-like eyes. Just to be certain, Pat showed me a second photo — he held it out for inspection so I couldn't get my grabby hands on it. It was a 35mm color shot of exceptionally high quality. The angle of attack was downward such that the photographer must have been at a position of high elevation relative to the target, most likely in a nearby skyscraper. The photo showed Bolochine standing on a street corner under construction scaffolding. He had on the same tweed sports jacket, light shirt, dark tie and tan slacks he wore yesterday. The sky was overcast and a puddle of rainwater lay in front of him. He grinned, his head turned slightly to his immediate left. He appeared to be talking to someone, but the identity of that person was a mystery because the photograph had been neatly cut in half. No mystery to me, however; I knew exactly who was standing next to Bolochine in that photo.

Yesterday, Bolochine and I had walked downtown along 6th Avenue and passed under scaffolding of a building being repaired. While standing on the corner waiting for the light to change, a taxicab roared through a puddle and splashed me.

My thoughts: *Motherfuckers! They should all die!* My words:

"Damn taxis." I wiped my pants leg. "They're so inconsiderate."

Bolochine shot me a grin. "They are alike the world over."

So I guess Pat's assurance that, "We won't be anywhere near you," really meant, *We'll be hundreds of feet away. You won't even know we're there.*

And that's what disinformation is: not so much lies as misleading truths. In this high-level chess match between Soviet espionage and American counterespionage, if a pawn like me ever hoped to escape being sacrificed, then I'd have to learn how the masters planned their moves. Get into their heads, so to speak. And Who said, *Won't be fooled again*?

Then Pat decided to share some background on Mr. Vladimir Bolochine: "Our new friend entered the country on February 9th. He's a scientist co-opted by KGB." According to Pat, the KGB frequently drafted people like Bolochine because many of their career officers lacked technical backgrounds. These co-ops were given rudimentary training in intelligence work.

Later, my own research filled in the rest: Bolochine had been co-opted to serve in Directorate T of the First Chief Directorate of the KGB. KGB intelligence officers and co-ops on foreign assignment were organized into components known as lines. Bolochine was assigned to Line X and charged with collection operations in science and technology. All KGB officers and co-ops assigned to Line X had academic or professional training in the sciences.[2] The GRU did not rely as heavily on co-opted personnel as the KGB. Further, the GRU did not have a separate cadre of scientific specialists like Line X officers. All GRU officers had technical backgrounds to go along with

2 Barron, John KGB: The Secret Work of Soviet Secret Agents, c1974, p. 107

their military specializations. For the approximately fifteen-hundred GRU officers who served abroad, scientific collection was an integral part of their work and a top priority.[3]

I asked Pat if this might be part of a concerted effort by the KGB and GRU. He said there was a strong rivalry between the two organizations. They had never operated jointly before.

"How can you be sure they're not doing it now?" I asked.

"Val has to report his contact with you to his superiors," Pat said. "If this is a screw-up, then they'll order him to break contact, that someone else is developing you."

If what Pat said was true, the implication was that these two fiercely competitive organizations dialog. If these fierce rivals really did talk to each other, especially about their assets, the most secret of secrets, then where and at what level? The answer to that particular question would be a long time coming — like two years later.

"So in other words," I said, "if Bolochine doesn't show up next Tuesday, then we know this is all a mistake?"

"There's another possibility," Mike said. "He could be doing this strictly on his own. Maybe word's gotten around that Michael has a hot prospect, and Val's looking for a piece of the action. If that's the case, then he'll continue seeing you strictly on his own—"

I finished Mike's sentence, "... without telling his superiors," but lacked his certainty. Then I remembered what Bolochine had said yesterday: that he didn't want word of our working together to get out among to his colleagues. Pat and Mike both nodded as if this was proof that Bolochine was acting on his own.

---

3 Suvorov, Viktor *Inside Soviet Military Intelligence*, c1984, p. 99

Conspiracy theories die hard; I held fast to serious doubts; the main one being that the guy walked up to me like he already knew me. "I still think that there's some kind of connection between these two guys," I told Pat and Mike.

Pat reminded me that I was scheduled to meet Michael this coming Friday. "Let's see what happens next."

KGB on Monday, FBI on Tuesday, and then the GRU on Friday, what a week! A spy's life that I wanted to go on and on and on…

Chapter 10
Greed Is Good — A Mantra For The 1980s

"Something is troubling me, John... Is it possible for two of your customers to order same document?"

***

Thursday, June 21, 1984

Today was another scorcher. At 4:15 p.m., I staggered through the door feeling like a wet mop that had been dragged through a chimney. Every free-floating, microscopic piece of grit that comprised New York's vast pool of air pollution had firmly attached itself to my clammy skin. The sooner I ripped off these filthy, sweat soaked, stinking roof clothes the better. After today, these rags could not be salvaged even in an industrial washer. Tomorrow, their destiny lay in a garbage can. But before I could shed these tatters and jump into the tub, the phone in the back room rang. Shit! It had to be him, he whom I was in no mood to deal with. So why did I answer? Because of the audacity of hope: he might be calling to say, *John, I will have very big order for you tomorrow.*

Instead, "John, is it OK if I stop by your place?"

Fatigue dropped its cloth over me: "You mean like... *today?...* Now?"

"Yes, but of course."

A day early! He had to be stopped. A trap had been planned, but one critical detail was missing. The objective: photograph Michael as he entered my building. The set up: a vantage point had been chosen, the kitchen window overlooking the entrance. Orange lace curtains were purchased and hung over the window on the odd chance that Michael would look up and see me aiming a camera at him. A telephoto lens had been dug out of the closet and attached to the camera. The screw up: no film in the camera. Asshole me intended to buy film at the very last minute; i.e. tomorrow at five when I got home from work.

"Michael," I said, sounding as limp as I felt, "I really had a tough day and—"

"I will be over in five minutes. Bye." *Click!*

Five minutes later my doorbell *thunked*, and Michael, all 6'6" of him, stood in the doorway smiling down at me. "You look well, I should think," he said.

How well should I look, torn white T-shirt, still in my work pants, and with no washed body parts? Even I could smell my own underarms. Bet he could too. He followed me into the living room. I walked with my arms tight to my torso.

"So what do you think of the place, now, huh?" I said, referring to the orange curtains that hung in the living room window so as not to draw special attention to the ones in the kitchen.

Michael looked confused.

"My curtains, what do you think of my new curtains?"

"Oh. They are quite nice." The words, polite, the tone: *Let's get down to business. I don't care a twit about your blooming curtains.*

"Nice! What do you mean nice. Last time you insulted my apartment. Called it a palace, so I try and make it look a little better and—"

"I never called your apartment a palace. I am quite sorry if I quite unintentionally hurt your feelings, John. Your curtains are lovely. They are exquisite. Now, what you've got for me?"

"Plenty and you better have plenty of money for me. That's the only way you can make up for this insult." I began carrying boxes stuffed with documents from the front room into the living room.

He asked if I had any plastic shopping bags.

"That won't help," I said. "You don't have enough arms." Then I had an idea.

It was way too hot outside for him to be struggling through the streets with a bag in each hand and a load under each arm. I lent him my duffel bag, vintage WW II and stenciled "USN" in faded black letters. Everything fit nice and snug inside.

"That bag belonged to my father, Michael. I also carry my hockey equipment in it, so please don't lose it" — *at your fucking embassy!*

A very large bag for a very large man: shoulder muscles rippled beneath his short sleeved, white shirt as Michael packed material into the bag. Watching him, I knew this guy could easily stuff me, Pat and Mike into that thing.

"Hot out there, huh?" An observation on my part, bet he'd spent most of *his* day in air-conditioning.

He nodded and gave me a look that hung on his face like melted wax on a candle. Then, "And how much do I owe you, John?"

The prospect of a rush of cool cash had me feeling a whole lot better. "$1,418.84," I happily announced. Tonight, I would *not* cheat myself. As for cheating him, I didn't give a rat's ass. He reached for his jacket, which was draped across an arm of the sofa, and pulled out a small white envelope. He removed a wad of twenty-dollar bills. He instructed me to count as he doled out the cash. I knelt on the floor, stacking the bills into neat little piles of one hundred dollars each. I counted out the first five hundred, looked up and saw another fistful of cash in my face. I counted out another five hundred, looked up and saw more bills. I counted out four-hundred twenty. When I looked again I saw two hands holding an empty envelope.

"Cleaned you out, huh? That makes me very happy, Michael."

He slapped his knee and laughed. "John that is what I like about you."

Greed is good — I like that about me, too.

He reminded me that he would be going on "holiday" in July, and I would not hear from him again until mid-September. I apologized for the mess in my apartment saying that I had planned on cleaning it tomorrow.

"Not to worry. I have saved you the trouble. John, you always say to me, 'Michael, I can get you anything.' So — use your imagination. Get me something interesting. This scrappy stuff," he said, flapping a limp wrist at the duffel bag, "means nothing to me. Is so you can make money."

We'd done this dance before, so I knew all the steps: the Bureau wanted me to get him to be more specific. "Like what, Michael? What are you interested in? I'll do anything, get you anything, but you gotta help me out a little."

He didn't. He just stared, expressionless.

By now, fatigue was like a ten ton weight pressing down on my mind and body. I wanted to get rid of him, so I could shower, eat and go to bed. But Michael wanted to chat. He smiled, leaned back on the sofa, and cupped his hands behind his head. "So, John, and how is your business?" Before I could respond, he dropped the bomb: "Have you picked up any new customers lately?"

That sure snapped me back to life. Calm, cool and collected: "As a matter of fact, I did. Got a call from a guy last week." No sense in lying to him because he and Bolochine might be comparing notes.

Michael's face hardened. He leaned forward, hands no longer resting comfortably behind his head. Now they were clasped together, hanging between his knees. His shoulders looked even more massive, more threatening. The big, bad grizzly bear had finally shuffled out of his den. The questions flew: *Bang! Bang! Bang!* He the hammer, me the nail.

"Who is he?" Michael asked.

"A chemist."

"What do you mean chemist?"

"What do you mean 'What do I mean?' The guy's a chemist. A chemist is a chemist."

"For who does he work for?"

"Uh… I don't know. Himself I guess."

"When did he call?"

"Last week sometime."

"Kindly be more precise."

Squinting like I was trying hard to recall: "Uh… Wednesday or Thursday… I think." (Overacting on my part. No Golden Globe for me tonight.)

"Why did he call you?"

"What do you mean, 'Why did he call me?' He wants me to do

work for him."

"What kind of work?"

"Information work, Michael, that's what I do, remember?"

"How did you find him?"

"I didn't. He found me."

"How?"

"He answered my *Times* ad, the same one you did." Oh no! My mouth had run a stop sign, one that I should *not* have missed. I blamed it on being asleep at the wheel.

"What is his name?" Michael asked.

I figured this question would come up eventually, so I had a prepared answer: "Sorry, Michael. I hold all my customers in the strictest confidence." I aimed an emphatic finger at him. "You included." Thinking the inquisition was over, and I'd won, I relaxed.

A mistake.

Smiling again, "John, I have a proposition for you. Suppose this other person orders something you think I might find interesting. Why don't you order an additional copy for me? He pays you. I pay you. What's the difference?" He shrugged.

Sure, great, a copy for him, a copy for Bolochine, and a copy for the FBI. A guy could make a nice living. But what if Michael and Bolochine were working together? And what if this was a test of my loyalty? If I sold out Bolochine, why wouldn't I do the same thing to him one day? But wasn't that what spies do, betray trust? Confused, I pulled an old strategy out of my back pocket: stall.

A tired, "Let's see what happens, Michael, maybe."

"You think it over," he said, neatly folding his jacket and putting it into his briefcase. Then he picked up the duffel bag, pretending like it was too heavy for him. "What will your neighbors think if they see me leaving your place with such a large bag? Will they think I am robbing you and call the police?"

"Nah! Everybody minds their own business around here. Besides, they won't call the cops because most of 'em are illegal aliens."

He lumbered to the door. "John, and what special gift shall I bring you back from Russia?"

"A ballerina would be nice."

He paused at the door. "Is not possible, you will simply be stuck with another illegal alien. Besides must fit in diplomatic pouch."

With that, he lifted and left.

And for me, finally, a long, hot bath. Luckily, I didn't fall asleep in the tub and drown.

***

Like a foul tide being excreted from bowels beneath the Upper Westside, out they poured: yuppies with six figure incomes and paying four figure rents. I watched them exit the subway station on Broadway and 86th. How many ulcerated stomachs passed by per minute? I used to envy these men and women: young, smart, aggressive, alphas all. Envy no more. Greed, and all that went with it back in the eighties, might have been good, but being a spy was better. A lot better. And I kept no *Rolaids* in *my* medicine chest.

5:30 p.m., early in the evening rush hour, and only a most confident, full-of-myself self waited on the corner. No doubt in my mind that Mr. Val Bolochine would show. As for Mr. Katkov, how much did he know about Val, and when did he know it? Perhaps there would be a new clue tonight, Tuesday, June 26th.

I spotted Bolochine's bald head bobbing and weaving. He came towards me mixed in with a crowd of Le Carrè's moronic masses crossing Broadway.

"Do you like seafood, John?" he said, smiling. "One of my colleagues recommended a restaurant nearby."

I said, "Sure," and we began walking south on Broadway. Pat once mentioned that the Upper Westside served as one of the Soviet's entry points for illegals into this country. Illegals were intelligence officers sent into a foreign country under deep cover. They were only activated in a time of national emergency; i.e. a break in diplomatic relations between our two governments. That meant the Soviet Union would have in-place spy networks when legal intelligence officers, like Michael and Val, were sent home. Pat said that Cuban intelligence was also active in the area. According to him it was difficult for the Bureau to operate up there. That made for many subterranean intrigues that flowed beneath one tiny, affluent New York neighborhood. And to this, all the natives were oblivious.

The weather was warm, mid 80s, so I wore a short sleeved sports shirt and slacks. Bolochine was dressed in the same clothes he wore last time. His clothing allowance must have been considerably smaller than Michael's. I never did see Michael in the same suit twice.

The restaurant was crowded, but not so crowded that we had to sit too close to other people. Bolochine led me to a small table near the kitchen and at the end of a row of tables. A flimsy room divider separated us from the bar. Noise from a nearby bus boy's station, clanking of plates, utensils and glasses, rendered our conversation unintelligible to eavesdroppers. We were, for all intents and purposes, secluded in a busy restaurant. Once again, Bolochine's tradecraft impressed me. Sitting with his back to the room divider, he looked far more relaxed than last time. I sat across from him.

I ordered spaghetti and scungilli with hot sauce, and a Coke.

"Two please," Bolochine told the waitress. He smiled politely and handed her back the menu. The genuine niceness of this guy began to nibble around my edges. I knew the end game this poor bastard faced.

Since I'd been born both Italian and coordinated, eating spaghetti did not pose a problem. I only needed one hand to twirl it around my fork before shoving it into my mouth. Not so Bolochine. He poked at the food on his plate as if it was a lab specimen. He went for the scungilli first, forking small pieces into his mouth. When they were all gone, he dared to take on the pasta. Out of the corner of my eye, I noticed him studying my spaghetti-eating methodology. When he was finally ready, he pressed the fork to the plate and, with the fingers of both hands, slowly began rotating it. Pasta coiled like a snake around the fork and partway up the shaft. Then, somehow, he managed to get it all in his mouth.

"Oops. Watch your tie there, Val… How's the food?" I asked, but he was concentrating so hard he didn't hear me. Louder: "*Val... How's the food?*"

"Is quite tasty. Reminds me of food from Georgia, one of our republics." Tasty or not, he pushed the dish aside. "I am not hungry today."

He politely waited for me to finish eating; then he handed me a new topic to search. The hand written list read: "new electrical insulating materials, insulators for high voltage electric power lines (1500-3000KV)." He told me to copy the list for myself. After I finished writing, he asked if it would be difficult for me to obtain the actual documents after I compiled a bibliography.

I smiled and gave him the standard spiel I gave to Soviet clients: "Not at all, Val, I can get you anything you want."

"This search is not part of my job at United Nations. It is for colleagues back home. We are willing to pay $40 for this first search. If it pleases us, we will have many more searches for you. You will make quite a lot more money."

Pat had it right, the KGB was cheap. It galled me that they expected so much for so little. The online costs alone might be close to $40. But, like I said, I knew their game plan, so I could afford to get tough with this guy. "Sorry, Val, but I'm in business to make money. I can't give it away. For $40 you're not going to get a comprehensive search." *And that my socialist friend is how capitalism works.*

He dropped eye contact. "I am prepared to pay as much as $50 if necessary."

"It's necessary."

We left the restaurant a little past seven. "If you would be so kind, John, shall we take a short walk? I have some further questions."

***

My ensemble the next day: a white T-shirt speckled with flecks of tar and hued brown from dirt that would never wash out, scruffy blue jeans with holes in the knees, and leather work boots scraped bare on the sides and toes. Needless to say, I was banging out a roof nearby. As the world turned, I decided to get another week out of my roof rags I wore last week for Michael instead of tossing them. I didn't get a chance to shop at Good Will.

I drove to the diner at New Hyde Park Road and Hillside Avenue in my Dodge Dart.

When I walked into the diner, everyone eating lunch must have looked at me and wondered: *Who's the homeless guy?* Not many of them in New Hyde Park. But I came here with a purpose: to set a crucial piece of the Katkov-Bolochine puzzle in place for two guys in suits. I didn't give a rat's ass how much spare change anybody had.

I spotted Pat and Mike seated at a booth that ran along a wall. I slid in across from them. We ordered, and before I could say a word, Pat informed me, "Headquarters is upset. You didn't tell them you were giving Michael floppy disks."

No way to gauge the Bureau's "true" dissatisfaction with me because Pat and Mike both put on their inscrutable cop's faces.

I was anxious to tell them about the short walk I'd taken yesterday with Val — as for Washington's hurt feelings regarding certain floppy disks — fuck 'em. Besides, the last want list I'd handed over to the FBI clearly stated that Michael wanted a whole bunch of blank floppy disks, both 5 ¼" (state of the art at the time) and obsolete 8". But this really wasn't about disks. These guys figured they could serve me a side order of intimidation along with a cheeseburger special.

While smothering the French fries with ketchup, I shot them a smirk. My thoughts: *Boo fucking hoo!* My words: "Too bad."

I could see that my attitude temporarily threw Pat off message; then he made a quick recovery: "You shouldn't have given him those disks without approval. I got chewed out pretty good because of you."

I hunched my shoulders, made a *What do you want from me?* face. After squirting some mustard between the cheeseburger and the sesame seed bun, I chomped down, bit off a chunk, chewed, swallowed, and wiped my mouth. Then I reminded him that, "I told you that I was giving him the disks. I even asked if you wanted me to order another set for the people in Washington. But you said, 'That won't be necessary.' Remember?"

That knocked him completely off his charger. Of course he remembered. He offered up a more conciliatory, "From now on everything you give Michael, even though it's in the public domain, has to be approved first."

I wiped my mouth again and grumbled, "Thought we had ironed this all out. Guess not."

"Remember FARA? We said we were willing to let you keep the money that Michael paid you. We don't do that for everyone. I stuck my neck out for you, had to convince the people in Washington. And then you pull something like this." Pat continued to preach what a good guy he was, that he was on my side, and how I'd let him down.

Fuck him and the horse he rode in on! I knew the truth about FARA, but knowledge is a power that must be carefully applied. I kept quiet, preferring to watch Pat dig a deeper hole for himself. When he finished, I paused mid-chew, then swallowed the lump in my mouth, leaned forward, and said: "You're not letting me keep the money because you're good guys. You're letting me keep the money because you want this to appear more realistic, like I'm not being subsidized. That's what you told me last time, remember?"

Pat held firm. "I don't want to argue about this. All I ask is that you let me clear everything with Washington before you give it to Michael. I know it all sounds like bull to you, but believe me there are reasons which, unfortunately, I can't go into."

What he couldn't go into was National Security Decision Directive #145 signed by then National Security Advisor, John M. Poindexter. By putting pen to paper Poindexter had created a new category of information called Sensitive but Unclassified. *NSDD-145* was a secret finding by the Reagan Administration that neither the general public nor I would find out about for another two years.

Putting all that bullshit about floppy disks and FARA aside, I said, "Remember when I told you guys about Michael's inquisition regarding my new client?"

That they admitted they remembered.

"And you guys agreed it's very likely that Michael knows about Bolochine?"

"I think we also said something about not jumping to conclusions," Mike added.

"Yeah, OK, you did say that… Anyway, you guys may not be ready to jump, but I sure am. Not only does Michael know about Val, but Val knows about Michael."

That sure put them back into their inscrutable cop-face mode.

A dramatic pause while I forked another fry, chewed, swallowed, and dabbed a napkin to my mouth. Then, "After we finished eating, Bolochine invited me for a short walk." Then I paused to sip more Coke.

I know how to play a scene, guys.

***

Last evening it was still light out when Val led me down 77th towards Columbus Avenue. He stopped in front of a row of townhouses across the street from a schoolyard; a wide open and highly observable area, just like the plaza at the J.C. Penney Building. It seemed to me like he had deliberately chosen this spot for a chat. The way I figured it, sneaky KGB bastards were hiding somewhere taking my picture. Admittedly, the thought of having high powered lenses on me made me feel even more like a spy. And a star, a star on a good hair day.

"I came here by metro," Bolochine had said, referring to the subway. Then he pointed to Columbus Avenue. "But I will take the bus home. Back in Moscow, the metro stations are so beautiful." His smile showed pride in his city.

"So I've heard." I'd ridden subways in Paris, where the stations were also beautiful. But no matter how old or how new, how clean or how dirty, how pretty or how ugly, all subways had the same smell: eau d' ozone.

Then Val got to the point: "Something is troubling me, John." He paused, his head down. When he looked up again he displayed a coolness that surprised me almost as much as the question. "Something is troubling me, John… Is it possible for two of your customers to order same document?"

The question caught me off guard, but I summoned up enough calmness to reply, "Highly unlikely. Why do you ask?"

He shrugged. "I am simply curious."

***

Back in the diner in New Hyde Park: "First Michael asks me to order him the same 'interesting material' my other client wants. Then Val asks me if it's possible for two clients to order the same thing. Like I said, I'm ready to jump. What about you guys?"

Their asses remained firmly planted in their seats. I'd expected an *Oh, wow!* moment. Instead, what I got from Pat was a deadpan, "That's interesting."

And from Mike: "Let's see how this plays out."

Mooks.

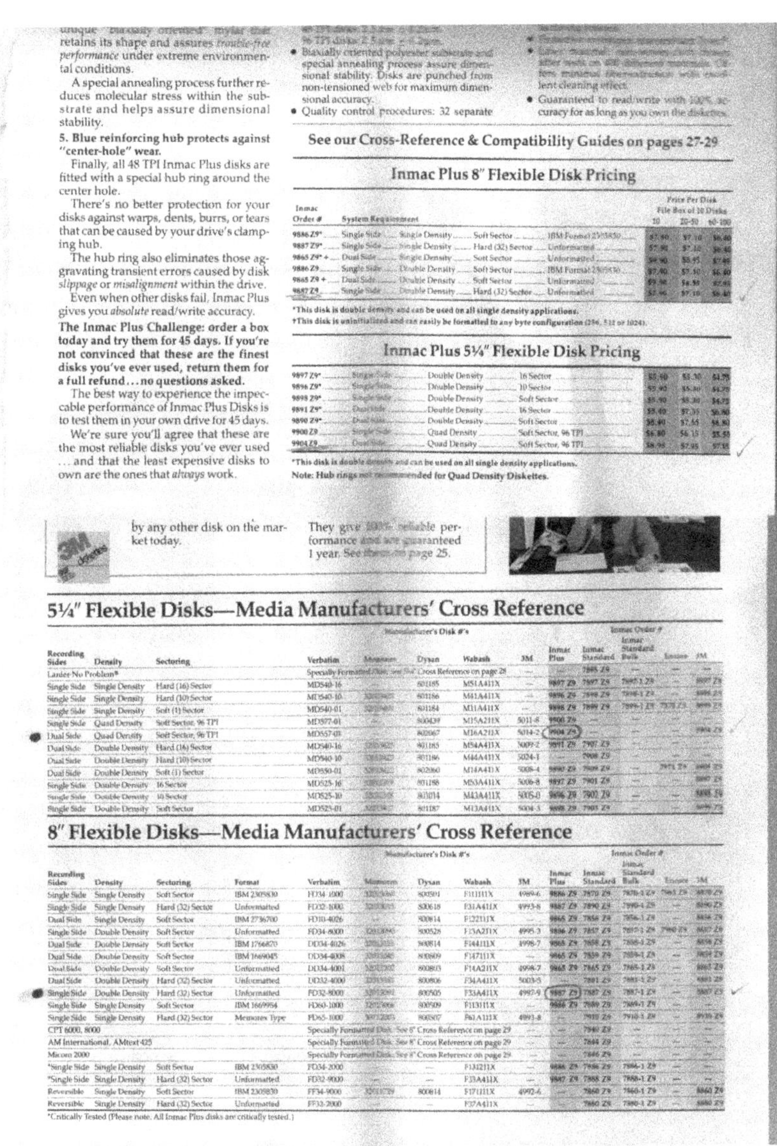

retains its shape and assures *trouble-free performance* under extreme environmental conditions.

A special annealing process further reduces molecular stress within the substrate and helps assure dimensional stability.

5. Blue reinforcing hub protects against "center-hole" wear.

Finally, all 48 TPI Inmac Plus disks are fitted with a special hub ring around the center hole.

There's no better protection for your disks against warps, dents, burrs, or tears that can be caused by your drive's clamping hub.

The hub ring also eliminates those aggravating transient errors caused by disk *slippage* or *misalignment* within the drive.

Even when other disks fail, Inmac Plus gives you *absolute* read/write accuracy.

The Inmac Plus Challenge: order a box today and try them for 45 days. If you're not convinced that these are the finest disks you've ever used, return them for a full refund... no questions asked.

The best way to experience the impeccable performance of Inmac Plus Disks is to test them in your own drive for 45 days.

We're sure you'll agree that these are the most reliable disks you've ever used ... and that the least expensive disks to own are the ones that *always* work.

- Biaxially oriented polyester substrate and special annealing process assure dimensional stability. Disks are punched from non-tensioned web for maximum dimensional accuracy.
- Quality control procedures: 32 separate

- lent cleaning effect.
- Guaranteed to read/write with 100% accuracy for as long as you own the diskettes.

See our Cross-Reference & Compatibility Guides on pages 27-29

Inmac Plus 8" Flexible Disk Pricing

Inmac Order #	System Requirement				Price Per Disk, File Box of 10 Disks: 10	20-50	60-100
9886 Z9*	Single Side	Single Density	Soft Sector	IBM Format 2305830	$7.90	$7.10	$6.40
9887 Z9*	Single Side	Single Density	Hard (32) Sector	Unformatted	[illegible]	$7.10	[illegible]
9865 Z9* +	Dual Side	Single Density	Soft Sector	Unformatted	[illegible]	$8.95	[illegible]
9886 Z9	Single Side	Double Density	Soft Sector	IBM Format 2305830	$7.40	$7.50	$6.60
9865 Z9 +	Dual Side	Double Density	Soft Sector	Unformatted	[illegible]	[illegible]	[illegible]
9887 Z9	Single Side	Double Density	Hard (32) Sector	Unformatted	[illegible]	$7.10	$6.40

*This disk is double density and can be used on all single density applications.
†This disk is uninitialized and can easily be formatted to any byte configuration (256, 512 or 1024).

Inmac Plus 5¼" Flexible Disk Pricing

Inmac Order #				10	20-50	60-100
9897 Z9*	Single Side	Double Density	16 Sector	$5.90	$5.30	$4.75
9896 Z9*	Single Side	Double Density	10 Sector	$5.90	$5.30	$4.75
9898 Z9*	Single Side	Double Density	Soft Sector	$5.90	$5.30	$4.75
9891 Z9*	Dual Side	Double Density	16 Sector	$8.40	$7.55	$6.80
9890 Z9*	Dual Side	Double Density	Soft Sector	$8.40	$7.55	$6.80
9900 Z9	Single Side	Quad Density	Soft Sector, 96 TPI	$6.80	$6.15	$5.50
9904 Z9	Dual Side	Quad Density	Soft Sector, 96 TPI	$8.95	$7.95	[illegible]

*This disk is double density and can be used on all single density applications.
Note: Hub rings not recommended for Quad Density Diskettes.

by any other disk on the market today.

They give 100% reliable performance and are guaranteed 1 year. See them on page 25.

5¼" Flexible Disks—Media Manufacturers' Cross Reference

Recording Sides	Density	Sectoring	Verbatim (Manufacturer's Disk #'s)	Memorex	Dysan	Wabash	3M	Inmac Plus (Inmac Order #)	Inmac Standard	Inmac Standard Bulk	Encore	3M
Lanier No Problem®			Specially Formatted Disk, see 5¼" Cross Reference on page 28				—	—	7885 Z9	—	—	—
Single Side	Single Density	Hard (16) Sector	MD540-16	—	801185	M51A411X	—	9897 Z9	7897 Z9	[illegible]	—	9897 Z9
Single Side	Single Density	Hard (10) Sector	MD540-10	[illegible]	801186	M41A411X	—	9896 Z9	7898 Z9	[illegible]	—	[illegible]
Single Side	Single Density	Soft (1) Sector	MD540-01	[illegible]	801184	M11A411X	—	9898 Z9	7899 Z9	7899-1 Z9	[illegible]	[illegible]
Single Side	Quad Density	Soft Sector, 96 TPI	MD577-01	—	800439	M15A211X	5011-8	9900 Z9	—	—	—	—
Dual Side	Quad Density	Soft Sector, 96 TPI	MD557-01	—	802067	M16A211X	5014-2	9904 Z9	—	—	—	[illegible]
Dual Side	Double Density	Hard (16) Sector	MD540-16	[illegible]	801185	M54A411X	5009-2	9891 Z9	7907 Z9	—	—	—
Dual Side	Double Density	Hard (10) Sector	MD540-10	[illegible]	801186	M44A411X	5024-1	—	7908 Z9	—	—	—
Dual Side	Double Density	Soft (1) Sector	MD550-01	[illegible]	802060	M14A411X	5008-4	9890 Z9	7909 Z9	—	[illegible]	[illegible]
Single Side	Double Density	16 Sector	MD525-16	[illegible]	801188	M53A411X	5006-8	9897 Z9	7901 Z9	—	—	9897 Z9
Single Side	Double Density	10 Sector	MD525-10	[illegible]	801014	M43A411X	5005-0	9896 Z9	7902 Z9	—	—	[illegible]
Single Side	Double Density	Soft Sector	MD525-01	[illegible]	801187	M13A411X	5004-3	9898 Z9	7903 Z9	—	—	[illegible]

8" Flexible Disks—Media Manufacturers' Cross Reference

Recording Sides	Density	Sectoring	Format	Verbatim (Manufacturer's Disk #'s)	Memorex	Dysan	Wabash	3M	Inmac Plus (Inmac Order #)	Inmac Standard	Inmac Standard Bulk	Encore	3M
Single Side	Single Density	Soft Sector	IBM 2305830	FD34-1000	[illegible]	800501	F111111X	4989-6	9886 Z9	7870 Z9	7870-1 Z9	[illegible]	[illegible]
Single Side	Single Density	Hard (32) Sector	Unformatted	FD32-1000	[illegible]	800618	F31A411X	4993-8	9887 Z9	7890 Z9	7890-1 Z9	—	[illegible]
Dual Side	Single Density	Soft Sector	IBM 2736700	FD10-4026	—	800814	F12211X	—	9865 Z9	7856 Z9	7856-1 Z9	—	[illegible]
Single Side	Double Density	Soft Sector	Unformatted	FD34-8000	[illegible]	800528	F13A211X	4995-3	9886 Z9	7857 Z9	[illegible]	[illegible]	[illegible]
Dual Side	Double Density	Soft Sector	IBM 1766870	DD34-4026	[illegible]	800814	F144111X	4998-7	9865 Z9	7858 Z9	7858-1 Z9	—	[illegible]
Dual Side	Double Density	Soft Sector	IBM 1669045	DD34-4008	[illegible]	800809	F147111X	—	9865 Z9	7859 Z9	7859-1 Z9	—	[illegible]
Dual Side	Double Density	Soft Sector	Unformatted	DD34-4001	[illegible]	800803	F14A211X	4998-7	9865 Z9	7865 Z9	7865-1 Z9	—	[illegible]
Dual Side	Double Density	Hard (32) Sector	Unformatted	DD32-4000	[illegible]	800806	F34A411X	5003-5	—	7881 Z9	7881-1 Z9	—	[illegible]
Single Side	Double Density	Hard (32) Sector	Unformatted	FD32-8000	[illegible]	800505	F33A411X	4997-9	9887 Z9	7887 Z9	7887-1 Z9	—	[illegible]
Single Side	Single Density	Soft Sector	IBM 1669954	FD60-1000	[illegible]	800509	F113111X	—	9886 Z9	7889 Z9	7889-1 Z9	—	—
Single Side	Single Density	Hard (32) Sector	Memorex Type	FD65-1000	[illegible]	800507	F61A111X	4893-8	—	[illegible]	[illegible]	—	[illegible]
CPT 6000, 8000				Specially Formatted Disk. See 8" Cross Reference on page 29				—	—	7940 Z9	—	—	—
AM International, AMtext 425				Specially Formatted Disk. See 8" Cross Reference on page 29				—	—	7844 Z9	—	—	—
Micom 2000				Specially Formatted Disk. See 8" Cross Reference on page 29				—	—	7846 Z9	—	—	—
*Single Side	Single Density	Soft Sector	IBM 2305830	FD34-2000	—	—	F13I211X	—	9886 Z9	7886 Z9	7886-1 Z9	—	—
*Single Side	Single Density	Hard (32) Sector	Unformatted	FD32-9000	—	—	F33A411X	—	9887 Z9	7888 Z9	7888-1 Z9	—	—
Reversible	Single Density	Soft Sector	IBM 2305830	FF34-9000	[illegible]	800814	F171111X	4992-6	—	7860 Z9	7860-1 Z9	—	8860 Z9
Reversible	Single Density	Hard (32) Sector	Unformatted	FF32-2000	—	—	F37A411X	—	—	7880 Z9	7880-1 Z9	—	[illegible]

*Critically Tested (Please note: All Inmac Plus disks are critically tested.)

(Fig 10.1) Ad for Michael's floppy disc order that upset The People Down South

25
Flexible Disks & Accessories

...or buy them in bulk & save 20%!

Now you can save up to 20% by buying your Inmac Standard Disks in bulk—without Tyvek® envelopes or filing boxes.

You get the same high-quality disks described on the opposite page... the same guaranteed 100% read/write accuracy.

Choose bulk packaging if you have a floppy filing system that doesn't require cardboard boxes. They're also ideal for extremely high-volume applications such as software distribution or nightly backup of your computer system.

Calculate how many disks you'll need over the next 6 to 12 months. Buying in bulk could save you plenty.

½ PRICE SALE ON ENVELOPES!

Fifty 8" Flexible disk Tyvek® envelopes. No. 7920Z9 (Reg. $19/pkg.) **Now $9.50**

Fifty 5¼" Flexible disk Tyvek® envelopes. No. 7921Z9 (Reg. $15/pkg.) **Now $7.50**

Bulk-pack Inmac Standard Diskettes are shipped in sealed, shrink-wrap packages.

See our Cross Reference & Compatibility Guides on pages 27–29.

Inmac Standard 5¼" Flexible Disk Pricing in Bulk

Inmac Order #	Recording Sides	Density	Sectoring	Price Per Disk (Units of 20) 20	40-100	120-200*
7897-1Z9	Single Side	Single Density	16 Hard Sector	$2.60	$2.35	$2.10
7898-1Z9	Single Side	Single Density	10 Hard Sector	$2.60	$2.35	$2.10
7899-1Z9	Single Side	Single Density	Soft Sector	$2.60	$2.35	$2.10

Inmac Standard 8" Flexible Disk Pricing in Bulk

Inmac Order #	Recording Sides	Density	Sectoring	Format	Price Per Disk (Units of 20) 20	40-100	120-200*
7870-1Z9	Single Side	Single Density	Soft Sector	IBM 2305830	$2.90	$2.60	$2.35
7889-1Z9	Single Side	Single Density	Soft Sector	IBM 1669954	$1.45	...Half Price Sale!	
7890-1Z9	Single Side	Single Density	Hard Sector	Unformatted	$2.90	$2.60	$2.35
7910-1Z9	Single Side	Single Density	Hard Sector	Memorex Type	$5.30	$4.80	$4.30
7857-1Z9	Single Side	Double Density	Soft Sector	Unformatted	$3.75	$3.40	$2.95
7887-1Z9	Single Side	Double Density	Hard Sector	Unformatted	$1.85	Half Price Sale!	
7856-1Z9	Dual Side	Single Density	Soft Sector	IBM 2736700	$1.95	Half Price Sale!	
7865-1Z9	Dual Side	Double Density	Soft Sector	Unformatted	$4.15	$3.75	$3.35
7858-1Z9	Dual Side	Double Density	Soft Sector	IBM 1766872	$4.15	$3.75	$3.35
7859-1Z9	Dual Side	Double Density	Soft Sector	IBM 1669045	$4.15	$3.75	$3.35
7881-1Z9	Dual Side	Double Density	Hard Sector	Unformatted	$1.95	...Half Price Sale!	
Reversible Disks							
7860-1Z9	Reversible	Single Density	Soft Sector	IBM 2305830	$4.15	$3.75	$3.35
7880-1Z9	Reversible	Single Density	Hard Sector	Unformatted	$1.95	...Half Price Sale!	
Critically Tested Disks							
7886-1Z9	Single Side	Single Density	Soft Sector	IBM 2305830	$3.75	$3.35	$3.05
7888-1Z9	Single Side	Single Density	Hard Sector	Unformatted	$3.75	$3.35	$3.05

*Higher quantity discounts are available.

Our bulk-packed Inmac Standard Disks can save you a bundle. Use them for software distribution or computer backup.

System courtesy of Computer Automation.

Prefer 3M disks? Get 'em fast!

Here are three good reasons to buy your 3M disks from Inmac:

We ship in 24 hours. No other source delivers them faster!

You get our 45-day trial guarantee. Just to make sure these disks live up to *your* expectations... as well as ours!

You get 3M reliability. 3M's durable lubrication makes these disks 32% less abrasive than the average floppy. You get reduced head wear, fewer errors and 100% accurate performance that's guaranteed for a full year!

We have a wide range of 3M disks now in stock for immediate delivery.

3M 5¼" Flexible Disk Pricing

Inmac Order #	Recording Sides	Density	Sectoring	Price Per Disk (Units of 10) 10	20-50	60-100**
8897Z9	Single Side	Double Density	16 Sector*	4.25	3.85	3.45
8898Z9	Single Side	Double Density	10 Sector*	4.25	3.85	3.45
8899Z9	Single Side	Double Density	Soft Sector*	4.25	3.85	3.45
8909Z9	Dual Side	Double Density	Soft Sector	5.60	5.05	4.55
8904Z9	Dual Side	Quad Density	Soft Sector, 96 TPI	6.50	5.85	5.30

3M 8" Flexible Disk Pricing

Inmac Order #	Recording Sides	Density	Sectoring	Format	Price Per Disk (Units of 10) 10	20-50	60-100**
8870Z9	Single Side	Single Density	Soft Sector	IBM Format 2305830	4.50	4.05	3.65
8890Z9	Single Side	Single Density	32 Hard Sector	Unformatted	4.50	4.05	3.65
8910Z9	Single Side	Single Density	Hard Sector	Memorex Type	7.25	6.55	5.90
8911Z9	Single Side	Single Density	Hard Sector	Wang	4.40	3.95	3.55
8888Z9	Single Side	Double Density	Soft Sector	RX02 format*	5.95	5.35	4.80
8857Z9	Single Side	Double Density	Soft Sector	Unformatted*	5.95	5.35	4.80
8887Z9	Single Side	Double Density	32 Hard Sector	Unformatted*	6.15	5.55	4.95
8856Z9	Dual Side	Single Density	Soft Sector	IBM Format 2736700	6.40	5.75	5.20
8858Z9	Dual Side	Double Density	Soft Sector	IBM Format 1766872*	6.40	5.75	5.20
8859Z9	Dual Side	Double Density	8 Soft Sector	IBM Format 1669045*	6.40	5.75	5.20
8865Z9	Dual Side	Double Density	Soft Sector	Unformatted*	6.40	5.75	5.20
8881Z9	Dual Side	Double Density	32 Hard Sector	Unformatted*	6.40	5.75	5.20
8860Z9	Reversible	Single Density	26 Soft Sector	IBM Format 2305830	6.40	5.75	5.20
8880Z9	Reversible	Single Density	32 Hard Sector	Unformatted	6.40	5.75	5.20

*This disk is double density, and can be used on all single density drives.

**Higher quantity discounts available.

(Fig 10.2) Page 2 of same floppy disc order

Chapter 11
Let It Bleed

Why did this guy decide to open a vein and bleed his life all over me? That almost, but not quite, killed my appetite.

***

Monday, July 9, 1984

Into the shower to scrub away today's accumulation of abrasive roof grime, and then to the mirror for a quick shave before slipping into clothes more suited for summer in the city: jeans and a red T-shirt. I got home from work at 4:35 p.m. I had to be downtown in a hurry to meet Bolochine at six. After a shower and shave the phone in the front room rang. Only two people called on that phone: the one who'd be waiting for me at Broadway and 86th, and the other guy who was supposed to be back in the U.S.S.R. on "holiday."

I picked up, hoping it wasn't Bolochine calling to cancel.

"Hello, John. Is Michael. Is it OK if I stop by your place in 40 minutes?"

"Thought you were… Never mind. I gotta business appointment. Gotta get out by 5:30."

"I shall try not to inconvenience you. Bye." *Click.*

Out of the T-shirt and jeans and into tan slacks, a blue short-sleeve dress shirt and red tie. I wanted to see how Michael reacted when he met Libraryman again.

Michael arrived at 5:10, huffing and puffing, like he ran all the way. “May I have a drink of water, please?” he gasped. When I returned from the kitchen, his hairy eyeball was checking out my ensemble. I’d told him the first time we’d met that would be the last time he’d ever seen me in a shirt and tie. Things change.

“You look very nice, John.” Then he pulled a clipping that described a patent out of his wallet. He handed it to me. “Can you have this for me by Friday?”

It was a British patent for an additive to aviation fuel called Avgard. Avgard reduced the tendency of aviation fuel to mist. That made it safer to handle and less likely to explode when undergoing shock; definitely dual use, both military and civilian.

“I am willing to pay one hundred-fifty bucks commission,” he said.

I figured the patent would cost me no more than twenty. Made for a nice profit, so I assured Michael he’d have it by Friday.

The next day, I called Pat and told him about Michael’s surprise visit.

“That’s interesting,” was all he had to say.

Then I phoned a company in Washington D.C. that specialized in retrieving patents from the Library of Congress. They assured me I’d have it by Friday — or Saturday the latest. I would’ve ordered a copy for the FBI, too, but Pat had specifically informed me, “That will not be necessary.” So much for approval from Washington. I was beginning to think those assholes were full of shit. I’d soon find out that the extent of the Bureau’s mass constipation would be truly astonishing.

When I got to the corner of Broadway and 86th, I saw Bolochine waiting. He asked if I felt like eating Chinese food. I said, yes, so we started walking uptown to a place on W. 90th. Along the way we passed a woman politicking for Walter Mondale for President. 1984 was an election year.

"Are you gentlemen registered Democrats?" she asked.

"I am. Don't know about my friend here." I turned and shot Bolochine a playful squint. "Are you a registered Democrat, Val?"

He suppressed a grin and shook his head, no.

"Well I'm gonna vote for Mondale," I told the woman. "As for my friend here, I'll do my best to win him over to our side."

When we were safely out of her earshot, Bolochine asked, "You are a supporter of Mr. Mondale?"

"Yes. Anybody's better than Reagan. He's a bit hard-assed when it comes to your country. And your country is a bit hard-assed, too."

"He calls us evil. Is to be expected, no?" His tone was tinted with a bit of a snarl.

A conversation that began in the street picked up again in the restaurant. "I am currently working on nuclear proliferation at United Nations. You will be surprised, John, how closely our two governments work in this area." He lectured that our nations had large nuclear arsenals and only we knew the consequences of their use. He said he doubted that we would ever use nuclear weapons on each other, "But there are other nations, India, Israel, South Africa, for example. It would be very bad if they, too, had nuclear weapons."

I agreed, adding Pakistan and Iraq (Soviet client-states at the time) to the list.

While we waited for our food to arrive — two orders of spareribs and fried rice — he handed me a slip of paper to copy. "I would like you to search this new topic: automation in coal mining. I would like it to cost fifty bucks, but I am prepared to pay more if necessary."

I glanced at the long list of keywords. "Be prepared."

He shrugged. "Is no problem, I spoke with friends at Institute. They seem interested."

I'm sure they are.

I gave him the superficial computer search I'd done on electric insulating materials on power lines. He glanced at the printout, smiled, and discreetly slid a white envelope across the table to me. The envelope contained five ten-dollar bills.

The food arrived and we dug in.

After wiping his fingers with a damp cloth, and before taking up another rib, he asked, "You are not married, John?"

Val's question hinted that I was a puzzle he needed to piece together: *John, you are young, reasonably good-looking and smart, so why don't you have a wife? Do you lack stability?*

To the KGB — and the GRU, FBI and CIA — stability was highly prized in their assets. Intelligence services constantly worry that an agent might flip out one day due to the pressure. In my case, being a controlled asset was fun. I felt no pressure. But I had to play my hand carefully: "Haven't found the right girl yet, Val. Besides, given that my financial situation is far from secure, I doubt any woman would have me. So it looks like I'll be a bachelor for a while — at least until I start making more money." I grinned. "Think you can help me with that little problem, Val."

Grinning back, "I shall try."

Figuring that I'd just put an end to it, I went back to the main course: greasy sparcribs in duck sauce.

And then, the guy playing this scene with me went silent. With no lines coming my way, I concentrated on eating, pouring more hot mustard on my fried rice. I loved hot mustard on rice, but sometimes, like now, it caused my eyes to water. A mouthful of cold water put out the fire.

"Damn, that's hot," I said.

"Has been long time since I was bachelor," Val said after wiping his mouth. He sounded like bachelorhood was not something he missed. "I have been married 14 years." A faint smile, "I met my wife at the Institute. We studied together. Eight years later, we married." And then he fell silent again. Val looked like a man who had stumbled into a secret room that held certain memories that cut like sharp objects. Not a place anyone should blindly rush into.

I averted my eyes. "That's nice," I mumbled. No way was I going to let him drag me into that room. Hey, comrade, this is business. Nothing personal allowed.

In my mind, and as far as this particular mini-drama sliced out of the Cold War was concerned, Michael, Pat and Mike existed only in the scenes we played together. The banter, barbs, quips and yuk-yuks we traded back and forth rendered them more cartoon-like than real to me. Not so Val. With a rib spanning the gap between both hands, his stare passed through me and far beyond the four walls of this restaurant. Standing alone in his secret room, what did he see? What special memories had been triggered inside him? And why did I let this happen? Me, a roofer stuck in life's sub-basement, a guy so low he had to look up just to see the bottom of the scale marked, *Those Who Really Matter in This World.* Hey, this was my movie-of-the-week! Watching Val connect with his own back story left me feeling alone and irrelevant, like a walk-on in the movie version of his life. Then a lid that I thought had been nailed down tight cracked open just enough to allow Val's images to slip into my mind like sunlight. Things I'd rather not see: two young students on the quad, walking hand in hand. Then a wedding: family, friends, lots of joy, and lots of vodka.

Cut to the future: Val being led into a trap by me! The FBI pounces: *"Spy for us, Comrade Bolochine, and we'll guarantee you more positive intelligence than you can handle. You'll be a big hit with your bosses back in Moscow. Soon you'll be a boss, too. The KGB? Don't worry, we'll protect you."*

Val was no seasoned intelligence professional. I didn't think he could handle the pressure; so I stopped there, slammed the lid back down and nailed it shut again. I wasn't in this to make friends or meet interesting people. All of us, me, Pat, Mike, Michael, and now Val, were simply the means to each other's ends. And I had to stay in character — a guy who only cared for money — because these two Russians might be comparing notes. So with a grin a bit too wide and in a voice a bit too loud, the strains of overcompensation, I said, "Fourteen years, wow! That's a long time. You're lucky, Val. You got somebody to cook for you, clean, do the laundry, and you get laid whenever you want. That's a lot better than bachelorhood, believe me."

Stare blank, I could tell Val's mind's eye was still in that special room. He pushed at a pile of fried rice around his plate with his fork.

"I'm going out with a dancer, Nanette." As I spoke the trailer of my own life story flashed across the big screen in my head: Nanette and I, holding hands. A big Italian wedding maybe, then all that comes with it: house, kids, etc. And then back to reality: "Always rehearsing, cares more about her career than she does me. Call her my Date of the Month because that's all I ever see her. Women! They give you nothing but aggravation." I wiped my fingers, and then threw down the cloth napkin.

Still staring down at his plate, "They bear children," he said in a voice so faint I could barely hear. When he looked up again, his eyes were red and glassy. "I have a son back in Russia. I love him very much."

He looked on the verge of tears. It crossed my mind to get up and get the hell out of there, forgetting all about Mr. Vladimir Bolochine. Leave him to his fate. Let the Bureau do with him as they choose, but without my help. But I didn't do that because alongside streams of conscience ran a darker, fouler tide. Self-Interest paddled alongside and reminded me:

If this guy is gonna bleed, let him do it on someone else. Why should I feel sorry for him? He entered this thing on his own. Nobody put a gun to his head. He wants what I want, a better life. He's using me like I'm using him. Shit, if I get arrested by the FBI, he'll move on to the next American! Too him, I'm a rung on a ladder to build his career.

"So, uh…" I turned away and coughed to clear a tight throat. "When will I see you again?" Rather than face him straight on, I took a sip of water and glanced at a couple of pretty girls sitting a few tables away.

That snapped him out of it. He shoved an appointment book across the table to me. At first I didn't think this was something an intelligence officer, even a co-opted one, should do. I saw that he had bracketed some dates and written the word "commission" in the right-hand margin. Only later did it occur to me:

These are his personal notes, so why are they written in English? Did he want me to see this for some reason?

We agreed to meet again on July 19th, at 6 p.m. at our usual spot, Broadway and 86th.

Outside the restaurant, we shook hands. I said, "I'd love to visit your country one day but—"

He cut me off with, "We'd love to have you." He shot me a warm smile. Obviously the guy loved his country every bit as much as me, Pat, and Mike loved ours.

I finished the thought with, "… I'm afraid of getting locked up." An inside joke because I knew I was really a spy, a spy spying on him and the U.S.S.R.

"Do you really believe we are all in jail?" The snarl in his voice rang out loud and clear this time.

"No, no, Val. You misunderstood. It was a joke."

A joke he did not appreciate. On that sour note the evening ended.

Chapter 12
And The Ear Makes Its Move

Click! *I get him coming.*

Click! *I get him going.*

Loaded the camera last night.

***

Thursday, July 12, 1984

I stood on the sidewalk at 120th and Riverside Drive, waiting, anxious to play the next scene. Behind me stood the massive Riverside Church where I occasionally attended service. I appreciated their liberal Christianity. Although not classified a cathedral, it was bigger than St. Patrick's in midtown. The church was modeled after the 13th Century Gothic *Cathedral of Chartes* in France. I always felt safe and watched over in its shadow. And I'd met Nanette at the Riverside Dance Theater.

Looking south on the Drive, I spotted a shitbox even uglier than my Dodge. Coughing, grumbling, and depleting the ozone layer, it was headed north. The car was a beat-up, light blue Ford LTD with a peeling dark blue vinyl roof. When it pulled up in front of me, I figured it for a gypsy cab. I waved it away. "*No voy.*"

Then I spotted Special Agent Mike Burns behind the wheel. When I got inside it was like jumping into a refrigerator. "This piece 'a shit has air-conditioning?"

He smiled proudly. "Sure does."

The time was now 6:55 p.m. Mike had called me at 5:05 to say he had to see me right away in regards to, "a matter of some urgency. The ground rules have changed. I have to see you tonight before you see our friend tomorrow." Then he'd asked if Michael's Avgard patent had come yet.

When I said, no, he seemed relieved.

We drove around the corner and parked. He left the A/C and engine running, allowing more greenhouse gases to escape into the atmosphere while simultaneously wasting a precious resource. Despite his steadfast refusal to tell me who he would be voting for in November, Reagan or Mondale, in my mind Special Agent Mike Berns would be indelibly stamped with the Mark of the Beast: Republican.

My guess: all of them down at #26 Fed Plaza were. I remembered reading somewhere that while CIA leaned democratic, the Bureau leaned republican. And CIA officers considered FBI agents dull police types.[1]

With his left arm resting comfortably on top of the steering wheel, Mike turned slightly in my direction and said, "If the patent comes tomorrow, we don't want you to give it to Michael. It has to be approved by the People Down South first." He added that because it was the weekend, approval from Washington wouldn't come until Monday. "So you'll have to stall him 'til then."

I checked a powerful urge to explode out of the car and slam the door. No patent for Michael meant no $150 for me.

"This is just a formality," he said, "to keep the People Down South happy."

Yeah, like their happiness meant so much to me.

1 In the 21st Century, since the FBI and CIA are on twice-impeached president Donald Trump's shit list, they're heroes to me. The times they are a-changing.

Mike squirmed in his seat like a guy sitting on his dick. More bad news: "We think it's time you told Michael about Val."

My head snapped back, and I shot him a WTF look. "You'd better explain this, Mike. And it better be good."

Apparently the Bureau finally concluded that Michael didn't know about Val. According to Mike, the FBI feared that when Michael returned home this summer he'd be called to explain why he didn't know that I was also being developed by someone else. At that point Michael would be in "a lot of hot water." (His cliché not mine.) The FBI feared that he'd be ordered to break contact with me.

Losing Michael scared me, too; especially if Val, whom I considered a dull academic type, might take his place. There went the high drama, not to mention higher payments. But still not quite convinced yet,

"Bullshit! Of course Michael knows about Val and vice versa. You guys even said so yourself. Remember?"

"We said we thought it likely that he knew, but we didn't want to jump to conclusions. Now we're sure, we're sure he doesn't know. There's very little chance that Michael's and Val's reports will cross here in New York, but back in Moscow they definitely will."

If, as Mike said, those reports crossed, then it would not be at the respective GRU and KGB Centers. The GRU and KGB would never share the most secret of top secrets: the identities of their agents. So when Michael and Val's reports did cross, it would have to be at another organ of Soviet government. Which one? How high up did this thing go on their side?

It took a while, but in August 1987, I would accidently find out. FBI Agent Mike Berns let something slip.

"Listen, Mike, I didn't tell him last time because I'd be breaking a professional confidence. That's very important in my relationship with him."

"That's all the more reason why you'll look good in his eyes. You know you're breaking a confidence, but you're doing it out of friendship. It'll increase your bond with him. You'll be saving him a lot of grief from his bosses."

"It doesn't sound right to me, Mike. What if Michael hadn't popped in so unexpectedly last Monday? Then, according to you, he'd be on the carpet right now."

"We had planned to initiate something like this in September when he got back, but his surprise visit presents a new opportunity."

None of this made sense. If, as Mike just said, they had waited until September, then Michael would've already been hauled up before a Soviet Inquisition and ordered to break contact with me.

"*New opportunity*?" I replied. "A minute ago, on the phone, you were telling me this was a crisis."

"I said urgent not crisis. Last Monday was historic because never before has someone in your position met with two Soviet intelligence officers in a professional capacity on two separate occasions on the same day. It's critical that we find out if the Soviets are employing a new technique." Then Mike laid out the plan as concocted by the People in Washington: I had to lure Michael up to my apartment without using the patent; if Michael couldn't be put off until Monday, then I had to ask him to stop by anyway. D.C. wanted me to say, *Michael, I know I'm breaking a confidence, but because we're such good friends, I have to tell you about my other client.*

Yeah right. Like Michael was really going to fall for that shit! He'd know right away that I'd been coached. Then what would he do? To me?

Mike said the Bureau wanted me to study Michael's reaction very carefully. According to their theory, Michael's jaw should drop into his lap, and his eyes should bulge out of his head. "It'll be like someone telling him that his wife's been screwing around with his best friend," Mike added, "and now she's pregnant."

A for-shit metaphor! "What! You want me to tell him that I'm screwing around with his best friend, and now I'm pregnant? Then check his reaction? I'll tell you his reaction. He's gonna throw me out the window. What do I do, take notes on the way down?"

Mike rubbed his forehead. "That's simply not the case."

Something was wrong. I truly believed that we were at risk of losing Michael. "OK, I'll tell 'im, but I'll do it my way. Frankly, your plan stinks. The arrogance of the People Down South; they sit in their safe, cushy, air-conditioned offices and make stupid rules." I put a thumb to my chest. "But it's my ass on the line. I take all the risks."

Guess Mike figured he hadn't completely won me over yet, because next came the schmaltz: "You're one of those rare individuals, John, who's able to step back and take a broader view. Most people tend to focus very narrowly. You're a bright guy. You can do this. Pat and I like working with you. We believe in you."

Sounded good, but then con jobs are supposed to.

"So what do you think he'll do after I tell him?"

"He'll tell you to break contact with Val." Mike sounded so damn sure he almost had me convinced.

Now seemed like the right time to drop a couple of bombs right in this guy's lap. "Know what I think, Mike? I think this approval stuff is a lotta crap. It's just another lie to control me."

Mike looked offended. "When have I ever lied to you?"

"I'm not talking about you individually; I'm referring to the collective you, the Bureau."

"When has the Bureau ever lied to you?"

"Plenty, and not only do you guys lie to me, but you think I'm stupid." I explained how it pissed me off when Pat showed me half a photo of Val. "That after he (Pat) promises me, 'We won't be anywhere near you.' Yeah, right. So you guys were a couple of hundred feet away."

"That picture was taken near their embassy. There's scaffolding there too. I can assure you, you weren't in that photograph."

"OK, what about that FARA bullshit. I've known all along about FARA." I told him about my discussion with the lawyer from Justice. "So your credibility is a bit suspect, if you catch my drift."

Mike look offended. He rpeated, "Well, I've never lied to you."

"Makes no difference, you work for the Bureau, and if I can't trust them, why should I trust you?"

"It's true that we use FARA as an instrument of control," he admitted, a bit too easily to suit me. "Although you were told that this is strictly an FBI operation, that's not entirely true. Certain counterintelligence operations, like the one we're running now, are funded and directed by the (Central Intelligence) Agency. They like us to use FARA on people like you for purposes of control." He was speaking about COURTSHIP, a program whose very existence would remain secret for a long time.

Mike continued, "Sometimes operations like this one generate a certain amount of positive intelligence. Years from now analysts will sit down, look at what's happened here, and make certain judgments. Analytically, this presents a rare opportunity to see which group takes pre-eminence, the GRU or the KGB."

That hooked my ass. Michael Berns, a fisher of men. As to whether or not I'd give Michael the patent, my only commitment to the Bureau was, "I'll play it by ear."

***

And the next day, Friday, July 13th, my ear told me, *If the patent comes today, Michael gets it.*

As for the FBI's *Michael, I've Got a Secret to Share* plan — worthless! I needed to come up with one of my own. Friday the 13th had always been my lucky day. I could only hope the streak continued. Dom was on his honeymoon, which meant it would be Bob, the helper, and me to finish a roof; more pressure, not what I needed.

Sixteen years I'd been banging out roofs, hard work and boring too. Slap a shingle down, nail it, and then slap down another — on and on and on and on for sixteen years. The only good thing about roofing was it cleared my mind while the body ran on autopilot, free to concentrate on other things. Like how to get Michael to my apartment just in case the patent didn't come; and, moreover, how to betray Val without it looking like a betrayal.

It took me a whole day of banging in the heat to finally figure out what to do: I wouldn't betray Val, he would betray himself. And it didn't take long after that to figure out a way to lure Michael up to my apartment. If the patent didn't come, I'd make a simple request: *Before you go home this summer, Michael, would you please be so kind and stop by and return my duffle bag? I really need it.*

If he was as anxious to please as Mike said, no way would he refuse. If he did, I'd just whine a lot.

Friday was payday, but I didn't even bother to pick up the cash. I jumped in my car, turned the ignition, and the next thing I knew, I'd parked in the garage. It was around 4 p.m. Then I immediately ran to the Post Office.

No patent. Good. Now to enact the *Duffle Bag Plan.*

***

RRRINGGG!

It's Michael asking about the patent.

I lie, "Haven't checked my post office box yet." I'm stalling. I don't want him showing up in five minutes. No way am I going to miss this time with my camera. Bought the film yesterday.

"Would you be so kind to go look," he says. He sounds annoyed.

"OK. Call back in 20 minutes."

Back to the Post Office just to make it look good in case someone is watching.

At 4:55 the phone rings again.

"It's not there Michael. By the way, I was wondering if—"

"Is OK. I will be over in fifteen, twenty minutes. Bye." *Click.*

Shit! He cheated me. A good plan gone to waste. Fuck, fuck, fuck!

At the kitchen window. Sitting on the stove. Camera ready. Loaded it last night. Sweat's running into my eyes, dripping off my nose. Heat, nerves, whatever.

Then I spot Michael. *Click* — I get him coming.

He's at the door panting. His tongue is hanging out. Bit heavy on the theatrics. He's a lousy actor. He asks for water. Drops his jacket on the sofa. Sits. Odd, he's not talking. Never is Michael not talking. His seated posture is aggressive: on the edge of the sofa, hands clasped, hanging between his legs. The grizzly bear is giving me a good look at his massive arms and shoulders. His eyes follow me. I feel like a bunny rabbit about to be squished.

"Fucking boiler is busted again, got no hot water. Gotta date with Nanette tonight."

After heating it on the stove, I lug a pot of hot water from the kitchen to the bathroom, and then dump it into the tub. I poke my head out the bathroom. "I told you about her, didn't I? The dancer who's always rehearsing. Well, she ain't rehearsing tonight." I shoot him a sly grin, then, "I apologize for having to wash up like this, but I gotta meet her at 7:15."

He waves a hand. "Not to worry." He leers. "I wish you good luck this evening."

"Thanks. I'll need it."

He's staring. Me, I'm babbling about Nanette, the boiler. I hear the monotony in my voice, like I'm forcing it. I change the subject: "Ya know, Michael, I wanted to ask you a favor," I call from the kitchen. Why waste a good plan? And besides, I really need the damn thing. "Think you can bring me my duffle bag back before you go home?"

"What bag?"

I rush into the living room. "What do you mean what bag?" I don't want to hear that he left my father's WW II duffle bag back at his fucking embassy!

He grins. Pulls something out of his briefcase. "Is this what you mean?" He hands me the bag. "I know how attached you are, so I made special effort to return it before I go on holiday."

Great minds think alike.

"Thanks, Michael. You scared the shit outta me. Thought you lost it."

I'm done dumping pots of hot water into the tub for washing up. He's still on the sofa, not talking. Looks like I got to make the first move. I sit down next to him: time to put the Val Plan into action. This is it, the big moment I've been rehearsing in my head all day.

"I was wondering about something, Michael… Did you happen to mention me to any of your colleagues at the U.N.?"

Calmly, "No, why do you ask?"

"Well, there's this guy I'm doing business with… A Russian… He works at the U.N. Sure you haven't said anything?"

Michael's eyeballs do not pop out of his head and roll around on the floor. His jaw is exactly where it should be: firmly attached to the bottom of his skull.

"Quite sure," he says.

I can feel his eyes bore into me. Better not fuck up now: "That's good because to tell you the truth, this guy's been giving me these scrappy little orders — and paying me shit! He promises and promises, but doesn't deliver. I was gonna tell him that if he doesn't start giving me bigger orders, he can take a hike. But I was afraid that he might be a friend of yours. I didn't want to offend *you*, know what I mean?"

Michael shrugs. "Your relationship with this other individual is no concern of mine."

So far so good: "So… If I drop this guy you won't be mad?"

"Of course not." He stands like he's ready to leave. "John, I am not going to tell you how to run your business. You may drop him or keep him as you wish. I can assure you that it will not affect our relationship."

I let out a sigh like I'm relieved. "Glad to hear that." *Damn. I should become an actor when all of this is over.*

"Was this the gentleman we had discussed earlier — the engineer?"

"Not engineer, chemist."

"Ah, yes, now I remember." His acting ability, mediocre at best.

Michael picks up his jacket and briefcase, getting ready to take his leave. His back is to me. Casually, "What is his name? Perhaps I know him."

I'm ready for this. Have an answer rehearsed and ready to go: "I can't say. He specifically told me not to say anything because he doesn't want his colleagues at work to know. While he's still my customer, I gotta respect his privacy."

Michael turns and grins. "But of course, you are like priest." He moves towards the door. He stops. "What does he look like?"

I grin. "Like a Russian. As a matter of fact, he looks a little like you. Like you guys are cousins or something. But you're much better looking. This guy's bald."

"Poor chap."

A concession to the People Down South: "Since we're such good friends, Michael, I'll tell you his first name. But you must keep this in the strictest confidence. It's Val, short for Vladimir."

"It seems to me that if you want to drop him, you should go ahead. I will give you plenty of big orders, John. You should not waste your time with him. But I am not telling you what to do. I am not telling you how to run your business, ya?"

Out of *friendship*, I throw him one last clue: "I'll be meeting him again next Thursday. That's when I lay it on the line for this guy."

I don't tell Michael the time and place, though; let's see how good he is at figuring it out.

Michael's left hand is on the knob. He says he will call me again next Wednesday, July 18th, to see if the patent has come. That's the day before I'm scheduled to meet Val. Then he leaves.

At the window again — *Click* — I get him going.

I continue to watch from the kitchen window. He casually flips his jacket over his shoulder. The guy looks like he hasn't a care in the world.

Later on the phone I tell Berns, "I think our friend was fishing."

"If he was, then he got what he came for."

Yeah, like no shit.

It all comes down to next Thursday, July 19, 1984. Will Vladimir Bolochine keep our meeting? And what about Wednesday, July 18th, how hot is Michael for that patent? Will he call? By Friday, July 20th, I'm going to know a hell of a lot more about where this thing is going than I do now.

(Fig 12.1) Top Left: My kitchen window with orange curtain & window fan

Chapter 13
Pavlov's Dog

Which Russian bear was coming back to me in the fall? The grizzly or the teddy?

***

A murky stream twisted and turned through the back waters of my mind in the summer of 1984. Serious doubts broke its surface like boulders impeding its steady flow. How was it going for my boy back in the U.S.S.R.? Was he tanning on a beach at a dacha on the Black Sea? Or was he at an unknown location in Moscow being grilled by an unknown organ of Soviet government?

"Tell us Comrade Katkov, this business with Comrade Bolochine has us confused. Would you be so kind, please clarify. Afghanistan is so lovely this time of year."

In mid-September, I called the FBI and asked for Pat.

"Pat's been reassigned to a special project. He's no longer on your case," the guy who answered the phone said. When my new case officer, Mike Berns, came on the line, I asked him what had happened. He said that Pat was a licensed pilot. The Bureau had few agents with that particular skillset and he was needed elsewhere. Later I read that navy spy John Walker had been under aerial surveillance, so I'd bet one of those eyes in the sky must have been Pat McKinney.

Near the end of September, the waters of that stream began to flow more clear and rapid. The big rocks that had been impeding its flow had been eroded to sand pebbles; because the more I thought about

Michael's body language back on that Friday the Thirteenth in July — the way he'd casually flipped his jacket over his shoulder and walked away with relaxed strides — convinced me he knew he would prevail over Comrade Bolochine. He'd be the one coming back. He came for information and, like Mike had said, he got what he came for.

On Friday, September 28th, Mike called to say "our friend" was back in town. He also relayed the latest plan from the People Down South: the Bureau wanted me to question Michael about Val. "It's a legitimate business question at this point," Mike said, "so it has to be asked now. Wait and see if he brings it up first. If he doesn't, then you'll have to."

"No problem. Val still owes me sixty dollars. So what do you guys think Michael's gonna say?"

"We're not sure, but we think it'll be a sore subject."

When I asked what the Bureau thought Michael would do about Val's debt, he said, "Probably offer to pay it."

"What do you think happened to Val?" I asked.

"He continues to be active," was all Mike had to say. That meant that Comrade Bolochine was still in their crosshairs. Poor bastard, but at least he was not a weight pressing down on my conscience anymore.

Good bye, good luck, comrade.

Three days later, on Tuesday, October 2nd, Michael breezed into my "flat" looking like a proper English gentleman. He was nattily attired in a well-tailored gray, pin-striped suit, dark topcoat, and English flap cap, or whatever that thing was called.[1] He handed me his cap and coat as a master would to a servant; very British. I let

1 It's called a herringbone flat wool Gatsby cabbie cap — thank you Amazon.

that slap to my class consciousness walk on by because I was so damn happy to see him. So instead of dropping them on the floor, I deposited both on top of the laundry wagon in the foyer.

My playful mood continued; as he was about to take his customary seat on the couch, I nailed him with: "And what special gift did you bring me back from Russia?" I shot him a big smile.

For a split second he froze, suspended in mid-air; then gravity took hold and he plopped backwards onto the sofa.

"Easy, Michael, the springs are weak."

After much wailing, gnashing of teeth and promising that, "I will bring you some very fine liquor next time," he smiled, thinking this would appease me.

When I replied, "I don't drink, remember?" he blinked.

I sat down next to him on the sofa. He rummaged through his wallet looking for something. I leaned closer and peeked. "Not much money in there, Michael. How are you gonna pay me?" I gave him an earnest look. Then he smirked. Then I grinned.

I spotted a *Mobil* credit card. "Hey, credit cards. So you got 'em too. You're just like us."

Merely an observation, no offense intended. But my socialist friend took it the wrong way. "What do you mean, just like you? We are all human. I merely use it for fuel."

Sometimes this guy made about as much sense to me as I did to him, which I suppose meant no sense at all.

"By the way, Michael, I got that patent you wanted so bad last summer, it came the next day. How come you didn't call back?"

He mumbled something about being "very busy"; then he removed a slip of paper from his wallet, an advertisement for a document called *The Directory of Persons Interested in Technology Transfer.* He handed it to me. "I will pay you fifty bucks for it, but you will keep it for reference purposes, yah?"

Not hard to figure what he had in mind: a directory for potential GRU targets. If he wanted me to be the conduit through which the GRU contacted these people, I'd yes him to death, then not do it.

From his shirt pocket he pulled out a 2" x 6" strip listing 16 reference books. It looked like a photocopy of a tiny section from *Books in Print.* (BIP was a bibliographic source that lists all books still in print in a particular year.) Something wasn't quite right, though. The boldface heading read, "Underwater Archeology." But the recurrent theme running through all the titles listed was underwater acoustics, as in sonar. Something else I thought odd: a large space between the heading and the first title. BIP would never insert empty lines like that, it's too expensive. The list had been composed, and the Russians had deliberately pasted-up the heading underwater archeology over books dealing with sonar. I knew that secrecy and distrust were endemic in Soviet society, but this seemed to raise it to a new level of absurdity.

Michael said, "It seems to me that you will maximize your profits if you merely borrow these books from the library and photocopy them."

More copyright infringement meant that Mr. Katkov thought it necessary to shave another layer off the coating that protected my moral fiber. That was *not* necessary. When it came to the Katkov Affair there was almost nothing I wouldn't do in the name of national security — except involve innocent Americans. Regardless, he was simply following SOP. Soviet intelligence officers were trained not to task their agents to do more than the agent's conscience would allow. Their job was to expand an agent's conscience gradually, such that an agent would do as the intelligence officer wanted, no questions asked.[2]

From his inside jacket pocket out came another list. At the bottom someone had written the word, "Thiokol." He said that I should use this keyword in a database search.

"What's Thiokol?" I asked.

"I believe is the name of company."

Later, I learned that the Morton J. Thiokol Corp. made booster rockets for the space shuttle.

Michael wasn't quite finished producing lists. Like a magician, he pulled yet another one from somewhere on his person. Made me wonder where he'd hidden the rabbit.

"These are my only copies," he said, handing me several long strips of paper. "I need them for reference. You may keep them for the time being, but you must return them when you are finished." He waved a finger at me. "You must not lose them, John."

Such important material merited closer examination. It looked as if someone had lined up individual 3" x 5" cards one on top of the other, photocopied the cards in long strips. How large was the pie this piece had been cut from? The cards were all handwritten in script lettering, and each contained a citation for an individual document. The documents were all unclassified government sponsored research and were available from the National Technical Information Service (NTIS) in Washington D.C.

Michael said, "I suggest that you try to locate them in a local

2 Copeland, Miles, Without Cloak and Dagger, c1974, p. 21

library. Columbia University may have these materials. You can make photocopies. Is better this way, yah?" Then he asked if I still had the listing of the floppy disks order he had given me last July, the same listing that had given the People Down South gas because I'd turned over the disks to Michael.

I went into the front room and checked where I kept his orders. "You're lucky, Michael. Found it," I called from the other room. "Haven't thrown it out yet."

"May I have it please," he called back. "I need it for my records."

I was happy to oblige. Interesting, though, because Val, a novice compared to Michael, never let me keep his lists. Did Comrade Katkov get a demerit for sloppy work back in Moscow?

Time was running out, it seemed to me that Michael would be leaving soon. Val had to be slipped into the conversation, but in such a way as to appear to be a logical progression from points A to B to Val. Not to worry, though, because Michael was about to lead the way. He leaned back, clasped his hands behind his head and smiled. "So how is business? Have you made any new contacts?"

I shook my head. "No. Business has been slow since you left town."

He stared for a moment, and then he leaned forward in a more aggressive posture. "Are you sure? Is there anything you want to tell me?"

I scratched the three days growth on the right side of my face pretending to give the matter serious thought. "Hmm… Don't think so."

Michael started to blink again. "What about that other fellow? You remember him." He paused to rub his forehead as if trying hard to conjure up an image, an image that I suspect had already been burned onto his CRT. "The engineer, that Russian chap, what is his name?"

"Oh yeah, *him.* That reminds me. There's something I wanna ask you about that asshole Val." I launched off the sofa like I had a Thiokol booster up my ass. I headed for the front room.

I returned with Val's computer search and handed it to Michael. The poor guy was about to have his gutters flushed by a torrent of obscenities: "That fucking, scumbag, motherfucker, know what that prick did? Stood me up! Orders this fucking search, says he's gonna meet me on July 19th at six, and never shows up. Never calls or nothing. Disappears, and I'm out sixty dollars — like I can really afford to lose that kind of money, right? Don't know why I ever bothered with the cheap bastard in the first place. How'd a shit like him ever get a job at the U.N. anyway?"

Michael looked lost, his head bobbing up and down like a rubber ball being carried in fast flowing sewage. Then I pooled my words into something more placid so he'd understand: "Michael, I was wondering if you could do me a favor?" I sat down next to him again. "Since you're both Russian, and you both work at the U.N., could you please find this guy for me and remind him that he owes me sixty dollars. His name is Vladimir Bol-Chine."

"I do not know him," he replied gruffly. "He is not with my group." He handed Val's search back to me. "We have many people working for us at United Nations. I am sorry, but I cannot help you."

Score one for the Bureau: Val *was* a sore spot. And Michael gave every indication that this matter did *not* concern him.

Tough shit! I'd make it his concern. "Guess I'll have to try something on my own, then."

That drew Mr. Katkov's attention. "What you will do?" Outwardly Michael showed no signs of alarm. But he had to be thinking: *What if this moodak does something stupid.* "John, it seems to me that because of our friendship, it will be better if I pay you for the search and you forget about the matter entirely, letting it drop altogether," he said, making washing motions with his hands.

Scored again! The FBI had been right twice on the same day, but so was a stopped clock. I was not impressed.

He removed three twenty-dollar bills from his wallet and casually asked, "How do you know his name?"

"Because he told me."

"Are you sure?" He looked at me as if I was hiding something. "Why did he tell you his name?"

Annoyed, "Because in America, when you do business with somebody it's customary to get their name. By the way, Michael, I'm not too sure about yours. What kind of a name is Ketco?" I had to somehow weasel his real name out of him just in case I ever slipped one day and called him Katkov.

"Is old Russian name," he mumbled, "so tell me, John, you always say that you keep your customers confidential." He pointed at his chest, "Including me." Then a challenging, "So why are you telling me his name now?"

A challenge easily met: "Because I wanted your help getting my money."

"But what of your oath? You told me, 'Michael, I am like priest, I say nothing.'"

"I *do* protect my customer's identity, but since this guy isn't my customer anymore, fuck 'im. And that priest stuff was a bad analogy anyway. I enjoy making sex with the ladies."

Michael laughed. "John, you have an insidious nature."

"Thanks, Michael. I take that as a compliment."

DIRECTORY OF PERSONS INTERESTED IN TECHNOLOGY TRANSFER

Contact: School of Business, University of California, Sacramento, CA 95819/ 916-454-6640

Contents: The Directory is a listing of more than 2,000 scientists, engineers, technicians, professionals, managers, etc., interested in technology transfer. Everyone included has agreed to respond to telephone calls concerning a technical question related to their area of expertise. More than 200 areas—ranging from acoustics to X-rays—are covered. The data base can be searched by geographical location or field of expertise.

Elements: The data base contains in excess of 2,000 entries. It is updated continually.

Services: Searches and printouts are available free of charge. The university will also generate mailing lists by zip code or area of expertise. Mailing lists are not compiled for advertising purposes. The Directory is also available in hard copy.

(Fig 13.1) Technology transfer directory

UNDERWATER ARCHAEOLOGY

Albers, V. M. Underwater Acoustics, Vol. 2. LC 62-8011. 416p. 1967. 49.50 (ISBN 0-306-37562-1, Plenum Pr). Plenum Pub.
Albers, Vernon M. Underwater Acoustics Handbook. 2nd ed. LC 64-15069. (Illus.). 1965. 20.00x (ISBN 0-271-73106-0). Pa St U Pr.
Andersen, Neil R. & Zahuranec, Bernard J., eds. Oceanic Sound Scattering Prediction. LC 77-3445. (Marine Science Ser.: Vol. 5). 859p. 1977. 65.00 (ISBN 0-306-35505-1, Plenum Pr). Plenum Pub.
Barkhatov, A. N. Modeling of Sound Propagation in the Sea. LC 74-136985. 91p. 1971. 25.00 (ISBN 0-306-10855-0, Consultants). Plenum Pub.
Caruthers, J. W. Fundamentals of Marine Acoustics. (Elsevier Oceanography Ser.: Vol. 18). 1977. 39.00 (ISBN 0-444-41552-1). Elsevier.
Clay, Clarence S. & Medwin, Herman. Acoustical Oceanography: Principles & Applications. LC 77-1133. (Ocean Engineering Ser.). 1977. text ed. 35.00 (ISBN 0-471-16041-5, Pub. by Wiley-Interscience). Wiley.
Committee On Underwater Telecommunications Division Of Physical Sciences. Present & Future Civil Uses of Underwater Sound. LC 76-606666. (Illus., Orig.). 1970. pap. 4.25 (ISBN 0-309-01771-8). Natl Acad Sci.
Cox, Albert W. Sonar & Underwater Sound. LC 74-15547. (Illus.). 1975. 16.95 (ISBN 0-669-95935-9). Lexington Bks.
DeSanto, J. A., ed. Ocean Acoustics. (Topics in Current Physics: Vol. 8). (Illus.). 1979. 37.40 (ISBN 0-387-09148-3). Springer-Verlag.
Flatte, S. M., ed. Sound Transmission Through a Fluctuating Ocean. LC 77-88676. (Cambridge Monographs on Mechanics & Applied Mathematics). (Illus.). 1979. 37.50 (ISBN 0-521-21940-X). Cambridge U Pr.
Keller, J. & Papadakis, J., eds. Wave Propagation & Underwater Acoustics. (Lecture Notes in Physics Ser: Vol. 70). 1977. pap. 13.30 (ISBN 0-387-08527-0). Springer-Verlag.
Lauterborn, W., ed. Cavitation & Inhomogeneities in Underwater Acoustics: Proceedings. (Springer Ser. in Electrophysics: Vol. 4). (Illus.). 319p. 1980. 36.00 (ISBN 0-387-09939-5). Springer-Verlag.
Officer, Charles B. Introduction to the Theory of Sound Transmission. (International Ser. in Earth & Planetary Sciences). 1958. 34.50 (ISBN 0-07-047612-8, 1, P&RB). McGraw.
Tacconi, Giorgio, ed. Aspects of Signal Processing. 2 vols. LC 77-3238. (NATO Advanced Study Institute: C. Math & Phys. Sciences 33). 1977. lib. bdg. 86.85 set (ISBN 90-277-0798-7). Kluwer Boston.
Tucker, D. G. & Gazey, B. K. Applied Underwater Acoustics. 1966. 23.00 (ISBN 0-08-011817-8); pap. 14.25 (ISBN 0-08-011816-X). Pergamon.
Urick, R. J. Principles of Underwater Sound. 2nd ed. 1975. text ed. 32.50 (ISBN 0-07-066086-7, P&RB). McGraw.
Worzel, J. Lamar, et al. Propagation of Sound in the Ocean. LC 49-4933. (Memoir: No. 27). (Illus.). 1948. 7.25x (ISBN 0-8137-1027-8). Geol Soc.

(Fig 13.2) Books in Print list

Aircraft On-Board Electrochemical Breathing
Oxygen Generators.
20-54 75A40861
Harrison J.W.
ASME, SAE, AIAA, ASMA, and AIChE, Intersociety Conf
on Environmental Systems, San Francisco, Calif, Juli
21-24, 1975 ASME 9P Refs RPT No. : ASME PAPER
75-ENAS-51 9p. Members Corp. Auth – General
Electric Co, Aircraft Equipment div, Wilmington,
Mass.

Analysis of a regenerable Polyethyleneimine
carbon dioxide and Humidity control System
20-54 75A40888
Lin C.H.
ASME, SAE, AIAA, ASMA, and AIChE, Intersociety Conf
on Environmental Systems, San Francisco, Calif, Juli
21-24, 1975, ASME 6p, Refs RPT. No. : ASME PAPER
75-ENAS-16 6p. Members, Corp Auth – Lockheeds
Electronics Co, Inc., Houston, Tex.

Electrochemical Carbon Dioxide Concentrator
Subsystem Math Model Final Report.
05-54 75A14467.
Marshall R.D. Carlson J.N., Schubert F.H.
LP240680 Life Systems, Inc, Cleveland, Ohio.
CONT. No. ; NAS2-6478 RPT. No. : NASA-CR-137565
LSI-ER-220-6 AVAIL NTIS 210p. HC.

Desiccant Humidity Control System Final report,
21.01.71 – 21.01.72.
08-54 75A17097
Lunde P.J. Koster F.L.
HD 304328 Hamilton Standard div, United Aircraft
Corp, Windsor Locks, Conn. Cont No.: NAS9-11971
RPT. No. : NASA-CR-115568 SVHSER-6040
AVAIL NTIS 330p. HC

(Fig 13.3) 2" x 6" strip list

Chapter 14
Life & Death in the Heights

The elderly make easy targets for those who prey on the weak and defenseless. And there are plenty of these carnivores in the Heights; hiding, watching, waiting.

***

Monday, November 19, 1984

After an especially hard day of roofing, I dragged my tired ass into the lobby of my building. It was 3 p.m. In a bad mood and with my brain idling in low, all I wanted to do was wash up, eat, and dump my bones into bed.

Two old ladies, one Greek and the other Dominican, waited at the elevator. When they saw me, they began squawking and picking at me like hysterical chickens. I smiled politely, thinking: *Whatever it is, ladies, I don't give a rat's ass.*

Then one of them grabbed my arm and yanked. "John! You were robbed!"

A shock wave of adrenalin exploded through out my body. I leaped the stairs in single bounds like superman, praying all the way that they made a mistake. When I got to the top landing, I saw my front door partially opened. Tiny needles pricked under the skin of my face and scalp; my stomach felt like it just dropped out of my ass. I moved to the left of the front door. Fear and indecision glued my back to the wall. I listened; quiet inside. A deep breath; then I pushed the door open just wide enough for me to squeeze through. The damn thing creaked. Shit! I bent low, made a quick left and grabbed a hammer out of the toolbox that lay on the floor just outside the kitchen. I flipped it over to its claw. With two skull-cracking steel spikes in my hand, I felt a little braver. I took cover behind the archway that led into the living room and peeked inside. I saw cut wires and a big empty space in the stereo cabinet where the receiver used to be. That receiver was a replacement for the one stolen two years ago. My computer lay on its side in the middle of the floor. The TV, that piece of crap with the broken rabbit ears and a Weekee-Watchee picture quality, sat unmolested on the white table. Twice robbed, and twice they left the damn TV!

I listened: still quiet inside.

By now my pulse rate had revved up to high idle. Bet my face glowed like a red lantern, because I realized that if the person or persons who did this were still in the apartment, then their only way out was through me. And what if said person or persons had something a lot more lethal than a hammer?

The smart move would be run downstairs to my friend's apartment and call the cops.

Then it hit me, an overriding reason to get in there and defend my property rights — the papers! Every scrap of information that linked me with Michael and with the FBI lay scattered in the front room. On the odd chance that the Russians had broken in, then they'd know everything. Even if it wasn't the Russians, then whoever robbed me would also know everything. What would they do with the information? Sell my ass to the DGI (Cuban intelligence)?

Suddenly a lot more than property rights were involved: my future was at stake. If my papers were gone — primarily my irreplaceable, detailed, and copious notes — then so too was my book, my movie deal, etc.

I may as well be dead, so WTF!

My mind screamed — *Die you motherfuckers!* I raised the hammer and charged through the living room and into the front room. If anybody was there, then they'd better be heading out the window. Luckily, I saw all my papers laid out exactly where I'd left them. I slammed open the bathroom door; nobody there either. Although I'd lost some stuff, I was glad the place had not been trashed, I had my papers, and my secret was still a secret. What I didn't have any longer, though, was the charcoal gray flannel suit I'd just bought to wear to a friend's wedding. And there would be no more pictures of Michael because no more camera. The bastards even took my *Gibson Hummingbird* guitar knock-off.

I called the police. Two cops from the Three-Four came over about an hour later to make out the report I'd need for an insurance claim. I told them I'd gone to work late that morning, about ten-thirty. My next door neighbor said he saw my door open around noontime, so the burglary occurred between ten-thirty and twelve. Speaking of my good neighbors on the 6th floor, it bothered me that my door laid open for at least three hours and no one bothered to call the police. At least there hadn't been a *Help Yourself to John's Shit* parade out of my apartment.

No doubt in my mind who'd done it. I told the cops about a guy named Moe who lived in 2E. Strange people were always going in and out of his apartment at all hours of the day and night. I figured him for a dealer, one of at least four who infested the building like fucking cockroaches. That made #515, otherwise known as Manor Court (yeah right!), something of a drug mini-mall. Even if it wasn't Moe, then it had to be one of his customers.

The cops agreed that it was probably an inside job. "Usually is," one of them said. "We'll check the roof and the basement. That's where they usually hide the stuff until they can get it safely out of the building."

Unless, of course, it was in Moe's place.

The other cop mentioned how bad the neighborhood had gotten lately. "There are a lotta bad asses living right up the block from you. Be careful around here, any one of 'em might be watching your movements."

After they left I called Mike Berns. He said he'd stop by as soon as he could.

"I'll meet you downstairs." Then making light of a serious situation, I added, "Try and look mean, like cops, so when people see us together they'll know not to mess with me."

Mike chuckled. "I'll bring my partner. He's real mean. Even scares the boss."

There was a specific group that I wanted Mike and his buddy to put some fear into: *The Watch Committee.* They were a bunch of winos that clumped together like a pile of dog shit outside the bodega right next to my building. Drunk or spaced out most of the time, but they saw all, told all.

About an hour later, Mike Berns and his partner, Tom Black, greeted me in front of the building. Mike was right; this guy Tom did look tough, but not so mean. I guessed from his accent that he was from out West somewhere, maybe Texas. Tall, lean, light complexioned and balding, he reminded me of a Texas Ranger. We stood outside chatting. Mike and Tom were dressed in suits and ties. Me, I still hadn't washed up or gotten out of my roof clothes. I figured my derelict chic look would show that I was not someone to be fucked with either.

Satisfied that the Watch Committee had a good look, I led the FBI agents upstairs. I showed Mike where the lock still hung from the doorjamb. The thieves had ripped the dead bolt from the door, which wasn't too hard to do because it had been so loosely attached. Something I'd been meaning to fix for months, but, as usual, I kept putting off.

Inside, Mike scanned the scene. "Really tore the place up, huh?"

Not really. The place always looked like this. My apartment never would make *Good Housekeeping*. No need to tell him that, though. Instead: "Yeah. So, think the Russians did it?"

"No, they don't operate that way. Besides, they have no reason to."

"Do you think it's possible someone saw Michael counting out all that money in the kitchen? Even the cops said someone might be watching me."

Michael's last visit had been four days ago, on Thursday, November 15th. That night he did something odd. I told Mike and Tom: "We were sitting in the living room. I'm giving him documents. When I finish, he gets up and walks into the kitchen. I followed. He paid me $1,000. *In the kitchen.* Weird, huh?"

"It's your house. You mean he just got up and walked into the kitchen?"

"Yeah. The lights were on so anyone outside could see what we were doing inside."

I explained to Mike and Tom that Michael, after helping himself to a drink of water, squeezed his extra large self into the chair to the immediate left of the window; that put his back to the wall. No one ever sat in that chair, he had to shove the table over two feet just to fit in. “So I ask him, ‘Why are you sitting there? No one sits there.’ ‘Not even your girlfriends?’ he says. ‘No,’ I tell him. So I make him take the seat opposite where we can both be seen.”

That piqued Mike’s interest. “Then what happened?”

“He looks out the window as he’s counting out the money. He says, ‘What if your neighbors see us?’ And I tell him, ‘Don’t worry about the neighbors. They’re eating dinner.’” I let out a sigh. “Stupid me, huh?”

Tom Black said, “It’s possible that someone knows your movements.”

And Mike said, “Hey, Tommy, don’t make him anymore paranoid than he already is.”

“If that’s the case,” I said to Mr. Black, “then Michael and I are both marked men, aren’t we?”

“Not necessarily,” Mike said. “They didn’t find any money, did they? You deposited it, right?”

“So what, just because they didn’t find any money this time doesn’t mean they won’t be back. I’m also worried about our friend. This is the wrong neighborhood for a well dressed white guy to be walking around at night; especially with a lotta cash in his pocket.”

Mike smirked. “Don’t worry about him. He’s a big boy; he can take care of himself.”

No doubt. After all, not only was the Russian grizzly bear big, but he was also an ex-paratrooper (Spetsnaz).

Mike continued, “If you have no objections, we’d like to record your next meeting with Michael.”

The FBI had been asking my permission for weeks, but I’d

resisted. I didn't much like the idea of having a government listening device on the premises. The only bugs in here had six legs. But now that my privacy had already been so severely violated, I finally agreed.

Mike and Tom looked about ready to leave — I suppose they had wives and dinners to get home to — so I thanked them for coming over on such short notice. Then Mike said he'd put in a request for the Bureau to pick up the tab for some of the damage.

"Thanks anyway, but I've been meaning to fix that lock. There's no one to blame but me."

Before they left Mike told me to expect at least one more meeting in my apartment. After that our friend would move things to a more "clandestine" location; i.e. a restaurant. I wondered why Mike thought a public place would be more clandestine than my apartment. He also told me *not* to mention the burglary. "It might prompt him to move your meetings to an outside location sooner than we'd like."

I agreed not to tell Michael.

***

"Michael! I was robbed!"

So much for being a closed-mouthed spy. Despite explicit instructions from the Bureau, when Michael called on Monday, November 25th, these were my first words into the phone. I knew I should not have done it, but I was worried for his safety. I added, "Be careful out there."

I'd said it, and I'd meant it.

"Do not discuss this on the telephone. I will stop by shortly." *Click.*

Michael wasn't scheduled to come until mid-December, so why a surprise visit?

I went to the window to watch for him. If he got into trouble, I'd grab a hammer, run down there, and save his ass. Despite his size and the fact that Michael was former *Spetsnaz,* I still worried. And it had nothing to do with protecting my economic interests, either. I genuinely like the guy.

Soon I spotted his tall, lanky figure walking on the south side of 183rd. Even in the daytime, that street was bad news. But after the sun went down, it became even more hazardous to a person's health. This was the block the cops had warned me about. Michael walked stiffly, carrying a briefcase in his left hand, his right hand in the pocket of his trench coat. He stared straight ahead. Many foreigners are told that to avoid trouble in New York, one must walk briskly with confidence and not look directly at anyone. Michael must have been reading the guidebooks. In the middle of the block, he crossed to the north side. Then I watched him traverse Audubon and enter the lobby of my building. At 5:40 p.m. my doorbell *thunked.*

Michael said he had stopped by to "clarify" part of his last order. "Do you've got the list I gave you? I would like to see it please." He meant the one he'd given me on November 15th. I went into the back room and got it. He tore off the top half. "You will make a copy for yourself please, because I will take this with me. I need it for my records."

After I finished copying, and whining about doing all this writing, Michael sat back and cupped his hands behind his head. Then with a big smile, he said, "So John. How is your life?"

"Whadda you kidding or what! I was *robbed*, Michael. Last week. Someone broke into my apartment, stole my stereo receiver—"

"But, John, you are—"

"— guitar, camera, brand new charcoal—"

"That is most—"

"— gray suit, dumped my computer on the floor, and," pointing at the TV with the broken rabbit ears, "they left that fucking thing, so I can't get insurance money to buy a new one!"

"That is most unfortunate. Did you call the police?"

"Of course I called the police."

"Did they question you why you own a computer?"

"Are you serious?" The look on his face said he was, so I figured the guy needed some serious enlightenment regarding life in these here United States: "Michael, America is an open society. A lotta people own computers." I enjoyed sticking him with that one. Then, "And it's all your fault!"

His face was easy enough to read: *What the Hell Are You Talking About!* But his mouth calmly stated, "How do you mean, my fault?"

"Remember last time? Counting the money in the kitchen, by the window? Someone must have seen us. How could you be so—" The word that best applied here was stupid, but instead I said, "—careless? You should've known better. After all, you're" — a trained intelligence officer — "supposed to be smarter than me."

"If you recall," he said, sounding a bit shrill, "I warned you to be careful, but it was *you* who said not to worry. People are eating dinner."

"Yeah, but it was *you* who moved us to the kitchen in the first place." The guilt I tried to smear on Michael wouldn't stick. His Teflon coating was as thick as President Reagan's.

"You say this little episode has upset you, yet you do not seem upset," he said matter-of-factly. "Next time I come, I will compensate you for your loss."

That soothed me a little.

"So, John, how are you progressing with my latest order?" He smiled.

His smile faded when I gave him the only thing I had, the *Persons Interested in Technology Transfer Directory*. "It seems to me, John, that you are neglecting your duties," he said, wagging a finger at me. "I ordered this, when, October? Why has it taken so long?"

Because Mike Berns told me to hold it back, that there were some names that the FBI wanted to check out. Mike also mentioned that the directory was continually updated. I had a pretty good idea what the Bureau was up to: they were going to toss a chunk of meat into the big grizzly's cage; i.e. drop a name into that directory hoping Mr. Katkov would gobble it up.

Couldn't very well tell Michael any of this; instead: "Because it's free they took their sweet-ass time and sent it 4th Class. By the way, you owe me fifty for it."

"But you said it was free?"

The other Michael, the one named Berns, had bitched just as loudly when I'd given him his copy; and using the exact same words: *You said it was free*; so I told both Michaels the same thing: *It was free for me not them.*

And then I reminded this Michael, the one sitting next to me, the one named Katkov, "I seem to remember you saying you'd pay me fifty for it."

After paying me, begrudgingly, he put the directory in his

briefcase.

"Thought you said that was for me?"

He pretended not to hear. "I think it is getting too dangerous for us to meet here. Someone might be watching. We should meet somewhere else, a restaurant, perhaps."

No way was I going to lug all those books around town. "Michael, if you wanna meet in a restaurant sometime to socialize, that's fine with me. But business is conducted here," I said, making pointing motions at the floor, "in the living room where I have shades."

Once again, he pretended not to hear. From the very beginning, he seemed in a hurry to leave. Michael kept looking at his watch while talking. Suddenly he stood up and said, "It seems to me that you are OK, so, if it's all right, I will go now."

I told him to be careful not to let anyone see him leaving. And I warned him to avoid walking down 183rd Street. I gave him a safer route. I also mentioned the strange phone calls I'd been getting all times of the day and night. "As soon as I say, 'Hello,' someone hangs up."

"It seems to me that someone is watching you, John. You should move — to New Jersey or maybe Queens."

"Can't afford the rent in those places, Michael, if you want me to move, I need bigger orders. And more money."

"Is entirely up to you, John. As I have told you many times, when you get me something interesting, I will be happy to pay you quite well."

"Kindly be more specific."

He smiled wryly. "You are a clever chap. Think of something."

At 5:55 Michael left. I closed the door, and listened. I heard the elevator ascending, then descending. I went to the window and looked. No Michael. I never saw him leave the building. Like a ghost, had vanished. Wish I knew how he did it.

***

Broadway and St. Nicholas Avenues, the two main north/south thoroughfares in the Heights, are not unlike the plains of Africa: hordes of people, like herds of grazing animals, peacefully going about their daily business. And like the Serengeti, there are hunters and those they hunt.

Although I'd see them every day, I only saw the elderly with my peripheral vision. To me, and most others, they were obstacles impeding the fast flow of life in New York City. We would weave past them as if they were slow moving vehicles plodding along on a highway. These old people were no longer able to keep up with the rest of the herd. Solitary, slow moving and with dulled senses, they made easy targets for those who prey on the weak and defenseless.

I have to admit that too many times I let myself get caught up in the importance of what the Bureau and I were doing. Then by November 1984, that all changed: a new perspective along with a raised consciousness. It began immediately after the burglary. I'd asked Mike Berns how important my personal safety was to the Soviet Union.

"Since you don't have access to classified information," he replied without missing a beat, "probably not very."

An inconvenient truth that I knew was right on. I felt like shit.

I began to wonder how important was the principle target's, Mikhail Katkov's, personal safety to the FBI/CIA? Judging by the way Mike and Tom Black had been acting lately, my guess: probably not very. And how important was *my* personal well-being to the People Down South? A whole lot less than probably not very.

Another shake to that pedestal I'd put myself on came when I saw Robert McGuire, a former New York City Police Commissioner, on *60 Minutes*. He said, "What does an elderly person living alone in New York City care about nuclear war, the Cold War, the Russians, when they must live behind ten locks and risk their lives whenever they go out into the streets."

But what really sent my aggrandized sense-of-self crashing came on November 28, 1984, only nine days after I'd been robbed. An old woman was murdered in her apartment by a thief who stole her TV set. (Stupid me making jokes about *my* TV not getting stolen!) The old woman lived just around the corner at 569 W. 182nd. Her death was a shock to my system; the old woman had been strangled; that's how lions kill, slowly. I felt a connection to her, a real person who had a real life, someone I'd never met, and never even thought about until now. How many other old, forgotten people that I passed on the street every day lived like she did, behind bolts and locks? And how many might come to the same tragic end?

That was when I came to a conclusion: on that great cosmic scale, how relevant were Katkov, Berns and Pansini? How relevant was the Cold War?

Definitely not very.

***

When I got home from work on Monday, December 10th, I faced a minor catastrophe. The elevator wasn't working, so I had to haul my tired ass up six flights. Passing the second floor I saw a line of cops spilling out of 2E like a long blue tongue. 2E was Moe's place. He was the guy I suspected had something to do with my burglary. Inside Moe was being grilled by detectives. His whiny, raspy voice echoed in the hallway. "I didn't do nothin'! I didn't do nothin'!"

Upstairs, when my neighbor in 6B saw me unlocking my apartment door, he told me that the cops had found the murdered old lady's TV set in Moe's apartment. Not hard to picture, Moe the killer: angry eyes, lean, hard prison muscles, tattoos, a shaved head and unshaven face. A Greek lady, one of my friend's aunts, used to call him "that dirty pirate."

Later I found out the truth: Moe didn't *do nothin'*. The cops arrested a 20 year-old kid named Reyes. I saw his picture in the *Uptown Dispatch*, a local paper. He looked like a clean-cut, All-American quarterback type; so much for judging evil deeds by evil looks. As for Moe, he disappeared from the neighborhood for a long time. Probably on an extended vacation upstate to Attica.

Chapter 15
A Trap Avoided?

"You mean you really didn't know what I was doing, even after I told you about the restricted documents?"

"No", he said. Then his face embellished: "No, asshole, I didn't!"

***

Thursday, December 20, 1984

"Michael, you look" — *like shit* — "very tired," I said. "The trains, huh?"

Mr. Katkov lumbered through the door looking like a communist Atlas carrying the entire weight of the un-free world on his broad back. He'd phoned at 5:15 to say he'd be over in twenty minutes. In the background I heard the unmistakable grumbling of the New York Transit Authority, so he must have been calling from a subway station. He arrived at 6 p.m.

Later when I told Berns about Michael taking the trains, Mike wondered out loud about our friend's sudden reliance on public transport. He said that on previous occasions Michael had driven to my place in his Sunbird. "We'd really like to know which of his buddies comes with him."

I led Michael into the living room, but not before showing off my new locks.

"It seems to me the best thing to do is move," he said wearily.

“This’ll cheer you up.” I disappeared into the front room and returned with an arm full of NTIS documents.

He removed a small white envelope, stuffed with twenty-dollar bills, from his breast pocket. “How much do I owe you?” he asked, flatly.

A tentative, “Twelve hundred?” Michael’s mood tempered my greed. No sense pushing the grumpy ole bear too far tonight.

He counted out five twenties at a time and handing them to me. At four hundred he stopped abruptly and motioned for me to return the money. He put the bills back in the envelope, and then handed it back to me. “I believe you will find $1,500 in there. I do not know which presents to buy you for Christmas. I think it will be better if you buy something for yourself. And I hope this will compensate you for your recent loss.”

“Thanks, Michael. Gonna buy a new stereo receiver.” I pointed to the empty space in the cabinet. “I can’t live without rock & roll.”

“You know, John, is very difficult for me to travel to your place. The metro is very bad. There is no place to park. I think maybe you should think about moving to Queens. Is very nice there, ya?”

“Queens is nice, but it’s also expensive. I need bigger—”

Michael held up a hand as if to say, *Enough already.*

He gave me my next order: a sample of a product called *Biobar* which prohibits the growth of bio-organisms in diesel fuel; then he asked me to do “a search on that underwater breathing device. That pay-tent (not *Avgard*) I asked for last spring.” Back then he’d given me a clipping that described the patent and the name of the device but no supporting documentation. Now he gave me a verbal order based solely on the clipping. I must have been as out of it as him because I thought nothing of it at the time. Then he proposed that we meet again sometime in early February; a cue to put my latest plan into action.

"Michael, you may have a hard time reaching me in February. I might be employed," I said, grinning, "so if you call and there's no answer, keep trying."

He leaned closer. I had his full attention.

1984 was fast coming to an end. Soon a new bus would roll into the station with a signboard that read, "1985." It came to carry me another year closer to Milepost Forty. At the time, I figured once a guy hits forty, it's all downhill from there.

I'd been a spy for a little over a year. Happy to bang nails while fighting the Cold War on the side, I dreamed of eventual book signings and movie deals. But what if this thing ended suddenly? Without a solid plot line I'd be lucky to land a magazine article. Then after my five micro-seconds of fame were gone, I'd be back banging nails until they put me in the ground. Bet I'd even have to hammer my own coffin shut. The way I figured it, I needed a backup plan just in case.

In early December, I'd thumbed through the Help Wanted section of the Sunday *Times* where a particular ad caught my interest. It said that the New York State Power Authority (NYSPA) in White Plains had a pressing need for freelance Indexers. A position I felt eminently qualified for. Since the ad said freelance, I figured I could work at home, transmitting and receiving data via modem and computer.

The following Monday I phoned the NYSPA. The woman I spoke

to said remote access would not be possible, that all indexing had to be done in-house. And then she told me why documents could not be taken home: "You'll be working with federal documents that are restricted to the building."

Only the words "federal documents" and "restricted" jumped from the telephone receiver into my right ear, vibrated my tympanic membrane, hopped onto a neuron and followed a super-highway marked "Straight To John's Brain." Once inside the matter, the words settled comfortably inside the conniving lobe: *If I get this job Mr. Katkov is going to be very, very, very happy.*

After I made an appointment for an interview, I called Mike Berns to fill him in on the details: "I'll be working with restricted federal documents. Provided I get the job, do you guys have any objections?" My motives seemed so transparent to me that I suspected Mike *would* object, loud and clear: *Don't do it, asshole!*

Then he surprised me: "Don't let your work with us interfere with your career. We'll work around it."

Good enough. I took this as tacit approval for what I had in mind. I decided to perform what's called in the intelligence trade a *dangle operation* on Mr. Katkov.

Back in my apartment, "Wanted to show you this anyway to see what you think, Michael." Then I got up from the sofa and headed into the front room to get the NYSPA ad.

When I handed it to him, he simply glanced at it before handing it back to me.

"Went for the interview already. Looks good, but I may not take it. You know how I hate office work." A certain lack of enthusiasm on my part was deliberate. I wanted to gauge his interest by faking my own disinterest. "Thought I could work at home with my computer, but they said everything had to be done in-house."

I searched his face for clues — *nada* — so I pushed a little harder. The absolute truth: I'd be working with *federal documents* that, for whatever reason, were *restricted* to the building. I gave Michael a slight variation on that truth: "Can't take work home because I'll be working with restricted federal documents which can't leave the building."

I'd given Michael, a seasoned intelligence professional, a dose of disinformation. He continued to stare blankly, so I squeezed a few more cc's into him: "When I went for the interview, they made me sign in and out, wear a badge and everything." I grinned, but Michael remained unimpressed.

That bold, risk taking part of me said, *Push harder.* But prudence warned, *Pull back. Don't seem too eager.*

Caution prevailed. We moved on to other topics: my plans for the holidays, and my current love life. "Got a Christmas card from an old girlfriend named Anne," I told him. We briefly chatted about my great expectations regarding Anne, and then, circuitously, he steered the conversation back to my professional growth.

"This job you speak about, is good opportunity, yah?"

"Maybe… They're offering $15/hour for a 30-hour week. They call that part-time — thirty-five hours is considered full-time — which means that I'm not entitled to any benefits. And I gotta schlepp all the way up to White Plains every damn day."

"The advertisement said Columbus Circle (in Manhattan)." He shot me a *Gotcha!* look.

Although the ad did say, "Dept. FLI-128, NY Power Authority, 10 Columbus Circle," I explained to Michael that people were supposed to submit résumés to that address. The actual job lay to the north, in the pastoral province of Westchester County, not mentioned in the ad. He'd taken in quite a lot of detail in such a quick glance. Amazed that he could memorize so much detail in such short order, and given the way his eyes sometimes turned inward when he spoke like he was reading from an internal script, made me wonder if Mr. Katkov had a photographic memory. Later I mentioned this possibility to the FBI.

"I will call you again in February," he said, smiling for the first time. "Who knows, perhaps our next meeting will be in very fine restaurant in White Plains. But remember, John, do not tell these people about our friendship."

"Don't worry, Michael. If I told them I was doing business with a Russian, I wouldn't get the job."

"And should you come across some material that you think will be of interest to me," he added, wryly, "I am sure you will be very happy to charge me for it."

"Quite a lot, Michael."

We both chuckled.

***

How high up did this thing go on their side? Mike told me that Michael's unscheduled visit on November 26th had confirmed something the FBI/CIA long suspected: that Michael acted strictly as a conduit between me and a group of persons who made the decisions regarding the materials being ordered. What group of persons? The VPK?

According to a 1982 CIA report, the Military Industrial Commission (the VPK) of the Presidium of the Council of Ministers "seeks one-of-a-kind military and dual use hardware, blueprints, product samples and technical documents to improve the technical levels and performance of Soviet weapons, military equipment, etc." The VPK, in turn, set collection priorities and tasked the collecting agencies: the GRU, the KGB's Directorate T and intelligence services of the Eastern bloc to acquire items of Western technology.[1]

Mike had mentioned that items wanted by the VPK were listed in something he called the *Red Book*. About the size of a New York City telephone directory, a copy had been obtained by West German intelligence. Soviet intelligence officers were required to recruit a minimum of four assets (assets recruited in excess of four were duly rewarded) and from these assets, officers were expected to obtain as much material as possible. When the FBI worried last summer that Michael and Val's reports would cross, I thought I now had the answer: they'd cross at the VPK.

Wrong! As I would learn much later, the Katkov Affair went a whole lot higher up the ladder.

***

Poor Mike Berns, thanks to me today, Monday, January 28th, got off to a bad start. With his eyes slammed shut, he rubbed his temples

1 Soviet Acquisition of Militarily Significant Western Technology: An Update. September 1985, p.2.

like a man on the verge of a colossal headache. "Wish you wouldn't tell me these things," he sighed. We were in the Red Oak Diner in Fort Lee, New Jersey — Jersey was where the Mob, and others, dumped the bodies. I wondered if he fantasized about a good place to dump mine.

He'd picked me up at the entrance ramp of the George Washington Bridge at 11 a.m. From there we headed west to Jersey for lunch.

The man severely disappointed me. He was FBI, not only the crème de la crème as far as cops go, but he worked in the Intelligence Division which raised him several notches higher. How could he look so shocked when I told him what I'd been planning?

I did get the job at the Power Authority. I'd be starting Monday, February 4th. I just finished explaining my little dangle operation to Mike. Not only did it set his head throbbing, but it apparently took him by surprise. "Thought you did it to advance your career?"

"Advance my career? You gotta be kidding. How's a bullshit job at the Power Authority gonna advance my career? Come on, Mike. You mean you really didn't know what I was doing, even after I told you about the restricted documents?"

His vocals were short and to the point: "No", but his face embellished. It said, *No, asshole, I didn't!* Mike worried that I might do something really stupid. "So far, neither one of you has done anything illegal, but if he tasks you for something that's restricted, he's breaking the law. And if you give it to him, then you are too. It could blow the whole operation." Mike added that if Michael should ask for a restricted item, approval could take as long as six to eight weeks. It had to pass through an alphabet soup: FBI, CIA, STATE, and not to mention the NYSPA.

"That should make the People Down South happy," I snarked, "at least they'll have something that really needs approval."

Mike did not appreciate the irony. "You can't tell him about a particular item in advance because then he'll wonder, *Why the delay in getting it?"*

I decided to employ a tactic that both Mike and Michael used on me. I changed the subject: "Remember that patent Michael had asked for last spring, the one for the underwater breathing device?"

"Yeah, the artificial gill, the *hemosponge*."

Mike's powers of recall were a lot better than mine. All I could remember was *hemosponge* and what I thought was the inventor's last name, Ventura. When I keyed those two words into the computer I got zero hits. I had to refer back to the original clipping Michael had given me that described the patent: the inventor's name was Bonaventura; and the device was cited in the literature under artificial gill, not *hemosponge*. Using a new search strategy, "Bonaventura OR artificial gill", the computer spit back several citations. If I had not saved the clipping, the search would've ended in failure. The problem: why would a person like me, a guy who cares nothing about what he's turning over to the Soviet Union, and a person whose only motivation is greed, save a clipping? (Unless he was writing a book.)

I told Mike, "I think this is a trap. Running the search with the only two keywords I remembered, I got nothing. If I give him a completed search, he might ask how I got it."

"I really don't think it's a trap, but you're the one who's dealing with him directly. We have to trust your instincts."

A major decision had to be made. Should I turn over the search I ran from the clipping and collect a tidy $350 fee or should I play it safe? Which brought up another question regarding Michael's odd behavior lately: "Why is he asking for his lists back?"

"It might have something to do with that business with Bolochine. Both of 'em acted very unprofessionally. They should've checked their indices to find your name. He might be feeling some pressure because of it."

Another clue: apparently my name appeared on a list that both the GRU and the KGB accessed. I still figured it had to be the VPK; but I was still wrong.

Then a shocker: according to Mike the pantheon down south thought I was a true believer, a squeaky clean, gung-ho type who consistently voted Republican.

"Did you tell 'em I don't pay parking tickets?"

"No we didn't."

"Did you tell 'em I'm a liberal democrat?"

"No."

Love to know how much shine these two Michaels put on me in their reports.

"Let me know if the Power Authority runs a security check on you," Mike said, sounding both frustrated and tired. "I'll make sure your name clears." He changed the subject: "Just saw a movie you'll wanna see: *The Falcon and the Snowman.* There's a scene where Dalton Lee (Snowman) feels betrayed by Christopher Boyce (Falcon). Lee said to Boyce, 'Thanks a lot, Julius.'" Mike chuckled. "Gotta kick outta that. I thought of you."

Later I saw the movie. The exact quote was, "Thanks a lot, Judas."

Mike may have mixed the names up, but his subtext was right on.

Chapter 16
Keeping It Real

"This is gonna get a lot of people in Washington very excited."

***

Friday, February 1, 1985

Mike called. We briefly discussed the NYSPA job that I'd be starting Monday, the 4th. Now he sounded happy for me. The guy was like a faucet where hot and cold water ran out of the same tap. He asked if he could stop by Sunday morning to install a tape recorder. Maybe that was why he was being so nice, he wanted something.

"Sure. Don't forget to bring your guns when you come into this neighborhood," I joked.

Sunday morning, February 3rd, at 10:30 a.m., was not a particularly dangerous time of day because all the bad guys slept-in on Sunday mornings; my doorbell *Thunked.* Mike and his buddy, Tom Black, came in from the cold.

"We want to show you how to set up the recorder," Mike said, unbuttoning his sports jacket. When I saw it, I took a step back. Tucked neatly behind the zipper of his pants, out of immediate view but within easy reach, was a .38 caliber revolver in a black holster. To me it looked like a cannon. Bet it blew big holes. Tom also had his weapon hidden in his crotch. If these guys sat down the wrong way, they might blow their dicks off.

After seeing Mike and Tom slinging their tools of authority as casually as I do a hammer on a belt hook, I had my first whiff of the java: these two guys were conduits between me and some powerful people I should not be playing games with. I must have turned a whiter shade of pale because Mike, the sensitive one, noticed. He put his gun in his briefcase. Tom stood there blasé with hands on hips like the marshal of Dodge City.

They showed me the best place to install the recorder: under the sofa with the tiny microphone (about the size of a thumbnail and attached to the recorder with an 18 inch chord) facing out. They said the Swiss-made recorder cost three thousand dollars and ran for 3 hours.

"The higher the (little) mike the better," big Mike said. "If this doesn't work, we'll try something else next time."

Not pleased, "Geez," I mumbled. "Had no idea this was gonna be an ongoing show."

Mike asked me to sign a waiver stating that I had authorized the Federal Bureau of Investigation to install a recorder in my apartment for the period of 2/3 - 2/10/85. Then I showed him the material I had for Michael. He took out a long sheet that looked like ledger paper and began noting the documents. While Mike wrote, I did some upside down reading: "Malus Pumila — Latin for evil dwarf; was that me? — #105 173 837." The top of the paper was stamped "SECRET." Not a particularly high level of classification, but it sure impressed the shit out of me.

"Technically, the recorder is only to be operated when you're in the room," Mike said, his head down, still writing, "but we realize you can't get up and switch it on and off every time."

I shrugged. "Who cares about his civil rights. What if he spots the mike?"

Big Mike stopped writing and looked up. "It'd be real hard for him to do that. He'd have to get down on all fours and crawl around on the floor."

"If he does that, just kick him in the butt and tell him to get back on the couch," the marshal added.

***

Monday, February 4th, my first day on the job: up at six, get dressed, catch the A Train to 59th, grab a quick coffee and donut from a nearby vendor, get on the van, get off at White Plains, and then index a bunch of Nuclear Regulatory Commission reports all day. At five, back on the van, back on the A, back home at seven. Then cook, eat, bed. And the next day would be the same. So would the one after that. And so on, and so on, and so on… In mathematics it's called an infinite series; in my case the sum of which was boredom as it approached an asymptote labeled "suicide."

This sure wasn't how 007 did it.

At 7:20 p.m., Michael called. He asked if he could stop by either tomorrow or Wednesday.

"Better come after seven," I said in a tired voice. "I got a new job."

"Better not to discuss this on the phone. Bye." *Click!* He sounded excited.

The next day, Tuesday at 7:30 p.m., "So, John, and how is your new job?" Michael casually asked.

"It sucks."

"I see… It seems to me it would be good for you to stay perhaps six months to build up your credentials."

"Michael, I've only been there one day and already I'm going nuts."

Like he wasn't listening: "Who knows, you may become company president." He smiled, showing rows of teeth, top and bottom. My new job made him a lot happier than it did me. "For how long will this job be for?"

Playing to the recorder chugging away under his ass, I waved my arms around: "A whole fucking year!" Wasted stagecraft on my part since this scene played in audio not video.

"Yah is good," he mumbled, nodding his head. "Do you think they will offer you a permanent position?"

"God, I hope not!" I said, clutching a fist to my chest.

"Did they check your background?"

"Said they did, but I doubt it." Then I began to rant: "Got no benefits. No health care, sick days, holidays, nothing. And the bastards are only paying me $15/hr." I shot him a serious look: "I'm being exploited, Michael."

"All Americans are exploited." Michael was blasé. "What do you expect from a capitalist society?"

"One day the workers will rise up," I said, shaking a fist in the air.

"Yes, John, we shall celebrate that joyous moment together." Then he looked at me like *Loony Tune*s ran in my head. "John? Are you on drugs?"

Guess acting natural was not my method. "No. Why do you ask?"

"Never mind. It seems to me it is good for you to stay there a while. Is better than sitting at home doing nothing, yah?"

"No it isn't, but I'll stay anyway. I endure this suffering only for you, Michael."

"Not to worry, I will compensate you for the inconvenience." He smiled. "So tell me, what type of materials do they've got there? Anything interesting?"

Poor Michael, I held the ropes on his cradle of disappointment. He had to be let down gently: "As you know, the only reason I took this job in the first place was because I thought I might run across something interesting."

He leaned closer, looking eager.

"But I don't think there is anything."

His face dropped a fraction.

"Most of the documents I'll be working with are NRC documents. Know what they are?"

He shook his head.

"Nuclear Regulatory Commission reports."

He brightened.

"Unfortunately, these aren't technical documents, and they're unclassified. The only reason the Power Authority restricts them is because they're afraid to let them out of the building because they might get lost. They're called NUREGS. They're rulings and findings by the NRC sent to local power companies. They're total bullshit — to us, anyway."

Michael's smile oozed into his lap. His shoulders slumped. A sad sight.

"Sorry Michael."

He made waving motions with two limp wrists. "Is OK," he said, sounding tired. "So, John, what you've got for me?"

I started bringing in piles of documents from the front room.

"I would like to check these against the original order to see if anything is missing. Please get it for me." When I returned with the want list in question, he put it in his wallet. "How much do I owe you?"

"Didn't really have a chance to tabulate it yet," I said, pausing to come up with a reasonable figure. I didn't want to cheat myself. "Let's say five hundred. And you're getting a bargain."

At first he threw up his hands and said I was being unreasonable; then he grinned, reached into his vest pocket and pulled out a small envelope. He flipped the envelope to me. "It seems to me you had a birthday recently. You will find $650 in there. Keep it."

Thirty-one twenty- dollar bills and three tens made for a nice, fat white envelope.

"When's *your* birthday, Michael? I wanna get you something nice."

He hesitated, caught between being too secretive or too informative. Finally, "March 29th."

"That *Haselblad* book hasn't come yet." (The book was published by NASA. When I finally got it, the book read like it had been written for 3rd graders.) "Tell you what, Michael. When it comes, it's on me."

He slapped his knee and laughed. "I give you one-hundred-fifty bucks for your birthday and you give me a scrappy little book that cost six bucks."

Earnestly, "Yeah, but I was gonna charge you a hundred for it."

He laughed even harder. "John that is what I like about you. Is there anything else?"

The "anything else" he referred to was the artificial gill search.

"Sorry, Michael, I forgot the name of the device and the name of the inventor. Had it confused with the other patent you ordered at the end of last summer, that aviation fuel thing (*Avgard*). Then I realized that wasn't what you meant. I usually throw away all your old orders when I finish with them — unless you tell me otherwise — so I had nowhere to look. If you want me to do the search, I need more information."

He stared at me and blinked; then, "Is called *Artificial Gill.* The inventor is Bonaventura from Duke University."

"That's it! Wasn't it called something else?"

"A *hemosponge*."

"Sorry I didn't remember, but now I can find it."

He shrugged. "Is your money."

Had I successfully steered clear of a trap? I'd played it safe, because Pat and Mike had always stressed that I should make this as real world as possible. And in the real world, I'd forgotten.

He gave me my new order: a large number of NTIS documents with a few ASME papers thrown in. Back in October I had asked Berns why Michael was so worried about me ordering materials directly from NTIS.

Mike had said, "The Soviets have a caveat about that. They're afraid that someone at NTIS might notice that a specific individual is ordering a large volume of material in a very narrow field." Then Mike stunned me by admitting that CIA did, indeed, have an asset at NTIS.

A *specific individual* mostly meant an American citizen like me. I didn't much like the idea that the Central Intelligence Agency spied on legitimate research done by Americans, no matter how narrow the topic. Further, I'd always thought that it was illegal for CIA to operate against American citizens within the continental United States.

Tonight, Michael Katkov surprised me when he cautioned me not to order all the documents directly from NTIS because someone there might notice that I was ordering large amounts of material in a narrow field. "You will draw attention to yourself," he said.

Amazing! Almost word for word. Was there anything each side didn't know about the other?

"Is better if you go to a place like Columbia University," he said. "They will photocopy them for you." Then he handed me an advertisement for something called a *stun gun*. The ad claimed the device was guaranteed to stop an attacker in his tracks by filling him with an electric, non-lethal charge. What page of the *Red Book* was that thing on?

"As you know, it is dangerous for me to come here at this hour," he said.

Not if he had that stun gun.

"So for our next meeting, I want you to do me a small favor: on the last Saturday in March, please stay at home until four p.m. and wait for my call. If I don't call, then do the same thing the following Saturday."

Later, when I phoned Mike Berns and told him about our friend's odd request, he said, "This is gonna get a lot of people in Washington very excited."

I had no idea why.

(Fig. 16.1) FBI Recorder on my kitchen table

(Fig 16.2) Ad for stun gun

Chapter 17
The Fat Spy Theory

"She's connected all right. Let's show John the picture of her pulling that plow."

***

As for me and the New York State Power Authority, the time had come to take this pot off the stove. I'd been overcooked. I'd reached the limp noodle stage. The thrill was gone, long gone. I'd left work early on a Thursday. Told the NYSPA that I had a pressing business engagement; in reality a pressing need to remain sane by escaping their office in White Plains. The next day, I called to say I'd be taking the entire day off. I did not bother to tell them why.

I came to work the following Monday, rested, refreshed and ready to endure another week in hell. As soon as I sat down at my desk I was told to report to the Big Boss Man. In his office, he was blunt:

"You will have to choose between your business and your work here with us."

I was equally direct. My reply came down on him like a hammer: "Since this job is part-time and for one year only, I'm sorry but there really is no choice. My business *is* my future."

A hint of spring blew in the smog-free air of White Plains. My banging arm twitched at night as I dreamed of new roofs to conquer. I could afford to take an attitude. To my surprise, Big Boss Man did not fire me on the spot. Guess there weren't many indexers out there with my qualifications: among my coworkers I was the only one with a Master's Degree in library science. Besides, there weren't many people out there who wanted such a crappy job.

***

Mike Berns called Monday night, February 25th. He sounded fairly convinced that the operational mode had shifted and Michael might start asking for hotter stuff. Then he added that our meetings would soon be moving to an outside location. “Especially if the meetings are gonna be on Saturdays from now on.”

“Last time you said the People Down South are gonna get all excited about that. What’s the big deal about Saturdays?”

“Now we’re getting into what’s called tradecraft, setting up meets and alternate meets. You read *Falcon and Snowman*, it’s in there. Moving to Saturdays will also make it easier for us to see which one of his buddies comes with him.”

“Think maybe my Power Authority ploy caused the shift?”

“I don’t think so. They’re just following a pattern.”

“So how will he react if I quit? Will he think I’m lazy, not such a hot prospect?”

“I don’t think so. So far you’ve laid a good foundation. Just say the job is tedious and not challenging.”

“And there’s nothing of interest there for him,” I said.

“I’d rather you not push that with him.”

A week ago Mike and I had discussed money. He’d said he put me in for five hundred dollars. That seemed fair to me: five hundred for each meeting with Michael plus expenses. Now Mike told me that I wouldn’t be getting five hundred for each meeting with Michael. More likely I’d be getting between three and five hundred and sometimes nothing.

"How's that?" I snapped.

"The money we pay you has to be justified according to how much time I spend debriefing you. Since we're letting you keep Michael's money," he added, sounding as tired of saying it as I was of hearing it, "we feel that you're making a fair profit. What you get from us is an extra bonus. What the Bureau decides to pay you is out of my hands, but I'll always try to do the best I can for you."

I was like a dog with a choke-collar around my neck. Michael B. on one end and Michael K. on the other. Both were trying to pull me where *they* wanted me to go. Now I like dogs and all of God's creatures both great and small, but *love* cats, especially their sense of independence.

Neither Michael knew they had a cat on their leashes, kicking and biting to get the fucking thing off.

***

March 1985, came in like a lamb. I called my old boss and asked if he had any roofs. "Sure do," he replied. He sounded happy, and that made me happy.

No more getting up at 6 a.m. On March 7th, after a little over a month, I left the New York State Power Authority forever. I was glad to wipe the dust of that place off my cheap sneakers.

On Monday, March 11th, I went to the Engineering Societies Library to photocopy some American Society of Mechanical Engineers (ASME) papers. The citations dealt with articles for spacecraft design. One in particular caught my attention. It came off the handwritten index card list. Someone had written in the word "em-dash" in a fancy script as part of the title. I thought nothing of it until I held the actual document in my hands. It contained a title and subtitle punctuated by what proofreaders call an em-dash (a long hyphen). Most computer printers circa 1985 could not print em-dashes or other special characters like Greek letters, subscripts in chemical compounds, and other scientific notation. Database vendors like DIALOG worked around this problem by printing out the name of the special character; i.e. in the case of this particular document, they printed "em-dash" as a part of the title. Therefore, the citations on this list must have come from an online search. And whoever copied these citations off the printout did not know proofreading symbols. He or she simply copied the title word-for-word. (See actual photocopy at the end of this chapter.)

This minute detail, coupled with a book I'd just read, answered a question that had been nagging at me for a long time: Why were so many of Michael's want lists handwritten? Now I had the answer: they were handwritten because in the communications center at the Soviet Mission to the U.N., the *referentura*, typewriters were not allowed. The Soviets feared that sounds made by striking keys might be monitored by the FBI.[1] And why did the GRU employ a technique as labor intensive as copying by hand citations from a computer-generated printout, then photocopying these handwritten lists, and cutting them into long strips? Because of the Soviet Union's warped sense of secrecy, no one must know that they had an interest in acquiring these documents. Thus, the list Michael had given me in November was a classified Soviet document; and because I'd turned it over to the FBI, that meant I was a real spy.

That made me realize that while I was not making the world safe for little old ladies sitting in their apartments watching TV, what we, the FBI and me, were doing was also worth something.

---

1 Shevenko, Arkady, Breaking With Moscow, Ballantine Books, c1985, p.39-40.

On Wednesday, March 2nd, at 2 p.m., I ate lunch with two clowns who should be cited for conduct unbecoming. This time I'd driven my Dodge Dart across the GW Bridge and met my FBI case officers at the Red Oak Diner. They were drinking coffee and waiting for me.

"Traffic," I said by way of apology. "Sorry to keep you guys waiting."

Things had gotten off to a good start when Tom Black expressed a special interest in the stun gun and Mike Berns made numerous references to Michael's shopping lists. Mike also mentioned that Michael had been in Staten Island last Saturday scouting out locations for a possible meeting with me.

"Took his wife with him," Tom added.

Soviet intelligence officers frequently took spouses along on missions pretending to be on family outings. Never seemed to fool the other side, though, so why bother?

"I don't wanna shlepp all the way out to Staten Island," I whined. "Why does he have to choose there?" For me, a trip to Staten Island meant two or three hours by subway and ferry, or one or two hours by car depending on traffic.

Mike grinned. "Why make it easy?"

"By the way, my father lives in Staten Island," I told them.

Mike and Tom exchanged glances. Did Michael know this, and was my father in the phone book? I answered yes on both counts, raising two sets of eyebrows.

Convinced that things were shifting to a more clandestine mode had Mike and Tom about as near to giddy as guys like them get.

"He wants to start meeting you on the outside," Mike said, "to get you used to it."

Tom chimed in with, "It's all part of the process."

According to Mike, with me in the bag, Michael looked real good to his superiors. "He'll do anything to protect you from drawing our (the Bureau's) attention."

Such a complicated and unjust world: here was Michael protecting me from *them*, and here I was already talking to *them*. I felt like a swamp thing crawled out of the slime.

Then Mike added a warning: "To be successful in your relationship with our friend, there are two things you must never do: lie to him or promise him something you can't deliver."

I asked why I was so important to Michael even though I hadn't produced anything "interesting" yet.

"It isn't often they get someone as willing to cooperate with them as fully as you have," Tom said.

Mike added, "You're just the type the Soviets like dealing with: long hair, beard (to protect my face from March's chill winds), and radical looking, not your ordinary Wall Street type. And young in appearance, like a student."

I asked Tom for his thoughts on the *hemosponge* business. He agreed it might have been a test. Then I asked, "When's Michael's birthday? He told me March 29th."

True, according to Mike. Mikhail Katkov was born in 1948, the same year as me, so at the end of the month he'd be thirty-seven. Mike added that older Soviet intelligence officers in their 40s whose careers had stagnated were the most susceptible to FBI/CIA inducements to *defect-in-place*; i.e. become moles. Positive intelligence provided by our side to these moles would give their careers big boosts. Add to that the promise of early retirement in the West and an ostrich-sized nest egg that they could sit on for the rest of their lives. No wonder many Soviets during the Cold War took this option. Would Michael? Mike and Tom said that our friend was still relatively young for an intelligence officer. Turning him would not be easy. So what enticements and/or pressures would the FBI/CIA inflict on Mr. Katkov? I'd have to wait and see.

In regards to my own future, I told Mike and Tom that I wanted to get out of New York and move to a place like Silicon Valley.

"If you do, and if the Soviets make contact with you again," Mike said, "when one of our guys comes to see you tell him you'll only talk to Michael W. Berns. You trust that guy with your life." Mike smiled. Apparently the Golden State appealed to him too.

"In all seriousness," Tom said, not sounding serious at all, "don't mention this to Michael yet, not even as a joke. He might have a heart attack at the thought of losing you."

"Too bad you guys will probably never get to meet our friend," I said, "you'd like him. He's a likeable kind of guy."

"You never know," Tom said, shooting a quick grin at Berns, "maybe in June, Mike and I will be waiting in your apartment. We'll introduce ourselves."

Tom's casual statement sent my brain into full-signal-processing mode, correlating certain disturbing facts with certain other disturbing facts:

The FBI knew that Michael was in Staten Island last week. That meant that they had a pretty tight net around him. Mike had even slipped and admitted that he had seen Michael recently; then he tried to cover that up by saying it was only in photographs. Innocently,

"Does he still have a mustache?" And finally, from case histories I'd been reading I knew that these things seldom lasted more than a year.

Guess they realized they'd said too much. To cover, Mike and Tom began to massage my ego, telling me how good I was handling Michael, how important this case was to our nation, how grateful the People Down South were, and how clever I'd been to discover the em-dash thing. They were being nice, too nice. It felt like a set up.

Careful analysis of the above data only raised more questions, the most worrisome being would the FBI interdict in June? If they did that would mean back to the tedium of regular life for me, not to mention I wouldn't have much of a tale to tell.

Plot is everything.

"Heard the tape," Mike said, "you were a little loud, but you did just fine."

"Thanks. Used a lot more *f-words* than usual. Always do when I get nervous."

Mike brought up Michael's Staten Island trip again. Then for some reason Mrs. Katkov became the main topic of conversation. Mike and Tom had taken an unexpected turn onto Nasty Lane: "You should see her," Mike said, grinning. "She looks like his mother."

They laughed, but I turned my head away and scratched the side of my neck. A swipe at Michael's wife seemed too personal, not to mention irrelevant. I felt obliged to nip this thing in the bud: "So she's not so young and pretty, but she *is* his wife. Gotta respect that."

That did nothing to quiet the two talking heads. On and on and on: wisecrack, wisecrack, and wisecrack.

"Maybe she's got some Party connections," I said in defense of a woman I'd never meet. Like Mr. and Mrs. Bolochine, I preferred Mr.

and Mrs. Katkov to remain one-dimensional in my mind, like Boris and Natasha. That was how I coped.

"She's connected all right," said Tom. Then he nudged Mike. "We should show John the picture of her pulling that plow."

A good one; despite myself, I cracked a grin.

These two were on a roll: low blow, low blow, low blow. Was this how they coped: Michael as clown, less than them, an object of ridicule? Their black and white world of good guys and bad guys seemed too simplistic. I was reminded of the complexity of the situation: Michael, Mike and me, participants in a game, a game we all chose to enter. The stakes were high, but so were the rewards. Each of us had our own reasons for playing. Cold but true: someone would win, someone would lose, and personal lives were best kept out of it. For me, that was the only way to play. But *these* two, if their intent was to dehumanize Michael, their antics only succeeded in making him more real and them less. The muscles that ran along my neck tightened. I rolled my head to get the kinks out. When I looked across at Mike and Tom, they were getting louder, sounding like a couple of locker room jerk-offs talking about a "dog" another buddy was dating.

Mike's behavior surprised me. Why was he acting like a total asshole? Was this the real Mike Berns? Maybe he wasn't such a nice guy after all. I wondered what his wife looked like. I remembered the way he once eyeballed a particular Red Oak waitress. Young with long, feathered blonde hair, she reminded me of Farrah Fawcett. Guess he preferred the *Charlie's Angels* look.

I figured that if I didn't join in their little reindeer games, then maybe they'd get the hint and shut the fuck up. They didn't. They simply moved to a new target.

Stomp, stomp, stomp!

Angry footsteps coming our way: something big; something menacing; something having a bad day.

Stomp, stomp, stomp!

She held a check in her hand.

Mike looked up. "Looks like she's been sampling most of the food here," Mike mumbled to Tom.

A five-foot three, two hundred pound waitress approached our table. She threw the check down on the table and turned to walk away.

"Excuse me, can we have two more coffees please." Mike smiled. She grimaced. I assumed things had not been amicable between her and the two agents long before I'd sat down. Listening to their razor tongues slice her up like cold cuts was none of my business. I'd asked her for an orange sherbet for no other reason than we were still talking, and I was still hungry.

After she was out of earshot, Mike said to me, "Tommy has a theory about fat people. Want you to know he's spent many a sleepless night formulating this theory. Tell him what it is, Tom."

Before Tom could give me his theory the waitress returned with the coffees and sherbet. She grabbed the check, added them in, and slammed the check back down on the table. Tom said to me, "That looks good, John." To the waitress: "Excuse me. I'll have a sherbet, too, please." He smiled.

The waitress sneered and stormed off.

"Should we leave her a fat tip?" Tom asked Mike.

"Nah, she's fat enough already." Mike chuckled.

"So what's the theory?" I asked Tom, but Mike answered for him.

"That fat people are more likely to sell out their country than skinny people."

"Look at Miller, a real porker," Tom said, referring to Richard Miller, the FBI agent arrested in October 1984, on charges of spying for the Soviet Union. Tom said he formulated his theory after carefully reviewing the facts in the Miller case.

"I gotta admit," Mike said to me, "I was a little worried about you, but Tommy over here" — he pointed at his partner — "says that, according to his theory, you're OK. You *are* OK, aren't you, Julius? You're not gonna prove ole Tommy wrong, are you?"

I grinned. "Does this mean I gotta start eating less, that you guys are gonna be watching my waistline?"

"You bet," Tom said.

***

The next day, at 4:30 p.m., I'd just walked through the door when the phone rang. Mike called to tell me he was almost positive that my next meeting with Michael would be on the outside. I asked him how sure he was.

"I'd be willing to bet on it." Then he instructed me to offer Michael a ride home in my car. "He'll refuse of course, but you question him. Try and find out how he got there." Then he said I should beep him once before I left and again when I got home, "So I'll know you haven't met with some kind of accident."

The Bureau's sudden concern for my safety touched me, although should I choose to pick up on it, I'd better wear gloves. I wouldn't want to be holding bullshit with my bare, naked hands.

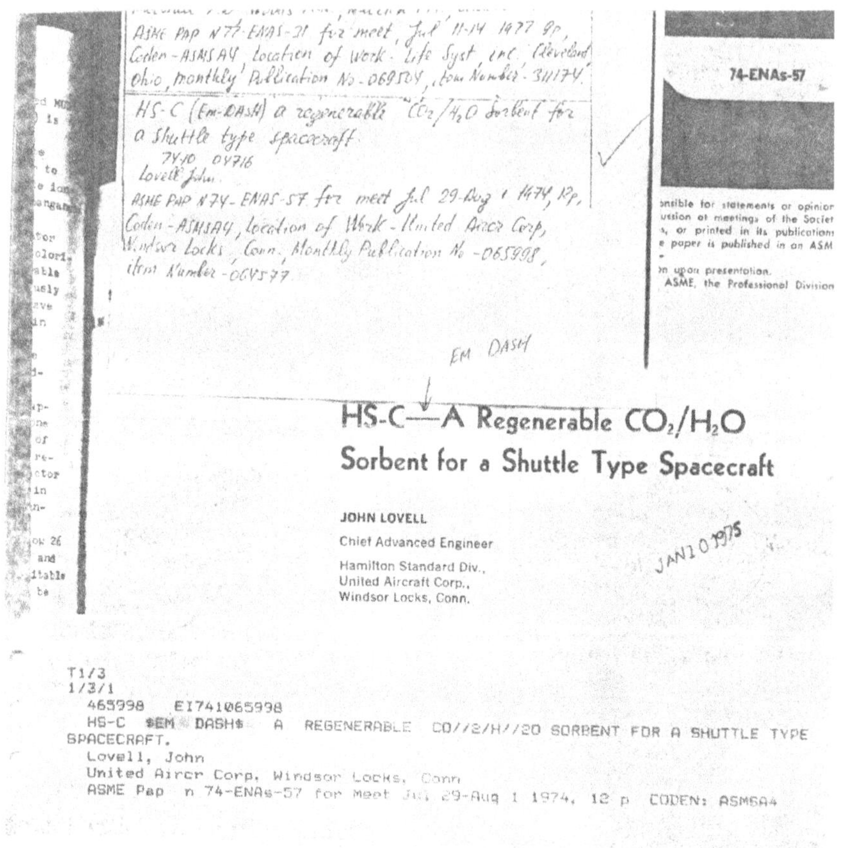

ASME PAP N77-ENAS-21 for meet, Jul 11-14 1977 9p, Coden-ASMSAY, location of Work - Life Syst, inc, Cleveland Ohio, monthly Publication No-069504, item Number-311174.

HS-C (Em-DASH) a regenerable CO_2/H_2O Sorbent for a Shuttle type spacecraft
74-10 04716
Lovell, John.
ASME PAP N74-ENAS-57 for meet Jul 29-Aug 1 1974, 12p, Coden-ASMSAY, location of Work - United Aircr Corp, Windsor Locks, Conn, Monthly Publication No-065998, item Number-064577.

74-ENAs-57

EM DASH

HS-C—A Regenerable CO_2/H_2O Sorbent for a Shuttle Type Spacecraft

JOHN LOVELL
Chief Advanced Engineer
Hamilton Standard Div.,
United Aircraft Corp.,
Windsor Locks, Conn.

JAN 10 1975

```
T1/3
1/3/1
  465998    EI741065998
  HS-C  $EM DASH$  A  REGENERABLE  CO//2/H//20 SORBENT FOR A SHUTTLE TYPE
SPACECRAFT.
  Lovell, John
  United Aircr Corp, Windsor Locks, Conn
  ASME Pap  n 74-ENAs-57 for Meet Jul 29-Aug 1 1974, 12 p  CODEN: ASMSA4
```

(Fig 17.1) Em-dashes in yellow highlights

Top: Handwritten bibliographic citation given to me by Michael

Middle: Title page of actual document

Bottom: Online bibliographic citation

Chapter 18
Real People

"What's the big deal?"

"The big deal is I don't wanna have to shoot somebody for stealing your briefcase."

***

My roofing buddy Dom wasn't the only close friend who knew about the Katkov Affair. A select group of others did as well. I had a few of them over for dinner one evening in mid-March. I mentioned that I'd let the government bug my last meeting with Michael.

"Wish I could get a copy of that tape for the book I'm gonna write, but the FBI would never go for it."

Please keep in mind that this was the mid-eighties and the technology at the time only allowed for print books supplemented by cassette tapes to provide sound. Even to the tech savvy of the eighties mp3 files, ebooks, QR codes, websites were all futurama. I might not have been able to divine the future back in those days; nonetheless, I was way ahead of my time. My vision of print to audio was for a reader to sit down with a cassette player handy. When the reader came to a section of the book, all they had to do was sequentially access a specific track on cassette tape to hear real spies in real conversations.

This had never been done before.

So when my friend Phil suggested that if I wanted tapes, I should buy a recorder at *Radio Shack* and make my own recordings. That excited me. Not only would these tapes substantiate my story, but they would make me a bestselling author!

When I was ready to start bugging my phone conversations with anyone and everyone connected to the Katkov Affair, I went to *Radio Shack* to buy a micro cassette recorder. I also bought a microphone with a suction cup that could be attached to the telephone receiver. I tested it on a conversation with my dad and it worked perfectly.

The first person to get bugged for the book was Mikhail Katkov on March 30, 1985. He called to tell me that he'd be right over.

(Audio 18.1) 0:13 seconds

Like I said on the tape, I should've taken that bet with Mike Berns.

***

In my apartment, Michael handed me a white envelope containing one thousand dollars for the documents I'd given him. Then he pulled out his wallet, and his band of the hand filled with even more cash. Joy to the world!

"It seems to me you said that you took the job (at the Power Authority) to please me," he said, holding out a hefty stack for the taking. "Here you will find an additional $900, because I am very pleased with you, John."

How pleased was he going to be when I told him I'd quit? Should I tell him the truth or keep my mouth shut and take his money? Tentatively, I made a small move for the cash. Then, with my own smile frozen in place, I pushed some words through my teeth: "Uh… Gee, uh, Michael, uh… This is a, uh…"

Pocketing the cash should've been no problem; seldom did this kind of money come my way so easily. But that fat stack of twenties carried with it its own sound track, a voice tinged with a Philly accent. What an inopportune time for SA Mike Berns to sneak into my head: *"Better not lie to him, asshole."*

"Michael, uh… I don't work there anymore… I quit."

Michael's face dropped like a rock; then he gave me a sad look like I had just run over his puppy.

My thumb and index finger closed loosely on the cash. Michael still held up his end. Instead of jerking the nine hundred back, he let go and shooed the money away with two limp wrists. Before he had a chance to change his mind, the money disappeared into my pants pocket. "Thanks, Michael. It was a boring, bullshit job anyway. Nothing interesting there either; if there was, I never would've left. Don't worry I promise you I'll get a much better job. It'll be easy."

"It seems to me you were quite concerned that you would get this job." His tone made me feel like I'd let him down. "It seems to me you should have stayed there a little longer to build up your credentials."

"In a place like that? No way. Believe me, the fact that I'm running a successful business looks a lot better on my resume than that job." I should've truncated it right there. Instead, eager to please because Mr. Katkov had paid me a whole lot of something for a whole lot of nothing, I added, "And besides I have an aunt who works at

Grummans. She's trying to get me in there."

Grumman Aerospace was one of the largest defense contractors in the country. The way I figured it, having a blood relative who worked there might put me right back on top of Michael's batting order. He'd have good news to carry back to his bosses.

Michael's eager response: "John, do you really think she will be able to help you obtain a position with that firm?"

"I sure hope so."

My aunt wasn't the problem, and neither was Grummans. Certain *others,* a powerful collection of small minds encased in concrete skulls, and all of them headquartered in our nation's capital, they needed to be convinced.

As he prepared to leave, busily stuffing documents into two Shoprite bags he'd brought with him, I turned the TV back on. Before Michael had arrived, I'd been watching a hockey game, Rangers vs. Flyers.

Michael briefly turned his attention to the TV. "Ah, yes, hockey, my favorite sport."

I let Michael's drop pass slide on by.

***

Mr. Michael Berns, along with the rest of his FBI buddies, they were wrong about Michael meeting me on the outside. I took great satisfaction in noting their mistake:

At the end of the tape, I told Mike I'd show him the hundred dollar bills, but he couldn't keep them. That was when he joked that I was being overpaid. That didn't bother me one bit. Given my blue-collar work ethic, and because I lived in a capitalist society like America, the way I figured it, little guys like me should grab all they can get.

(Audio 18.2) 1:37 seconds

***

At breakfast the next morning at the Star Diner on Broadway & 179th Street, I told Mike Berns and Tom Black that Michael said hockey was his favorite game.

Mike said, "Did you ask him what position he played?" Then he shot his partner a grin.

"Not this time," I replied. "I know better now."

The waitress delivered the food: I had a western omelet; I forget what they had. Then I delivered the bad news: "I told Michael about my aunt at Grummans."

Until now, she had been a tightly held secret between me and the FBI. I did not tell them her name, however. Judging from the looks that now came my way, Mike and Tom were not happy.

"Had to, he made me feel like shit for quitting the Power Authority." I sunk deeper into my seat. "I made a mistake. Sorry."

Sorry, but not that sorry. By my calculus now that Michael knew about my aunt at Grummans, the FBI could place me there without drawing Soviet suspicion. Time to plead my case: "So how about it? The People Down South can do it."

Both of them shook their heads, no. Mike said, "They're not gonna go for it."

"How you gonna trap Michael without bait?" If they didn't want a lot of whine with their eggs, they'd have to come up with a more detailed explanation.

According to Mike, having John Pansini a librarian at Grummans was not in the government's interest because: "Ideally, what our friend wants is for you to present him with a menu of classified documents from which he can pick and choose. Not what our side wants. We learn nothing this way. There are analysts down south who do nothing but go over lists that you, and people like you, give us."

Tom added, "One day he'll ask you for something the government's unwilling to give up. When that happens, an order you can't fill, that's the last you'll see of our friend."

"Makes sense, so I guess I should just keep banging nails for a few more years?"

"That's not what we're saying." Mike sounded pissed-off. "We want you to do what's best for *you*. People are always looking for work. Hell, if someone offered Tommy and me seventy-five grand a year you'd never see us again."

"Try not to get too caught up in this," was Tom's advice. "This is just a small piece of a much larger pie. Michael could suddenly be gone. Don't let him become the most important thing in your life."

Michael could suddenly be gone —that was his text; but what was his subtext? Interdiction maybe? If that happened, then John Pansini went back to being just another tiny nail in God's Great Cosmic Pouch. Rather than dwell on that depressing thought, I began telling Mike and Tom about a minor culture clash Michael and I had yesterday.

As soon as he'd walked through the door, I said, "Happy birthday, Michael," and handed him his gift, the stun gun. "This'll keep you safe when you come to visit."

I truly liked the guy, so my concern for his safety was real. I didn't want him to fall victim to a street predator. For whatever reason, though, Michael did not strike me as being appreciative enough. He went deadpan. "It seems to me you are merely protecting your money, John." He put the stun gun in the pocket of his jacket and sat down on the sofa. Then he wanted to know, "Will I have to register this device with the police?"

"You gotta be kidding." Then pointing at the *deadly* weapon, "For that fucking thing?"

"I am quite serious," as was the look on his face. "Remember, John, it is for you that I am concerned. What if the police should question you why you bought it? What happened to it? Did you lose it? What you will say?"

"Michael, this is New York not Moscow. We don't have a KGB here."

Shrilly, "Don't tell me about your country, John. I know more about your country than you do."

Back at the diner, I asked Mike and Tom, "Is he for real, or what?"

They both grinned and shrugged.

We left the diner, and Tom drove us to 181st and Broadway. He parked in a bus stop. Foot traffic was always heavy this time of day. I felt a thousand eyes on us. Not hard to guess what those eyes were seeing: cops and an informant, not a healthy combination up here in the Heights.

Mike sat up front next to Tom. I was in back. Discreetly, I passed the tape recorder wrapped in a newspaper to Mike. Yesterday's meeting with Michael had also been bugged. Then Mike let his left arm drop behind the seat-rest, and he backhanded me an envelope containing three hundred dollars. I put the envelope in my briefcase.

"Put it in your pocket, Julius," he said in a cold tone that surprised me.

I shrugged. "What's the big deal?"

"The big deal is I don't wanna have to shoot somebody for stealing your briefcase."

Chapter 19
Kiss of the Spider Woman

"The opposition is not a single individual, but groups of individuals who not only outnumber you in their collective brain power, but they're also professionals with a great deal more experience playing the game. You're fooling yourself if you think you can compete with them at their level."

***

Saturday Night, May 4, 1985

A symphony of happy feelings surrounded me in quadraphonic. (Quad was big back in the 70s and 80s.) At 7 p.m., I drove my '74 Dodge Dart east over the 181st Street bridge that connects upper Manhattan to the Bronx. A full moon hung in the eastern sky. It reminded me of an old Dean Martin song: something about the moon hitting you in the eye like a bigga pizza pie, "*That's Amore.*" Anne, the ex-girlfriend I'd mentioned to Michael, had invited me to her place for dinner. The moon that lit the way not only triggered Dean Martin, it hovered low as if God Himself had dropped a giant beacon just above the bridge to guide me.

But joy can be such a fleeting thing: I aimed the Dart down the incline and onto the entrance ramp of the Cross Bronx Expressway at 172nd Street. The Cross Bronx is a sunken highway with three lanes in each direction. Tan brick retaining walls, with streets on top, ran along each side of the Expressway. At the bottom of the ramp I ran smack into a long, red ribbon: the ass-ends of a thousand other cars stuck in stop and go traffic.

I let out a "Damn!" and pounded the steering wheel. Then I maneuvered the Dodge into the queue and began the creeping crawl to Anne's multi-storied apartment building. She lived on 204th Street, within walking distance of the Bronx Botanical Garden. If traffic didn't thin out soon, I might be late for dinner.

Tall, slim, with curly big, black eighties' hair and round, dark eyes that appeared to be all pupils, Anne was more than sexy and attractive, she had brains, too. We'd met in 1980 when we both worked for the H.W. Wilson Company. I was an indexer on the *Applied Science & Technology Index* — a job I hated — and she was a struggling writer/poet who clerked at Wilson — a job she hated. The other indexers at Wilson ("professional" librarians with Master's Degrees) treated her (a mere baccalaureate) as if she was a creature who had only recently crawled up from the primordial ooze. Soon Anne and I became great friends; however, once our relationship progressed to a more intimate level the trouble began.

We hadn't seen each other in over two years. Not that she was ever out-of-sight out-of-mind. So when I received a Christmas card from her in December '84, I immediately called her. The sultry, breathy, calm sound of her voice brought back many memories, both good and bad.

Our former relationship could best be likened to a manic mountain bike race: mad cycling at break-neck speeds, the exhilaration as we careened from high point to high point before the inevitable fall. We'd tumble off our bikes after hitting one rut too many. Bruised and wounded, after a short respite, we'd get up and try again. Our past relationship could be best described as two smart people too stupid to know they weren't right for each other.

Was this still true? Was it time for us to mount up one more time for one more try? As for me — living alone, eating alone, sleeping alone — what did I have to lose?

Anne told me that she'd been married, but was now recently divorced. She currently worked as an English teacher at a business institute in Manhattan. I said I was a self-employed consultant who still roofed on the side. I did not mention who I consulted for.

For the next few months we peddled slowly, carefully avoiding past mistakes. We traded phone calls; went on a few coffee dates or lunched, and enjoyed an occasional night at the movies. In the beginning, I'd always offered to pick up the check, but she would politely insist on paying her own way. As she grew more comfortable being with me, she allowed me to pay for the both of us. And when I was short on cash, which was more often than I cared to admit, she would gladly pay for me, too.

Could two people who had been so wrong for each other suddenly morph into a happy couple? Apparently, Anne and I thought so. She had finally invited me over for dinner. We were both taking a big risk. What if we both fell back into our old being mean to each other ways? I was ready, willing, and able; after all, I had nothing to lose. But what about her?

Since our re-re-re-acquaintance was still in its early stages, being late meant being rude. If I drove more aggressively than usual — speeding up and cutting in and out of lanes — I might get there by eight, dinner time. I hit the accelerator and made my first cut, jumping two lanes from the far right into the far left. Then I ran out of free lanes to jump in and out of. One good thing about sitting in traffic and inching along in the Dart, it gave me time to think. By the time I got to her apartment building and parked (at about 8:45), I'd come to a decision. The following commandment had been chiseled onto the

Great Stone tablet I held in my head: *Keep-eth thy mouth shut-eth!* Set and cured, I promised myself that I would not break it no matter what. To share my secret life as a spy with her would give her power over me, something she already had more than enough of.

A jittery me rang the doorbell. Tonight was like our 100th first date. If it did not work this time, it never would. I stepped into the overly polite personae I occasionally used to cover-up high stress. Then I heard the approaching sounds of high-heels clicking on a wood floor. I knew even before she opened the door that Anne would look stunning. As for me, not too shabby, either: black on black, slacks and turtleneck sweater, topped by a tan camelhair sports jacket made for a sharp dressed man back in the 1980s.

The footsteps stopped just short of the door. The peephole slid open, and then closed. I heard an unsnapping of a multitude of locks that people lived behind in New York City. Anne opened the door and smiled. One of her top front teeth slightly overlapped the other, a smile I'd always found quite endearing. Her dress was a pale blue and yellow floral print. The two blue straps that held it up accented her smooth, olive-skinned arms and shoulders. I remembered that lying next to her was like snuggling with a warm, satin comforter.

When we embraced, I caught her scent: *springtime*. Would tonight be a new beginning for both of us? All those storms that had once gushed between us in the past, would they now be like old weather reports?

Then I stepped back, smiled, and held her right hand in my left. With my right hand I pressed the wine bottle tight to my chest.

Smiling, "Anne… You look beautiful."

"Thank you, John. So do you — look handsome, I mean." A

shy smile and slight stumble of words made me realize that she was nervous too.

I handed her the wine bottle. “My roof-buddy, Dom, recommended it. He knows the right wine for the right occasion.”

“Oh, thank you, John,” she said, “and thank you so much for coming.”

“Thanks for inviting me, Anne. Sorry I’m late, damn traffic.”

She waved it off: “Not to worry. I don’t drive, but I do understand.” Stepping to the side, “Come in.”

In the deep background, the simple beauty of eighty-eight keys tapping out a classical piece on the stereo. The room lighting was subdued. Not only had Anne put together a wonderful dinner of chicken Kiev and wild rice, but she had chosen to set an intimate mood. We sat at a small, drop leaf wood table in the middle of the living room, so close our knees touched. The aroma of two plates of food mixed with the scent of a burning candle. She had set two wine glasses on the table. I poured; her first, of course.

Was it the romantic lighting and intimacy of the moment? Or, perhaps, the need to impress a beautiful woman? My guess the latter because Anne moved from the *Does Not* to the *Does* column. That tablet in my head was made of clay not stone.

When I finished telling her, she believed me, but not without certain reservations. “Why would a Russian spy be interested in someone like you?”

“To begin with, Anne, he’s *not* a spy. He’s a Soviet intelligence officer. His job is to recruit spies, Americans willing to work on behalf of the Soviet Union.”

As soon as I released them I knew the words that came out of my mouth made me sound condescending, but I didn't care. And she knew me well enough to know that this was how I reacted when challenged — especially by her.

"You say the material you're giving him is unclassified, correct?" Her question had an edge that cut against my grain. "Why doesn't he simply purchase these documents himself instead of paying you ridiculously high prices?"

"Because he's not buying the documents, he's buying me. Thinks he owns me."

"What does he expect for his money?"

"He wants me to get a job at Grumman's (Aerospace) or some other defense contractor where I'll have access to classified documents." My tone hardened, and so did my facet: "He thinks I'm in *his* trap. But I'm only the bait. The People Down South have—"

"The who?"

"FBI, CIA headquarters. They have a rope around his neck, and he doesn't even know it. Sooner or later — Geez, it could be as soon as next month! — they're gonna start pulling, choking, make him an offer he can't refuse: 'Work for us or else.'"

She looked at me squint-eyed. "You mean become a mole?"

"That's only in spy novels, Anne. In the real world it's called to *defect-in-place.*"

"What happens if Michael refuses their offer?"

"Then his career in Soviet intelligence hits a wall. The guy came off a cooperative farm. He's now in the top 2% of his society." My eyes widened, and I nodded to emphasize the point. "Yeah, it's true. The FBI told me. They know quite a lot about him. They even said he's not well like by his colleagues." I scratched my freshly shaven chin and speculated out loud: "Makes me wonder who's *their* source; has to be another Soviet, someone on the inside. Probably another GRU officer." Turning my attention back to the question at hand, "Anyway, he'll be sent home. Probably spend the rest of his life behind a desk. Never leave the SU again."

"And if he accepts?"

"They'll pay him $1,000,000 up front. Then they'll guide his career. Make him look good to his superiors. After all, the higher up he goes, the more interesting information he has access to."

Anne leaned forward in her chair, tightly wrapped in a sitting fetal position. A shiver, a sip of wine, and then: "It's all so sordid. This may sound naive, but I'll ask anyway: what if Michael agrees to become a mole and the Russians find out?"

Anne had opened a door I thought I'd locked up tight, a harsh truth I'd rather not think about. But now she had forced me to step through. "Then he's a traitor. Know what the GRU does to traitors? Ever hear of a guy named Oleg Penkovsky?" A short obligatory pause, because, outside of those select few with a specific interest in Cold War intelligence, very few people ever heard of this guy.

I answered my own question: "He was a GRU officer who defected in place in the early 1960s. During the Cuban Missile Crisis he supposedly fed secret information to the West. I say supposedly because I read in another source that Penkovsky was really a double agent feeding disinformation to the West.[1] Hard to know what's the truth in this business; anyway, according to another book I read, when the GRU found out that he was a traitor, they burned him alive.[2] The

1 Wright, Peter, Spy Catcher, Viking Penguin, c1987, p. 305.
2 Suvorov, Viktor, Inside the Aquarium, McMillan, c1986, p.3-5.

GRU made it into a motivational film to show it to all new recruits. 'This is what will happen to you, comrade, if you ever betray us.'"

Anne shivered again. I had to admit Michael being strapped down and melted in a blast furnace gave me the creeps too. "But that was long ago," I said, trying not to dwell on the unimaginable. "The Russians are more civilized now[3]. Hopefully, they only shoot people."

"This puts you in a difficult spot." Anne had a strained look like she was grappling with information way above her weight class. "You pretty much know the whole scenario. Do they know you know? And by *they* I mean *our* they."

"Yeah, and I know what you're thinking. A defector-in-place is the ultimate to these FBI, CIA types. If Michael accepts, it becomes a top, top secret known to only a few highly placed individuals," a sly grin, "and one lowly roofer."

That caught her by surprise. "Why would they tell you?"

"They won't," I said, sounding like a pompous asshole again, "but I'll figure it out eventually."

"You do and your life won't be worth much."

"I am aware of that possibility, and I'm taking the necessary precautions." Before refilling my own wine glass, I made a move towards hers.

She shooed my hand away with her fingers. Then, "You're not thinking of a little blackmail are you, John?"

That remark pushed me back in my seat: "Of course not. I'd never blackmail the United States of America. How can you even suggest that? Besides, blackmail is stupid. And I'm not stupid."

"Oh, but you are," she said sharply. "Stupid, I mean. Except for

3 Tell that to the Ukrainians.

fulfilling a middle-aged, juvenile fantasy, I can't for the life of me understand why you involved yourself in the first place."

A middle-aged juvenile fantasy! Oh yeah!

Then she frowned. "What if Michael becomes a mole? Not only will he be putting his own life in jeopardy, but yours as well."

An emphatic, "First of all... *Anne*... I don't think Michael will ever betray his country no matter what kind of pressure they put on him."

"You don't know that! You don't know what kind of man he is. You've just finished telling me deception is his stock and trade."

Right again. I did not come here to fight with her, especially a fight I was already losing on points. Instead of jabbing back, I appealed to her area of expertise: "You're a writer, so how's this for a metaphor? We have a chess match. The USA is white, the USSR red."

"Congratulations on your first cliché, John." She smirked and motioned for me to continue.

While my mind spun in a grumbling overdrive mode, I bounced over her speed bump and my mouth continued on its merry way: "I'm the pawn. The USSR thinks the pawn is theirs, but in reality, the pawn belongs to the USA — sort of."

"Why sort of?"

"Because the pawn has some moves of his own in mind. For now, though, he lets the chess masters move him along, rank by rank. But when he reaches that final rank, the 8th, the pawn becomes a queen, the most powerful piece on the board. When I reach that 8th rank, Anne, I'll be someone both sides will have to reckon with."

"Your little chess analogy is somewhat interesting," she said, downsizing my metaphor. "This is indeed a multi-dimensional game, but I don't think you fully appreciate the precarious position you're in. You're at a distinct disadvantage. The opposition is not a single individual, but groups of individuals who not only outnumber you in their collective brain power, but they're also professionals with a great deal more experience playing the game. You're fooling yourself, John, if you think you can compete with them at their level. I think a better metaphor would be someone involved in an illicit love affair. You're infatuated with the adventure, the danger, and the excitement."

Her metaphor sent me bouncing my chair in my seat, "Absolutely! That's much better than my chess thing."

"I've known writers who have tried to live their fiction. It's not only foolish, it's dangerous."

A quizzical, "I don't understand. How is it dangerous?"

"You think you can manipulate real people and real events to create your own fiction. One day you might set something in motion that neither you nor anyone else can control."

Being lectured by someone who had no idea what the fuck she was talking about annoyed the shit out of me. The only thing she was right about was that my life had become like a movie, written, directed, and starring me. A movie came to mind that the two of us had just seen: *Kiss of the Spider Woman.*

In *Spider Woman*, the character played by William Hurt is locked inside a South American prison. His only escape comes from stories he conjures and shares with his cell mate, a political prisoner played by Raul Julia. At the end of the film, the authorities set only Hurt free. Their plan is to use him to get at Julia's people. When he's released, Hurt is tasked by Julia to deliver a secret message to them.

Unfortunately, because Hurt has been held captive so long inside the walls of his own imagination, he's ill prepared to deal with the real world. Hurt innocently leads the authorities to Julia's people. Hurt along with a lot of other folks get killed.

Me, John Pansini, the amateur spy, am I going to let myself be set up like that asshole Hurt in *Spider Woman*? Will Michael, me and everyone else involved in this mini-series come to a bad end because of something stupid that I might do?

"That's not going to happen, Anne. Besides, the FBI severely underestimates me. As a matter of fact, they probably think I'm a clown, a real jerk. Let 'em. That's to my advantage."

"Advantage, you have no advantage, John! Your cavalier attitude frightens me. I need some time to think."

"About what?"

From Anne, silence. She wouldn't even look me in the eyes. Instead, she held herself tight again and her mind folded deep inside itself. Me, I just sat there like a schmuck.

Her body language was easy enough to read, but it's my nature to question even the obvious. "Would you like me to leave?"

She nodded. "Be careful, John. I worry about you. And please don't call me again. That road you're so intent on romping down, I'm not sure I want to join you."

It was for the best. Anne and I were like two ships steaming past each other in turbulent seas. The distance between us was now so great that we might as well have dropped off opposite ends of the earth. At thirty-one-years-old and recently divorced, for her stability was all she wanted. And stability was something I could not give her.

Chapter 20

Dirty Deed Done Dirt Cheap

"When they're strapping you in the (electric) *chair, you'll look out and see two familiar faces. And I'll be saying to Mike, 'What did you say that guy's name was?' "*

***

Monday, August 12, 1985

TECHNICAL LIBRARIAN

EDO Corporation, a major defense contractor is currently seeking a qualified librarian to handle all the functions of a technical library.

Position responsibilities are to catalog all material, purchase books, documents and periodicals, research subject material using on-line information system, INMAGIC and DIALOG database; and the acquisition of technical information and documents from a variety of government agencies. Will also have responsibility for handling a Document D Control Center.

We require a M.L.S. degree and a minimum of 3 years experience with a defense contractor in a similar position, with a good understanding of security regulations as they relate to handling of classified material.

U.S. citizenship required. We offer a salary fully commensurate with experience, and 100% company-paid benefits, including pension and stock plan, tuition reimbursement and more! For immediate consideration, call the Employee Relations Manager, 718 [illegible], or send resume in confidence to EDO Corporation, 14-04 111th Street, College Point, Queens, NY 11356-1434.

An Equal Opportunity Employer M/F

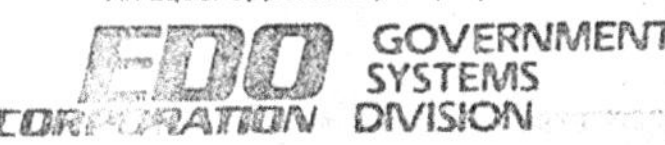

EDO CORPORATION GOVERNMENT SYSTEMS DIVISION

(Fig 20.1) New York Times Help Wanted, July 14, 1985

Nine o'clock in the morning and already a scorcher. The sun beat down on shiny, white-hot metal roofs. If there really is such a place, then this must be it, where all bad roofers go when they die. Imagining what it would be like to roof on a frying pan for all eternity, I vowed to lead a more righteous life henceforth.

What brought me here on such a God-awful day in my three-piece, winter-weight Yves St. Laurent suit: the previous Help Wanted ad in the *Times*. A job at EDO would be a hammer with which to chisel at Mr. Katkov and sculpt him to my liking. Today was the interview.

The EDO plant, located in College Point, Queens, was an R&D center as well as a manufacturing facility. The complex looked like a cross between a military base and a machine shop: prefabricated buildings all lined up in neat little rows, lots of new construction going on, and mud everywhere. Last night's rain did nothing to cool things off, though; it only added to the mugginess and pushed up the mercury on my irritability scale. I walked from building to building, and hopped from puddle to puddle, trying to find the personnel office. Mud splattered on my newly polished shoes. Here less than five minutes and I already hated the fucking place.

A lot of foot traffic outside, and all of it male, engineer, and wearing white short-sleeved shirts, dark pants, dark ties and black wing tips. Five thousand horny guys, and if I got the job there would be 5001. If I still had Anne, this place might be tolerable. But I didn't, so it wasn't.

Despite $28,000/year — not to mention certain fringe benefits to be gained from the USSR — second thoughts regarding EDO laid flat in my mind like the mud that surrounded me. A well-rounded peg like me would be a miserable fit in a square hole like EDO.

Somehow, I finally found the personnel office. After presenting my less than enthusiastic self to the receptionist, she led me to the office of the man who would be my king. He was in his 50s, tall, dark hair, and wearing black horn-rimmed glasses. He had the paunch and drooping shoulders of a man who had spent too many years with his ass planted in a chair. Another cause for pause: this could be me one day.

Boss man led me to the library located in another part of the building. Along the way he explained that EDO's work involved mostly sonar and ASW (anti-submarine warfare) equipment for naval vessels, and mechanical release devices for aircraft weaponry.

The library, not much bigger than my apartment, was a single room: dark, dingy, cramped, and with all the ambiance of a tomb. A large reading table sat in the center of the room, and a desk stacked with papers was shoved into a corner; the librarian's desk, no doubt. There were also a few racks thinly populated with documents. In surroundings like these every minute that passed would seem like an eternity. No doubt about it, this was Librarian's Hell. I wanted to run out screaming. And then I spotted them, several very large, very gray file cabinets. Each one had a steel bar running down the front and a huge padlock. Not hard to figure out what delights were contained within.

Yes, yes, I wanted this job!

The next day I called Mike and filled him in. "Unless you people have any objections, if they offer it to me, I'm gonna take it."

"We appreciate you letting us know, but we want you to do what's best for you."

Carte Blanche from the FBI? Not quite. What the government

giveth, two days later (Wednesday, August 14th), the government taketh away: "If you do get the job," Mike informed me, "we don't want you to tell Michael yet. There're a few cards we'd like to play first."

Michael was back from his summer holiday in the USSR. He had returned about a week ago, hence the necessity of today's luncheon at the Red Oak Diner with Mike Berns and Tom Black.

Mike continued, "We wanna see where he's gonna take you. He's probably been given an evaluation back home. Has he been told, 'You have this guy (meaning me), now get moving with him. Bring back something interesting.'"

"If that's the case," added Tom, "then he's gonna start pushing you more aggressively towards meaningful employment."

A frustrated, "Whadda ya think he's been doing."

I reminded them what had happened the last time I saw our friend.

My last meeting with Michael, before his summer vacation, had been on Saturday, May 18th. He'd asked me if I'd spoken to my aunt about a position at Grumman's. I told him I'd asked her to get me an application. Then I mentioned that the job was out in Bethpage, and it would be easier if I had an apartment out there.

"But I have no intention of giving up this place here," I told Michael. "It's gonna be renovated soon. Besides, I like living in Manhattan. It would be foolish to give up this 'palace' as you call it." He nodded, so, emboldened, I continued: "Therefore, I think it only fair that you pay the rent on the other apartment, the one on Long Island. Before I do anything, I must know whether you agree to this."

"Is no problem," he said casually.

"In that case, my car is old and—"

Annoyed: "First get job. Then we talk." Then he felt a need to insult my intelligence: "John, you must be careful not to tell anyone at Grumman's of our association."

"Michael, if I ever mentioned I had a Russian friend, not only would I *not* get the job I'd probably get a visit from the FBI."

He waved a finger at me. "Precisely, that is why you must be careful not to draw the attention of the authorities."

Sharply, "I know that. I'm not stupid, you know." Then loud and clear for the benefit of those tiny ears under my sofa where the Bureau's recorder chugged: "Besides, I hear the FBI are a bunch of assholes, anyway. They don't scare me."

"John, be afraid. I worry for you."

Four months ago, Michael had begun to put more pressure on me. Now the time had come for me to put more pressure on the Bureau. "So? How about you guys get me in at Grumman's or EDO?" I said to Mike and Tom.

Mike nearly leaped out of his seat. "Hey, if we thought the time was right, we'd put you in there tomorrow." He settled down. "But we need a lot more information before we give away the store." According to Mike, the FBI wouldn't even consider placing me in a job with access until the fourth year of Michael's tour. "He's been very happy with what you've been getting him. We see no need to allow him to get his hands on anything else."

Solid logic, so maybe I was behaving selfishly. Maybe I would end up in Roofer's Hell after all. "OK, so I'll let this Grumman's business drop. Let Michael think I'm trying to get a job there."

"We already told you," he said beating on that dead horse again, "do what's best for you, not what you think Michael wants you to do.

Don't let him take over your life."

"Yeah, OK. Hey, Mike," I shot him a big grin. "Know what I did?"

Mike turned to his partner and sighed. "Don't think I wanna hear this, Tommy."

"Tell you what, Mike. You go like this" — I put my fingers in my ears — "and I'll tell ole Tommy over here." A laugh, then, "I was at a copy machine in the engineering library at Columbia (University) with a roll of dimes and a NTIS report on microfiche. Then it hit me: why bother? So I dropped the fiche into my notebook, and it accidentally-on-purpose follow me out the door."

"You mean you stole it?" Mike said.

"I don't see it that way. More like I borrowed it. How was I to know it would end up in the Soviet Union forever?" I smiled.

"You stole it," he repeated, smirking.

"Yeah OK, but it was for a good cause. National security." Then to Tom, "Know what Michael said when I told him what I did?"

Mike was busy rubbing his temples (another headache, no doubt), so Tom had to play the straight man: "What did he say?"

"He shakes his finger at me and says, 'That was very, very naughty.' Then we both cracked up."

Dirty deeds done dirt cheap, the fiche cost about a dollar-three-eighty, but Mike looked at me as if I'd just admitted I ate puppies. "Don't ever do it again," he said.

I laughed. To Tom: "Hey, that's exactly what the other Michael said." To Mike, "Don't have to. It only has to be done once. Scored some big points with our friend, turning that stolen fiche over to him was my way of saying, 'See Michael, I did this for you, a Russian. There's no limit to what I'll do for you if you pay me.' Just playing the role, Mike, and that's what I have to do to be successful with our friend."

Seemed logical to me, but Mr. Berns didn't appreciate the subtlety, so I asked, "If you wanna trap this guy, you gotta give him something, right? A piece of the store, no?"

"Not necessarily," Mike countered. "The Russians are well aware that most English-speaking countries share certain intelligence. Being expelled in one is tantamount to being expelled from all of 'em. Even if he did report our overture to his superiors, while he wouldn't be punished, most likely he'd be sent to some hole somewhere. And believe me, there're plenty of places like that."

"Afghanistan, for one," opined Tom.

Mike continued. "For all intents and purposes, he'd be washed up."

"You mean he already *is* washed up, isn't he?"

I certainly didn't need *their* confirmation. I already knew that I had helped kill a man's career, a family man, a man who trusted me and who wanted to protect me from the very same people who now sat across the table from me. And then, like the guy who works a garbage truck, I pulled a lever and all guilt and conscience rolled out of my head. What I didn't know at the time, though, was that instead of being dumped into a landfill to be gone and forgotten, *Guilt* and his buddy *Conscience* sat on a loading dock rotting, stinking, and gathering flies. They awaited the right opportunity to let themselves be forklifted back in my head.

I went on the offensive asking questions about how they intended to *turn* (recruit) Michael. Mike said it was a long, tedious process that involved piecing together bits of information gathered after each one of my meetings with Michael. Mike cautioned that entrapping him with the hot stuff was "only one path. There're many forks on this road. We have a few surprises in store for our friend."

The May 18th meeting with Michael had been taped. With that in mind, I reminded Mike to pay particular attention to the part of the tape where Michael mentioned President Reagan's visit to Bitburg. He had begun by telling me what a crazy and confusing country America was. Then he mentioned Reagan's visit to the S.S. cemetery at Bitburg and the snubbing the Soviet Union got at VE Day celebrations. "We lost 20,000,000 people," he said, sounding like each and every one of them was a friend or relative. "More than any other nation. And after this we are not allowed to participate!"

"Don't blame you for feeling that way, Michael, but Reagan's a stupid old man, so don't let it bother you. Russians really hate Germans, don't they?"

"I harbor no ill feelings to those Germans born after the War. But the others, I have no regards for them whatsoever."

"Based on his Bitburg remark," I said to Mike and Tom, "my guess is our friend will never go for your deal."

"That might be true," Mike said. "He's still a rising young corporate executive. It's the guys in their early forties whose careers have stagnated who are the most susceptible."

"Also the guys who have lived in the West for longer periods of time, and who like it here," Tom added. "One of our inducements is an offer of asylum at some later date."

I warned them that if the day ever came when the FBI asked me to hand over a classified document to Michael, "I'm not doing it without written approval from the People Down South. Their verbal approval means shit as far as I'm concerned."

"That's not a problem," Mike said.

Then I added, "Know what, sometimes I think you guys don't trust me."

Mike turned to his partner and grinned. "I dunno, Tommy. What do you think? Is he still lean enough?"

Tom stared, carefully measuring me against his *Richard Miller Fat Spy Theory*. "Yeah, he's still OK."

Time to play with their heads a little: "If I recall," I said, elbows resting on the table, hands held together like a church steeple (an attempt to look intelligent), "Mr. Miller said he was trying to infiltrate the KGB. Is that true?" An absurd claim by Miller's defense; a hostile intelligence service is not penetrated from the outside, it's penetrated from the inside by compromising one of the service's own officers. In the Miller case the only infiltrating was of the FBI by the KGB.

Both Mike and Tom smirked, and Mike assured me that Miller was "not working for us."

I expressed my sympathy for Miller's wife and children. "He betrayed more than just his country. He betrayed his family too. In my opinion, that's worse. How are they gonna live with what he did? While I do favor the death penalty—'

"That's good to know," Tom broke in. "When they're strapping you in the chair, you'll look out and see two familiar faces. And I'll be saying to Mike, 'What did you say that guy's name was?' "

"But not for *treason*. And that's why I want everything in writing so nobody will be strapping me into nothing."

Mike and Tom exchanged grins. Then Tom asked, “So how much you gonna charge our friend?”

That summer I did something very uncharacteristic. My grandmother’s death threw me into a depression. To compensate I spent a whole lot of money, all on myself. $2,000 worth of clothing had been charged to my American Express card. I intended to pay for the new wardrobe by splitting the cost between the two Michaels.

“About eleven hundred after deducting the eight hundred he (Michael K) already gave me.” A reasonable price, one that guaranteed a tidy profit yet still was within bounds of what Michael would willingly pay.

“Is that all? You have a whole summer’s worth of documents to give him,” Mike said. Call him Johnny Apple Seed because that was what the guy just did; plant an idea in my mind.

“Well you guys are the experts,” I replied, “you saying I should charge more?”

“That depends. How much would you charge a normal customer?” Mike asked.

“I don’t have any normal customers.”

“OK, so how much would you charge a guy like ole Tommy, here?”

I pointed a finger at Ole Tommy. “Who *him?* More. And I mean a *lot* more.”

Mike turned to his partner and smirked. “Still think he’s on our side, Tommy?”

Chapter 21
Horror Behind the Wall

"But of course I bought these clothes for your benefit. What am I gonna do, wear them on the roof?"

***

Wednesday, August 28, 1985

Michael Katkov's call to tell me when he'd see me again:

(Audio 21.1) 0: 48

My call to Mike Berns the next day to tell him what Michael had said. Mike and I spoke of many interesting things:

(Audio 21.2) 3:20

***

On Friday, August 30th, at the Three Star Diner on 179th St: Mike looked like he was about to up chuck his cheese sandwich. At least I had the decency to wait until he was finished eating before reminding him about a dead rat that had been entombed in my wall beneath the kitchen sink.

(Audio 21.3) 1:40

Although we had briefly discussed this on the phone yesterday, today I felt a need to embellish:

"Stunk up the whole apartment. You should've seen it. It was all black and corroded with these disgusting hairs sticking out all over the place." Then I noticed Mike's nausea. "And the tail on that thing! Long, pink, and as fat as your finger." I grinned. "What'sa matter, no rats in Jersey?"

"We don't keep 'em in our homes."

"I can assure you that rodent was not there by my invitation. He was wedged between the pipes. Probably died a slow agonizing death; bet he got half-eaten by relatives."

Mike made a face and turned away.

I smiled. "Tragic, isn't it?"

Mike changed the subject: "If you read the *Times* this morning you'll see that we're not gonna get a raise this year. Military is. So are the postal workers."

No sympathy from my side of the table.

Then Mike had some explicit instructions for me regarding our friend: "We want you to pin him down. What does he mean when he says 'something interesting'?"

"But it's understood, 'something interesting' means something classified."

"Not good enough. When dealing with foreigners, Americans are too easily intimidated. We don't ask questions. If they (the foreigners) clam up or look out the window, we simply let it drop. We want you to put it to him, press him for answers."

"Let me handle Michael my way. I learn a lot more by keeping my ears open and mouth shut. Our friend does not like questions."

Mike asked if I'd heard anything from the EDO Corporation.

"Got called back for a second interview last week, but it doesn't look good. The guy asked me some strange questions."

"Like what?"

Instead of answering his question, I ignored it and said, "Also found out the choice is between me and two women. He'll probably pick one of them. Since I probably won't get the job anyway, can I tell Michael? Let him know that at least I'm trying."

An emphatic: "*No*. You already raised his hopes once before only to quit that job at the Power Authority in a week."

"It was a month."

"Yeah, but it seemed like a week. He's liable to start thinking: This guy can't hold a job." Besides," he paused to sip his coffee, "you still might get it. You're certainly qualified."

I asked Mike why he wanted a sample of the plastic shopping bags that I sometimes gave Michael to carry documents in. He repeated what he told me on the phone yesterday: after Michael leaves my apartment he heads straight home. Since Michael was forbidden to take documents home with him, he had to pass them off to someone else. That person then brings the material back to the GRU residency.

"He'll only pass them off to another GRU officer," Mike added. "We wanna know who this person is. We want to follow the bags if necessary."

I'd decided to make it easier for the Bureau. My cousin owned a store on Long Island. The possibility of there being other bags like these on the entire island of Manhattan on any given day was next to nil.

"See what we can accomplish when we work together, Mike," I said passing the bag to him. "And don't worry; I have a lot more of these at home."

Mike said, "It's crucial that we have a tape of your next meeting with Michael."

"Why? What's gonna happen?"

Mike made like he didn't hear the question, and I didn't press him.

We left the diner and walked around the corner to where Mike had parked a late model, blue sedan. It never ceased to amaze me how he always managed to find parking in this neighborhood, an impossible feat for ordinary humans.

I sat up front. Mike reached under his seat and pulled out an *Associated* shopping bag. The bag contained two small, cheap-shit stereo speakers. He proudly showed me what the "boys in the lab" had come up with. Inside one of the speakers a recorder and mike had been duct-taped into place. After turning on the recorder, all I had to do was screw the speaker shut using four Philips-head screws. The government was even kind enough to supply me with a Philips-head screwdriver. I wondered aloud how many hundreds of dollars they paid for it.

"I know you're a little afraid of Michael," Mike said. "He's a big guy. But don't worry, for him to find this thing he'll have to take this speaker apart."

"If Michael does find it, he won't have to throw me out of the window, I'll jump."

"Please don't do that. The paperwork involved would be enormous."

I asked Mike for his thoughts regarding all the GRU and KGB officers the Soviet Union had turned loose in America to steal our technology. I expected him to give me much the same Evil Empire bullshit that came out of the White House. Instead, "Both sides can blow each other up ten times over. What we have here is simply one economy desperately trying to catch up with the other. It all boils down to building a better washing machine."

"You mean I'm risking my ass so some Russian housewife can get her clothes 50% brighter?"

Mike nodded.

That was a downer.

My *Dumb Roofer Ploy* must have been working better than usual today because Mike felt the need to go over how to operate the equipment. I assured him that the two years I studied engineering qualified me to turn on a tape recorder and screw a speaker shut. Not convinced, he kept going over in minute detail each step. While he droned on and on, my eyes meandered around the interior of the car. My thoughts: *So this is where my taxes go. Complains about a pay raise! Plush. AC, stereo — what the fuck!*

When my eyes landed on it, my brain signaled: *RED ALERT!* On the dashboard, in a neighborhood with the highest homicide rate in New York City, sat a huge sign: a black NYC Police shield surrounded by a border that read, "Federal Bureau of Investigation." To the immediate left of the shield were large letters that said, "Police identification permit." Below was written, "This vehicle is on official police business."

To all felons, drug dealers and crazies in the immediate vicinity the sign screamed an open invitation to *Come Shoot the Two Assholes In This Vehicle*.

I sharply interrupted Mike's dissertation: "Get that sign off the dashboard and don't tell me I'm being paranoid either!"

He fumbled for the sign and shoved it into the glove compartment. "Sorry about that," he said, looking embarrassed. Then he offered to drive me home. I refused.

"The less time I spend in this vehicle the better. You wanna die so bad, why don't you just paint a bull's eye on the door?"

I got out and slammed the door shut. I walked away shaking my head. I couldn't believe that an FBI agent as sharp as Mike Berns could make a cavalier mistake that put both our lives in danger — or maybe just my life since I was the guy who had to walk these mean streets alone and unarmed.

The next day, Saturday, at 10:26 a.m., the phone in the living room rang. I reached for the receiver.

"Hello, John, is Michael. I will be over in one hour."

I turned on the recorder, screwed shut the speaker, and placed both speakers on the floor behind the blue chair and next to the TV table. A three-hour tape meant plenty of time, so I turned on the FM oldies station to relax me. The station was playing *A Salute to Elvis*.

Michael arrived at 11:25 a.m. looking like the Great Gatsby coming off safari: designer glasses that rested on top of his head, not on the bridge of his nose; khaki slacks and a khaki shirt wide open at the neck exposing a pink, hairless chest. He seemed relaxed and happy. Guess he got a good evaluation back home.

"You look good, Michael. Get that nice tan at a beach in the Baltic?"

"No, at Nassau Beach (on Long Island)." He stretched before sitting down on the sofa. "I was on beach looking at all the pretty girls. They assaulted my morality. I thought of you, how much you would appreciate such a sight."

Anxious for business not bullshit, I began bringing in documents from the front room and piling them onto the blue chair.

He motioned for me to stop and sit next to him. "We will get to that later. Let's chat." He launched into another one of those long, scripted speeches. This one dealt with the sorry state of the American economy. The picture as painted by Mr. Katkov came right out of 1930s Middle America: a dusty bowl about to get even dustier. "You should look to your future, John, to a job with more security. I would like to see you with better things. I would like to give you $50,000 commissions, but not for this scrappy" — he pointed at the material on the blue chair — "how do call it?"

"Shit."

"Precisely, this scrappy shit. And how are you progressing with your search for a position at Grummans? Have you spoken to your aunt?"

"She said she might be able to get me a job, but not necessarily a library job."

"Is no problem, you should accept any position. With your talent and abilities, and our help of course, we expect you to advance quite nicely."

Our help and *We expect* — the first hints that Michael spoke not just for himself but also a group of persons with a special interest in my career. My relationship with the GRU was solidifying. I felt so happy and important that I made a mental note to jack up Michael's already jacked up bill. After all, he had to pay his fair share for my new wardrobe.

Michael gave me my next order: a software package called *The Microdynamo*; a computer search on PAN carbon fibers; an ad that looked like the Russians had clipped it out of the *National Inquirer.* The ad described a device called a *Voice Changer* sold by mail order outfit in Florida.

The new order also included two government publications: *Military Tire & Rim Data Book, 1975-1982* and a *Dictionary of U.S. Army Terms*. These items seemed innocent enough, but, as Anne had warned, they did set in motion something that neither I nor the Bureau could control.

Michael told me not to use NTIS. Rather I should go to the library and photocopy each of them a few pages at a time.

"And don't steal them either," he said wagging a finger at me and grinning. "I will pay you $350 for each."

My mouth dropped open. This was a ridiculously high price even for him.

My Russian buddy seemed in such a jolly good mood that I figured the time was right: "You know Michael, I've been giving a lot of thought to your suggestion about developing more contacts — for our mutual benefit of course. Know what I did?" I got up, walked to the closet in the foyer and began removing articles of clothing and hanging them on the chinning bar that spanned the entrance to the living room. "Look what I bought. One must dress well in order to create a favorable impression, yah?"

He smiled and complimented me on my good taste.

"By the way, Michael, the bill for all that stuff over there," I said pointing to the documents on the blue chair and stuffed into two Village Luggage bags, "is $2,535. Less the eight hundred you gave me last spring, you still owe me $1,735."

Michael's head snapped back like he'd been kicked in the face. Then, in an odd tone that tossed anger, pleading, and incredulity into the same salad bowl: "You told me the material will cost only $800. For which I paid in advance. I brought another $800 for additional costs."

"Not additional enough, I'm afraid. Sorry, Michael. And besides" — my turn for a memory lapse — "I don't remember saying any such thing."

"John, if you would be so kind to explain how you arrived at such ridiculous figure."

My calculations were based on:

1) The FBI's not too subtle hints;

2) What Michael just said about the USSR's interest in my professional growth;

3) And what had happened in the case of Johnny Walker the Red.

When I'd asked Mike Berns what Michael's "problem" was — Why the delay between his return to the United States and contacting me? — Mike said it was too sensitive to discuss on the phone. So I asked him again yesterday when we were at the Star Diner. Mike had said because of the Walker Family Spy Case, "The Soviets are standing-down. He won't mention Walker, so you don't either."

(John Walker began spying for the Soviets in 1967. He was arrested by the FBI in 1985.)

And I didn't mention Walker, not by name, anyway. "Michael, let me remind you that these are dangerous times. I could get into a lot of trouble if my government knew I was doing business with a Russian. Besides, see all that stuff hanging over there." I pointed at the clothing. "You don't think I'm gonna pay for all that shit, do you? It's only fair. I bought all that to help you."

He shook his head and laughed, more amused than angry. And why not? Agents are supposed to be greedy by nature, the character flaw every intelligence service hopes to exploit. I was merely being a perfect spy.

"John, please do not insult me. I am genuinely sorry that I do not have enough money to pay you at this time."

"That's OK. I trust you. You can pay me next time."

"But please do not say that you bought all this beautiful clothing for my benefit. Is simply ridiculous."

"But of course I bought these clothes for *your benefit*. What am I gonna do, wear them on the roof? Please, Michael, now *you* insult *my* intelligence."

I think I was starting to believe my own bullshit.

"I feel bad," Michael replied. "Next time I will pay you an even $1,000." Then he raised an arm and pointed across the room. "I feel so bad that I want to jump out that window."

"Don't do that, Michael. Then I'll never get paid."

***

I'd slipped back into that lazy habit like it was a comfortable old sweat shirt: at 5:50 p.m. on Wednesday, September 4th, Mike and I met for dinner at the *Three Star Diner* on 179th Street. We were becoming familiar faces there, and you never knew who saw what up here in the Heights.

When I ordered a salmon steak dinner, Mike made a mental note of another one of my comfortable habits: "You sure do like salmon. Is that all you eat?"

Since salmon steak was pricey, "Only when the government's paying, Mike."

Until his remark, I'd never realized that for Mr. John Pansini it was always a western omelet for breakfast, a cheeseburger deluxe for lunch, and a salmon steak for dinner. Mr. Berns was drawing a bead on me; so was the other Michael. How could someone as predictable as me compete with these people? I vowed to make certain changes, at least as far as my menu was concerned.

Normally, I was the one who always preferred getting right down to business, but tonight Mike and I reversed roles. He seemed keyed up, tense, like a guy trying to do ten things at once. He mumbled, "There're a lotta people vying for a piece of my time." After ordering a tuna club on rye and a coffee, he pulled out his note pad and shot me a *Let's Get Going* look.

"How much did he pay you?" Mike asked without looking up.

His pen moved rapidly across the page with my eyes following right behind. All I could make out was, "John 9/4 5:50." I thought it read kind of biblical.

"He had $800 in one of those little white envelopes. Then when I gave him the bad news, he pulled another one hundred dollar-bill out of his wallet."

"Knew it!" Mike slapped down his pen. He wore a grin that stretched almost up to his eyebrows.

"Knew what?"

"He's skimming, knew it."

Outfoxed! Tricked! Used! That obnoxious grin that by rights belonged to me now creased Mike's face. That I was $100 richer did nothing to soothe my ego. "Very clever of you guys to get me to overcharge him to see what he does. You're a lot smarter than I thought. I'm impressed."

Mike didn't respond. He just kept on writing. And smiling. So Michael skimmed a little, what was the big deal? For Soviet intelligence officers stationed overseas, this was just another perk; maybe so their wives can buy better washing machines. Soviet intelligence officers were allotted funds to pay their assets. Since no written receipts passed between officers and assets, a Soviet could dole out the cash as he saw fit; therefore, "If Michael has been skimming all along," I said, "then those bonuses he's been giving me came out of *his* pocket, right?"

Mike's obnoxious grin dropped off his face and fell into his lap. "It's important that he keeps you happy. Just remember, all that money is supposed to go to you anyway. It's your pocket he's picking."

With emphasis: "*I don't see it that way.*"

Suddenly Mike's beeper went off. He grabbed his briefcase and borrowed a quarter from me for the pay phone. He left his note pad open on the table. I leaned over for a better look: Mike's notes were equally unreadable even right side-up. While he was away making his call, the waitress came and served the food. Too hungry to be polite, I was nearly done eating when he returned.

When I showed him the clipping for the VC (*Voice Changer*), Mike chuckled. "The boys down south will really get a kick outta this one," he said. "The Soviets have equipment like this. It's not beyond their technology. What they're gonna do is tear the damn thing apart to see if the Japs have made a better one."

Later, I learned that the VC was a far more complicated piece of hardware. And it wasn't made in Japan, either, it was made in Israel. The VC was a hot item from the *Red Book;* for me to acquire it would prove formidable.

***

No suit every day, no tie every day, and no wing tips, either. But no apartment on Long Island, no new car, and no access to *something interesting* because no job at EDO. The day after my meeting with Mike at the Three Star Diner, I found out that EDO gave *my* job to someone else. Not that I didn't see it coming. A second interview with Boss man had not gone well. He'd asked me an odd question: "If there's anything in your past I should know about, please tell me now."

I assured him that nothing in my past need concern him. I did not mention that it was my present he should worry about. Boss man wasn't satisfied with my answer. He said, "I had someone working for me, a fine young man who did excellent work. Worked for us about a week. Then the FBI found something." He paused. "I had no choice.

Had to let him go. It was a shame." He shook his head. "Are you sure there isn't something you want to tell me?"

"Positive."

Had Johnny Apple Seed and his cohorts down south dropped kernels of my destruction into this guy's cranium?

On Friday, September 6th, Mike called at 8:45 a.m. to tell me, "There's a problem with the tape. We listened for the first ten minutes. You forgot to turn off the radio. All we could hear was Elvis Presley."

"No, no! I told you. Only the first hour is Elvis. As soon as Michael arrived, I turned the damn thing off. Just keep listening. You'll get there eventually."

(Fig 21.1) FBI recorder & its hiding place

Chapter 22
A Man With a Plan

***

The headline said, *"Five years ago these mikes would cost you $5,000. If you could get them."*

Michael wanted this one, shown below.

(Fig 22.1) Ad for Voice Changer

This may sound odd," Mike Berns said, "but I'm gonna have to ask you to delay giving Michael the Voice Changer." He explained that getting approval for electronic hardware and software takes a little longer. Odd, though, that he did not mention delaying the MicroDynamo, a piece of software. Something was up with that damn VC.

"I have no intention of getting it for him," I replied, "not yet anyway. I called and found out that they accept only *VISA* and *Master Charge*, two cards I don't have. So if he wants it, he's gonna have to pay me in advance."

"OK. Order one for me too. You should be getting a check from us next week. It'll include an extra two hundred for the *Voice Changer*."

The VC cost $175. I was not happy with the markup, but I kept it to myself.

The next day, Friday, September 20th, Mike called back. "We're having a little trouble finding an address for that outfit (who sold the *Voice Changer*)."

"I know. They sound a bit sleazy. When I first called to place the order, the operator wouldn't give me any details. Said she had no connection with the distributor. She only took orders over the phone. There's something fishy about those guys."

"Nah, there are hundreds of little outfits like that out there."

"Yeah, and most of 'em are crooks."

When Berns called back Monday morning, on the 23rd, I asked, "When will I be getting my money?"

"Soon as I clear up some paperwork." Then he asked how much the material I gave Michael cost, how many hours I spent gathering it and how many hours did I spend debriefing him. "Doesn't have to be exact, an approximation is good enough. I'm gonna send it all down to Washington, so you can get paid."

Approximation was a dangerous word to use on a guy like me; especially since the Bureau had to pay their fair share for my new wardrobe. I told Mike $750 for the material and 100 hours gathering the material. I waited while his mind crunched the numbers: at my current rate of $50/hr the entire bill came to $5,750. I eased the receiver away from the side of my ear. A degree of separation would spare me the howl I expected to hear.

Instead, "OK. I'll send it on down." Mike sounded like his concentration was still focused on pushing a pen across the page like a farmer plows a field. What words did he seed it with? My guess: *This fucking guy is nuts if he thinks we're gonna pay that.*

The next few days rolled by and a preposterous idea began to germinate in my fertile imagination: *The FBI will be so grateful for my help in discovering the em-dash thing that maybe I am going to get, if not all, then most of the money.* Hard to say where the notion came from: the power of prayer, perhaps? Then on Friday, September 27th, I figured that if there was a God, He didn't give a rat's ass about me. A check for $600 arrived, $200 of which was for the *Voice Changer.* Not what I expected. And speaking of gods, those of the lower-case who did dwell inside the J. Edgar Hoover Building in D.C., they would soon feel my wrath. I'd done a computer search on PAN fibers for Michael. Washington wanted a copy too. Theirs was ready, but I'd been holding it back until I decided how much to charge. Had I gotten a $5,750 check, it would've cost the People Down South nothing. Now it was going to cost them plenty.

The search had yielded a ton of citations with abstracts, too costly to print online on a modem that processed 1200 bits per second. When it came to computer time, back in those days things like free and unlimited access were Orwellian. I would have had to pay $90 per hour broken down into seconds. Instead, I had the results printed offline on one of DIALOG's high-speed printers. DIALOG then mailed the search to me in a packet containing fifty pages. I took the pages to the local library, photocopied them at 15 cents/pg for a total cost of $7.50. The pages along with a bill for $502.40 ($500 for the search, $2.40 for postage) were stuffed into a large manila envelope. I walked to the Post Office and shoved it down the chute.

On Tuesday, October 3rd, I called Mike. He apologized that he was only able to get $400 for me instead of the usual $500.

"Mike, I was expecting a lot more than $500; I was expecting five thousand," I said, carefully focusing my anger on them, the People Down South. I gave no indication that I considered *him* one of *them*. "Did you get the computer search I sent?"

"Yeah, thanks," he replied.

Firmly, "And I expect to get paid, too. I'm billing the government for the information — *and* my services."

"If I put it to them on that basis, Julius, they'll say, 'Since he's already being paid by our friend, have him *Xerox* the pages for us.'"

"That's exactly what I did. It's the information they're paying for. It has intrinsic value. That value being what Katkov & Co. is willing to pay."

Mike said it was a tough world out there, and I should remember I was dealing with a government that had run up a huge deficit. I replied since they didn't seem to care, why should I?

On Friday afternoon, November 29th, I received the following greeting from Mike Berns when I joined him in a booth at the *Three Star Diner* on 179th: "Hey, it's Jonathan Pollard the 2nd."

Time Magazine had dubbed 1985, "The Year of the Spy." With good reason, because in addition to the arrests of Soviet spies Richard Miller and John W. Walker, Jonathan Pollard had been caught spying for the Israelis.

Unusually cheerful, even for him, Mike added, “I’ve got 2,000 things to do and only a couple of days to do ‘em.” He paused, then, with one of his biggest, brightest smiles, he announced, “I’m gonna be a dad in another week or two.”

A first time daddy! I was genuinely happy for him. “That’s great. Congratulations. If it’s a boy, you gonna name him Michael?”

“No way, maybe his middle name.”

The waitress came over to take our orders. She said to me, “It’s not nice to keep this young man waiting.” Obviously Mike had passed the time making a friend. She was in her fifties and probably wanted to adopt him. Mr. Berns was definitely a people-person kind of guy.

I said to her, “He doesn’t mind. He’s gonna be a daddy.”

“Congratulations! I’m so happy for you!”

After the waitress left, “You gonna leave *her* a fat tip?” I asked, referring to his and Tom Black’s obnoxious behavior towards the waitress in the Red Oak Diner back in Jersey.

He grinned, and took out his notepad. Back to business: the Reagan-Gorbachev Summit in Geneva ended recently and with it so did another GRU stand down. Katkov’s latest visit had been a week ago, on Saturday, November 23rd. Hence today’s debriefing.

***

“What you’ve got for me?” Michael had said after taking his customary seat on the sofa. I sat next to him, smiling and full of myself because I had over fifty pages of citations for him. But when I handed him the PAN search, his sharp look pierced my bubble.

"You mean after three months all you've got is this scrappy little, excuse my language, shit. How much will it cost?"

Squirming on the hot seat, "Five hundred?"

"Five hundred bucks for this!" he said, waving the papers in my face. "You know, John, I think I have spoiled you."

No shit, but so what? Then I went into full-whine mode: "But you said you'd give me five hundred."

"I said five hundred maximum. It seems to me — how much did it cost you, one hundred bucks?"

"One fifty."

"In that case I will pay you three hundred."

An emphatic, "I am not happy, Michael."

"You have doubled your money, John. Be happy." He skimmed through the pages. When he looked up again something caught his eye. His mood swung 180 degrees: "Who is that?" he said, smiling and pointing.

I glanced over and saw my new roommate standing in the hallway that connected the living and back rooms. He sniffed in Michael's direction.

"Oh, that's Stinky, my new cat. Went to a party in September, got him from a couple who are moving to Florida." I smiled. "He's only 9 months old. Looks like Morris, doesn't he?"

"Who is Morris?"

"A big orange tabby."

"Oh." Michael made some clucking noises and stretched out his hand.

Stinky's nostrils flared. After a good whiff, he turned and scampered into the back room to hide. I laughed. "Guess he doesn't like Russians."

"He simply does not like strangers," Michael said, his dark mood reappearing.

It turned as black as the tar I smeared on a roof when I told him, "If you want me to get the MicroDynamo it's gonna cost you $1,000."

Michael shot me a look as if I just farted.

"Listen, Michael, I could get into a lot of trouble for selling a piece of software to a Russian." My inference was to all the Americans who would soon be on their way to prison for spying for the USSR. "It's risky business, so I feel I should be adequately compensated."

He threw up his hands. "I see I *have* spoiled you. I could go to store and buy all the software I want." He shook a finger at me. "You overcharge me on the pretext of my nationality."

There was a crooked man who gave a crooked smile: "So what?"

***

Back at the diner, Mike said, "I hope you didn't mention (Johnny the Spy) Walker?"

"You told me not to, so I didn't. But he reads the papers. He caught my drift."

Mike mentioned that Michael had left the Soviet compound at 11:09 a.m. that day. The compound, across the river in Riverdale, the Bronx, was only a five minute drive to my place.

Michael had driven to a subway, parked, and spent the next three hours sanitizing himself; i.e. eluding surveillance, successfully too, because the FBI had lost him. Mike grudgingly admitted that Michael was "a good spy." He added that on other occasions when Michael had met me during the week between five and six p.m., he would leave work at three. Therefore, even knowing Michael's starting and ending points the Bureau still could not attach a tail to him.

For intelligence officers on foreign assignment, be they CIA, GRU or KGB, their first obligation is not to hide their own identity; it doesn't take the other side long to figure out who's who. Job #1 is to protect the identity of their assets.[1] Hence,

"Poor Michael going through all that shit to protect me. It's a little sad, isn't it?"

Not in a philosophical mood, Mike simply noted that Michael never delayed after a meeting. "He's usually back home within half an hour. This is pursuant with his getting down to business personality. In that sense the two of you are alike."

I slid two 8 1/2 x 11 typed carbon pages — in poor condition like they'd passed through a lot of hands — across the table to Mike. The latest order from Michael consisted of 43 government reports numbered with the prefix PATR (Picatinny Arsenal Technical Report). All the reports dealt with explosives and munitions. Michael said he would pay me $2,000 for all the items on the list, plus an extra $200 if I had them all for him by our next meeting. He also warned me to be careful not to draw attention to myself.

Mike said, "I want 'em (the pages) when you're finished. We'd like to compare them to other samples we have." He handed the pages back to me.

Judging from the titles, many of the items, if not hot, sure looked warm.

1 Rositzke p.174

Five of the PATRs also had NTIS accession numbers, so I ordered those directly from NTIS.

On December 11th, I received a memo from NTIS stating that my order had been delayed. That never happened before. I remembered that Mike had said CIA had an asset there. Was the delay deliberate? Was the government trying to slow me down? From the very beginning both Pat and Mike had been telling me that things were moving too fast, that I should think about holding some material back from Michael. When their requests made sense, like with the technology transfer directory, I did as requested; but when it seemed arbitrary, I did what I wanted. Therefore, this memo made me wonder if the government intended to control the flow of unclassified information between Michael and me.

On Thursday, December 19th, I let my fingers do the walking: I dialed the Picatinny Arsenal in Dover, New Jersey. I gave the librarian the following cover story: I was an automotive engineer doing research on the design of an armored personnel carrier. I had a list of reports published by the Arsenal dealing with projectiles and explosives. They were old, published in the 40s and 50s, but still relevant to my work. Was it possible for me to order them directly from the Arsenal?

The librarian told me the Arsenal had all the reports. Then she added that even though the reports were old, they still might have restrictions on them. "And you know the Army, be prepared to answer a lot of questions."

(Audio 22.1) Time: 2:20

I told the interim librarian, even though I was not a terrorist, I decided not to bother with Picatinny anymore. I called two document delivery services: CAROLIB (The University of North Carolina) and IOD (Information on Demand). Both were very large and very prestigious. I wondered if the Army would ask them a lot of questions. I'd done business with these companies before, and I knew they would protect my identity. But just to be safe, I ordered only two PATRs from each.

As for the *Voice Changer*, I managed to track down the Israeli who sold it. I spoke with him on the phone. He said that he was currently out of stock but was expecting a new shipment soon. Then he mentioned that the price had dropped from $175 to $129, a bargain that I would not pass along to the People Down South. I ordered two, one for the good guy who paid his bills on time and the other for the cheapskates in D.C. who still owed me money.

As for the *Dictionary of Army Terms*, I'd ordered that through a company in California I'd stumbled upon by accident, *Newport Aeronautical Sales.* But on January 2, 1986, I'd received a memo from them that said the dictionary was currently out of print and in revision.

Desperation is a choke hold, its tightest grip on those who haven't got their shit together. The only thing I had for Michael was the MicroDynamo. My ass was on the line, and I had to do something to save it. Then a seed blew in from the West Coast. It nestled in the coldest, most calculating, most self-serving part of my soul.

On Monday, January 6, 1986, it blossomed.

First the cover story: "Hello, Bob. This is John Pansini from CIR. I'm calling to check on the status of the Army Dictionary." Then the real reason for this phone call to Newport Aeronautical: "Bob, I'm having difficulty locating some documents for a client of mine. I know where they are, the Picatinny Arsenal in Dover, New Jersey. But you know the damn Army. They're going to make me fill out a whole lot of forms — *in triplicate*. I remember you once told me that you could cut through red tape. Think you can help me out here?"

"Why su-rrre," Bob replied. "Back when I was an air force pilot, I used to fly materiel in and out of there all the time."

The way I figured it, air force pilot meant air force officer. Officers had connections. Then my conscience laid it out for me: *You might be getting this guy into some deep shit. Better tell him to forget the whole damn thing.*

Instead, *I* told Bob, "Thanks. Whatever you can do will be appreciated."

The next day, one of my other assets, *Information on Demand*, called and said that The Defense Technical Information Center (DTIC) and Picatinny had the reports, but neither would release them to IOD. I would have to submit a written request for the documents, and they would be released only on a need to know basis.

The DTIC is a clearing house of government sponsored research restricted to defense contractors and others with special security clearances. When all restrictions on a document are removed and it is approved for public release, the document is then transferred to NTIS for distribution. Proof positive: some of the reports on Michael's list were either classified or restricted.

On Wednesday morning, January 15th, Mike called. First I congratulated him on the birth of his daughter, and then down to business. I told him about the difficulty I was having getting the PATR reports. I explained to Mike that library/information science is a lot like police work. Once the cops have a positive ID on a criminal, it's only a matter of time before they nail his ass. Same thing with documents: once a person has its citation (author, title, publisher, date, etc.), whether the document is restricted or in the public domain, it's only a matter of time before it can be acquired. That raised an intriguing question: how did the Soviets come up with these citations?

Mike said, "CIA probably knows, but they aren't sharing that information with us because we have no need to know," his implication being that *we* also included *me*.

(Audio 22.2) Time: 3:26

What about Bob at NAS? He seemed so confident. What had I gotten him into? I'd intended to play it safe and order only two PATRs with him, but I let myself be talked into ordering eleven altogether. (I still held a few back.) For this, selling restricted information to the Main Enemy, Bob wanted $15/document plus costs, hardly the wages of sin.

By January, 1986, I'd build up quite a library of micro cassette tapes. But the only recordings I had of Michael were of the "I will stop by in twenty minutes" variety, all less than 30 seconds. Not enough time to capture the man's essence for the book I planned on writing.

I'd been making tape recordings of my meetings with Michael for the FBI on a regular basis. The Bureau had even stopped asking me to sign waivers. And then one day it came to me: why should the People Down South have all the golden memories? I wanted a few of my own. That made me the man with a plan.

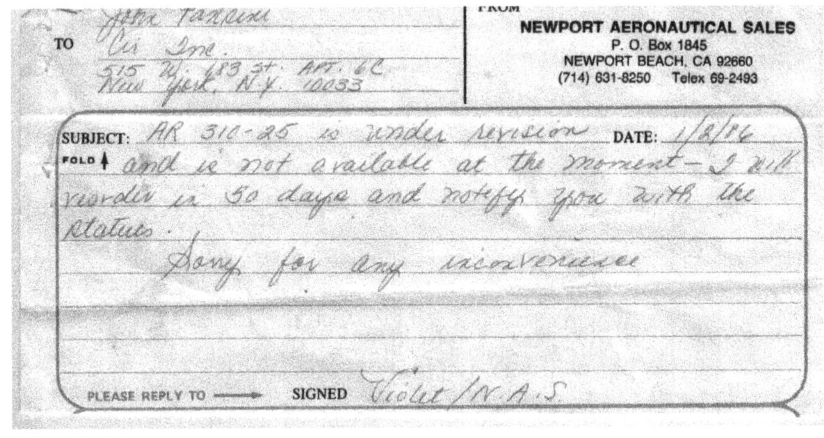

TO John Taranu
Cii Inc.
515 W. 183 St. Apt. 6C
New York, N.Y. 10033

FROM
NEWPORT AERONAUTICAL SALES
P. O. Box 1845
NEWPORT BEACH, CA 92660
(714) 631-8250 Telex 69-2493

SUBJECT: AR 310-25 is under revision DATE: 1/8/86

FOLD ↑ and is not available at the moment - I will reorder in 30 days and notify you with the status.

Sorry for any inconvenience

PLEASE REPLY TO → SIGNED Violet/N.A.S.

(Fig 22.2) Note from NAS saying dictionary of army terms is under revision

1. S.Kogan, Effect of RDX Granulation on Properties of Composition B, Picatinny Arsenal, PATR 1433, 1944, U S A.

2. P.B.Tweed, Effect of RDX Granulation on Properties of Composition B, Picatinny Arsenal, PATR 1458, 1944, U S A.

3. O.E.Sheffield, Establishment of Optimum Granulation of RDX for Use in Cyclotols, Picatinny Arsenal, PATR 17-09, 1949, U S A.

4. D.C.McLean, A Study of Various Solvents and Solvent Mixts for RDX and Investigation of the Effect of Surface Active Agents of the Viscosity of High RDX Content Cyclotols, Picatinny Arsenal, PATR 1793, 1950, U S A.

5. M.Baer, Investigation of Methods for Determination of Viscosity of Composition B & Other Binary Explosives, Picatinny Arsenal, PATR 1803, 1951, U S A.

6. S.J.Lowell, Cast Loading of Composition B with Heated Probes, Picatinny Arsenal, PATR 1978, 1953, U S A.

7. S.J.Lowell, P.B.Tweed, Investigation of Surface-active Agents for Reducing the Viscosity of Molten Composition B and Cyclotols, Picatinny Arsenal, PATR 1983, 1953, U S A.

8. L.Jablansky, Evaluation of 70/30 and 75/25 Cyclotols for Use in HE and HEAT Projectiles, Picatinny Arsenal, AD 017 262, 1953, U S A.

9. S.Fleischnick, C.E.Jacobson, Development of Improved Methods for Cast-Loading RDX/TNT Compositions and Comparison of Composition B and 50/50 Pentolite as HE Filler for 2,36 Inch M6 Rocket Heads, Picatinny Arsenal, PATR 2008, 1954, U S A.

10. A.Nordio, The Cooling and Solidification of Molten Composition B and Causes of Shrinkage Cavitations in Cast Loaded Shell, Picatinny Arsenal, PATR 2190, 1955, U S A.

11. S.Lowell, A Study of Grit and Exudate as Possible Causes of 75mm T50E2 Shell Premature, Picatinny Arsenal, Feltman Research Lab., 1955, U S A, AD 061 692.

12. E.Scettini, N.Baron, Evaluation of Fragmentation, Safety and Functioning Characteristics of Composition B, 75/25 Cyclotol in 105mm HE Shell, Piaatinny Arsenal, Feltman Research Lab., AD 089 567, U S A, 1956.

13. M.Margolin, C.Hartman, Investigation of Composition B and Cyclotols for Use in 60mm M49A2 HE Shell, Picatinny Arsenal, Feltman Research Lab., AD 107 580, 1956, U S A.

14. J.D.Hopper, Results of Penetration Tests of HEAT Ammunition Containing Octol Bursting Charges, Picatinny Arsenal, Feltman Research Lab. AD 132 847, 1957, U S A.

15. A.M.Anzalone, Bibliography on the Flow and Viscosity Properties of Cyclotols, Composition B and TNT, Bibliography N°4, Part 1, Picatinny Arsenal, 1957, U S A.

16. C.E.Jacobson, et al, Evaluation of Materials for Use as Desensitizers in Composition B, Picatinny Arsenal, PATR 2433, 1957, U S A.

17. M.Margolin, E.A.Scettini, Ammunition Loading Technique, Expl Dev Sect Rept 43, Picatinny Arsenal, 1958, U S A.

Orde rec 11/23/85

Chapter 23
The Other

"He made me feel inadequate, like I had let him down. I was desperate to say something to please."

"Don't worry, it was a good move."

***

Friday, January 24, 1986

At 4:40 p.m., the phone in the front room rang; that had to be Michael. Really big balls would be needed, but each time the phone rang mine got smaller and smaller. Pretty soon I'd be carrying a sack of pea nuts between my legs. The equipment was good to go, but the man with the plan could not get going. What if I'd overlooked a detail that might bring one of Katkov's massive fists down on my skull? Worse, what if he spotted the recorder? Unlike the FBI's $3,000 recorder — again hidden in one of two speakers lying on the floor behind the blue chair — my $55 worth of equipment had certain limitations. Since the micro cassette tapes ran for only sixty minutes per side, every second was precious if I hoped to capture the entire conversation. I couldn't very well stop in the middle and say, "Hold that thought, Michael. Gotta change sides." Also, when the tape ran out there was an audible *click*; therefore, the recorder and the mike could not be in the same room. But the microphone cord was only 4 feet long.

A problem I'd solved after much thought: the kitchen and living room windows were only a few feet apart, forming an inverted L. Perfect. I placed the recorder outside on the kitchen window ledge and had the mike pressed up against the glass inside the living room window. Shades were pulled, curtains drawn; Michael's voice would filter through while his eyes were kept out. On the odd chance that a neighbor might look out their window and see a tape recorder on my sill, I secreted the recorder inside a roach motel. The little buggers infested the entire building. On cool evenings I bet they liked to congregate outside on my sill to chat: "Ate some crummy tuna fish sauce and spaghetti in 6C tonight. Is that all that guy eats!"

The phone continued to ring every ten minutes. Finally, at 6 p.m., sick and tired of playing Hamlet, I picked up: "Hello… Yeah, OK. Come on over."

Minutes later, from the kitchen window, I watched a tall figure, draped in a dark trench coat walk briskly into the building behind three other people. I noticed something odd: Michael did not carry his attaché case; his hands were in his pockets.

Thunk!... Click!... Slam!... The doorbell… The recorder… The window.

***

"Is this all you've got for me?" Mr. Katkov said, after I handed him the MicroDynamo software.

Michael's degree of pissed-off-ness showed on his face. "You are neglecting your duties, John. I have spoiled you." Then he paid me $300. "What about those other documents? (The PATRs). Why haven't you've got them yet?"

That was when I panicked and told him about NAS — something I had not intended to do. "I ordered the PATRs through them. This guy Bob said he may be able to get them for me." Eager to please, I shot him a smile.

Michael's face displayed little enthusiasm either for NAS or me. I showed him the memo NAS had sent me regarding the army dictionary. He looked at it, then folded it and put it in his breast pocket. But later, on three separate occasions, he asked me for more detailed information about the company in general and Bob in particular. Then he surprised me by saying, "Is better if you cancel your order with this company since we don't want you to take any unnecessary risks and do anything illegal." Then he took the PATR list from me. "You will forget about this too." He folded it and put it into his breast pocket.

Later, after I replayed the recording, I knew the window setup would not work. The mike picked up too much ambient noise; i.e. one of my neighbors blasting their stereo. I'd have to come up with something better next time.

(Audio 23.1) 1:50

***

The next evening I met Mike and another agent in the Red Oak Diner in Fort Lee, New Jersey, for debriefing and a side order of dinner.

"I'll have a Swiss steak, please," I said, handing the menu back to the waitress.

"What?" said Mike, grinning. "No salmon?"

"Not tonight. Gotta keep you guys off balance."

He grinned.

"Been reading a book about the GRU, pretty soon I'm gonna be as smart as you guys." I said, pointing across the table at Mike and his new buddy Kevin, late 20s, dark hair, friendly face.

Mike grinned at Kevin and reached down into his briefcase. "You mean this book." He held up his copy of *Inside Soviet Military Intelligence* by Viktor Suvorov.

Kevin said, "Don't believe everything you read in a particular book, John."

"I don't. I read several sources. Get differing viewpoints. Then I match that against my own personal experience and what you people tell me."

Mike said, "You gotta watch this guy, Kev. Sometimes he thinks we work for him."

Well, I was a taxpayer, so I suppose, theoretically, he did.

I told Mike the pressure was starting to get to me. "I beeped you this morning at three." If I couldn't sleep, why the hell should he? "I wanted to talk. Why didn't you call back?"

Mike smirked. "Contrary to popular belief, I don't sleep with the thing under my pillow."

"Michael said I look terrible. Do I look sick, or what?"

"I dunno," Mike snarked, "maybe you should try getting more sleep." Then Mike took out his notepad and asked, "So what happened?"

"To begin with, Michael took back that PATR list, but don't worry, I made a photocopy for you guys." And one for myself, too; my little secret. Then I apologized to Mike and Kevin about practically handing Michael my source at NAS on a platter. "He made me feel inadequate, like I had let him down. I was desperate to say something to please."

Mike said, "Don't worry, it was a good move."

Kevin added, "It's always a good idea to tell us everything you tell the other guy."

Exasperated, "Always do, but I had no intention of telling Michael in the first place." I turned to Mike. "I don't wanna make trouble for this guy (Bob)."

Mike, scribbling in his pad, mumbled some dry wit: "That's OK. We'll arrest him later tonight."

When Mike finished writing, he looked up and asked me if I knew anything about the guy from Picatinny who'd been missing for the past five weeks.

"We're looking for him," Kevin added.

"Heard it on the radio this morning," I said. "Maybe that's why he took the list back. Bet it's getting pretty hot over there with federal agents crawling all over the place."

The missing person Mike referred to was an engineer named Gary Gnibus, age 31. Gnibus had been working at the Army Armament Research & Development Center at Picatinny since 1980. He had access to top secret information. He was last seen on December 16, 1985, when he left home for work. Ten days later, on December 26th, his wife filed a missing persons report. Both the FBI and Army were looking for him, but neither would comment on whether they suspected espionage.

Picatinny Arsenal, a base with 6,000 civilian and 300 military employees, was the Army's primary center for R&D on gun armaments, munitions, tools and equipment used to maintain weaponry. It was also the site of at least one SDI project, or "Star Wars" as dubbed in the press. SDI (the *Strategic Defense Initiative*) was a Reagan Administration program intended to put a missile shield in space.

Four days after my meeting with Mike and Kevin, events at Picatinny turned grisly. On January 29th, Col. Alfred Crumpton, age 45, the director-commander of the Fire Support Center, was found hanging from a banister in his home. A spokesperson for the Army said that Crumpton had been the subject of an investigation for "travel improprieties" allegedly committed during a previous assignment. Crumpton had been posted to Picatinny in December 1984, and one of the 1,000 civilians under his command was Gary Gnibus. So by late January, 1986, federal agents were like lice crawling all over the Arsenal. (I never did find out how the story turned out.) No wonder Michael worried about me ordering documents from there.

"He's protecting himself as well," Mike said. "He'd be at just as much risk if you ever handed him anything classified."

What Mike had said about me handing Michael a classified document was true. Suvorov writes in his book that the GRU had a preference for dead-drops (i.e. tin cans in Jersey) or brush contacts when passing the hot stuff, not face-to-face meetings in apartments. Besides, Michael was a Viking, a top-notch officer. The GRU would never risk having a Viking caught with classified material on his person. Other, less productive, officers called *borzois* (which means dogs in Russian) were used for that. They were the ones who went sniffing under rocks, and if they got caught, so what.

I told Mike and Kevin, "Michael is continuing to press me about getting a job at Grummans. He said he doesn't expect me to get a job with access right away, but with 'our help' he tells me, 'we expect you to work your way up.' Now I don't want to presume to do your thinking for you, but—"

"Don't you believe a word of that, Kev. He's always trying to think for us." Mike grinned.

"This represents a unique opportunity for us to string him along. To see exactly how the GRU is going to help me." I paused, then, "So, whadda ya say, huh?"

Mike gave me a tired look. "We've already been through this, John." Then to Kevin, "Seems like a hundred times." Back to me, "Right now it's just not in the cards."

Then he told me something interesting about Mr. Katkov: "While he was in London, he was so industrious, such a good company man, that he was not well liked by his Soviet colleagues."

In a secret society like a Soviet compound overseas, how did the FBI come by such intimate knowledge regarding Michael's relations with his fellow GRU officers? One thing about secret societies, they also possess secret informants. Which Soviet fed information about Mikhail L. Katkov to the People Down South? One possibility might have been Oleg A. Gordiyevsky, the KGB Rezident in London and a defector-in-place for the West for two decades. He was spirited out of a Soviet prison and granted asylum in Britain in September, 1985.[1] Gordiyevsky was stationed in London the same time Michael was. As KGB Rezident, one of Gordiyevsky's duties was to spy on the GRU. Still, if I was a betting man, my money would be on an unknown GRU officer also stationed at London's GRU residency at that time.

1 *New York Times*, September 29, 1985.

I might even double-down that this GRU source was still *in place* in January 1986.

I learned early on when dealing with the Bureau, and by extension CIA, that these people did not think like the rest of us. They had what's called in the trade a *clandestine mentality.* When they shared specific intelligence with me it was like a chess move, it had a purpose.

I also suppose they'd learned something about dealing with me as well: *From now on, be careful what you tell this asshole.*

Pat had once hinted that I might not be the only harpoon in Michael's side. Today Mike made no allusion, he was quite specific: the FBI/CIA did have another controlled asset feeding them intelligence about Mr. Katkov. When I asked for more information about this person, Mike replied, "I'm not at liberty to say."

Then why say it in the first place? Because this move was meant to warn me, *You're expendable, Julius, so behave yourself.*

Proof positive when Mike followed up with: "From now on we don't want you seeing our friend on a moment's notice. Next time he calls and wants to stop by in five minutes you say, no, it's inconvenient."

Michael was *my* client, so whatever was convenient for him I'd make convenient for me. As for weaning Michael off the five minute rule, "I'll try," I told Mike, with no intention of doing so. The more control of the situation Michael believed he had the less likely he'd throw me out a window.

***

The following Monday, January 27th, at 5:15 p.m., I called my contact at NAS. "I think it's best that we cancel the order, Bob. Found out that Picatinny won't release the reports to a third party to sell to me. They're restricted to defense contractors only."

"Doesn't mean a thing, I can get them. *I am a contractor.* Think positive, John. The government has shut-off repositories to the general public. That eliminated 90% of the Freedom of Information requests. But a lot of stuff is still available for legitimate business purposes. A government contractor can write in and order from a government repository, but not every Joe Blow."

What about Joe Blowsky? That be me, of course.

"We provide services to companies like you, John, small outfits that aren't government contractors but want to bid on government contracts. We do business with guys like you every hour. It might take a while, but I'll let you know the availability. Remember, we're in business because we know how to extract information from the government."

Great pitch, but I still had my doubts: "I wouldn't want to do anything illegal, Bob. Know what I mean?"

"You worry too much, John. I can assure you, it's all perfectly legal."

***

As disturbing about using an innocent like Bob and NAS was, it was not the only thing that troubled me. A new squatter made itself at home in my head: *Who is the FBI's/CIA's other controlled asset? And is this squatter a risk to me?*

Twenty-seven years later, in 2013, I'd finally have the answer. And this person was not what I'd expected.

Chapter 24
Prowling the Periphery

"... so whadda ya gonna do, lock me up?"

"Yeah, you bet I will," *he shot back.*

I smirked. "I don't believe you."

***

Monday, March 31st, 1986

On Monday, at 5 p.m., Michael pulled an envelope out of the left breast pocket of his navy blue sports jacket. It was fat with cash. He flipped it to me. *Splat*! It hit the Formica top of the kitchen table; there it lay. I stared, eyes slowly widening. I imagined myself tip-toeing through a patch of tulips with petals of one hundred-dollar bills. Ah, the sweet smell of money. Could life get any better?

Whatever this guy wanted for his money, I'd worry about it later. I scooped up the envelope and peeked inside. Shit, fuck, and all profanities in between. Fifties! A rain cloud dumped on my field of dreams turning it into a big slush of mud.

"Here is $700," he said. "We would like you to go to California to meet with that chap we spoke of before." That had to be Bob at NAS.

As quickly as it came, the rain passed; the sun shined again. An all expenses paid trip to California. That made me a secret agent on a secret mission. Could life get any better?

Michael continued, "You are to establish a business relationship with him." When I asked him to be more specific, he replied I would know what to do.

After Michael left, I beeped Mike. He called back, and I told him about the trip.

(Aud 24.1) 1:35

***

April Fool's Day, so I should've expected something like this to happen. Mike called this morning before 8 a.m. He told me I'd have to turn all $700 over to the FBI.

(Aud 24.2) 2:13

Again shit, fuck and all profanities in between.

"Don't worry, Julius. I'll explain when I get there. I'll be over in one hour." He said he would bring another agent with him to house-sit the painters while I was gone. For obvious reasons, I didn't want unattended workmen left alone in my apartment, especially with $700 in cash in the top drawer of my dresser.

From what Mike told me yesterday, and what he said today, this had to be important to the Bureau; important enough for me to dig in. Not only did I hold all the money, but all the cards too. Mr. Berns was going to have to persuade me.

The agent Mike brought with him, also named John, rang the front doorbell. He wore glasses and looked like an accountant. I sat him down in the kitchen. Then I went into the front room where the painters were working and took out my accounting ledger.

"Don't mind the guy in the kitchen," I said to the painters, "he's my accountant. He's gonna look over my books." A grin, and then an aside: "Hope he doesn't take too good a look."

The painters laughed.

I checked in the top drawer on my way out the door. A fat white envelope stuffed with $700 lay beneath a stack of jockey shorts. With an FBI agent on the premises, I was not worried about it getting up and walking out the door. Besides, these painters did not look like the kind of guys who would rummage through another guy's underwear.

I met Mike downstairs. We drove in his car to 190th Street & Amsterdam and parked.

"So what's the big deal that you had to see me this morning?" I said.

"First tell me what happened, word for word, as best you can remember." He took out a notepad. When I finished telling him, Mike smiled. "By tasking you to travel outside his twenty-five mile limit and contact someone on his behalf, he's just broken one of the espionage statutes."

"You gotta be kidding."

"I'm not. We have grounds to PNG (expel) him right this minute if we want." Then he added that the People Down South had no intention of doing that, not yet anyway.

A challenging, "So why can't I keep the money, then?"

"Because Michael wouldn't be the only one breaking the law, you would be too if you took his money."

Remembering when the Bureau tried to pull that FARA bullshit on me, I smirked. "Like I really care, so what are you gonna do, lock me up?"

The curtains on Mike's easy going role play ended and the curtains dropped. I caught a glimpse of a threatening guy as he stepped out from behind them. His head bobbed up and down like one of those little kewpie dolls that ride in the back of cars. "*Yeah, you bet I will*," he shot back.

I smirked. "I don't believe you."

He saw his threat had no effect, so Mike's tone went into charm mode. He said the FBI had every intention of *allowing* me to go to California, only they'd be the ones to pay for it. Since the Katkov Affair had just ratcheted up several notches on the clandestine scale, I'd be a fool to blow it now.

"OK, I'll give you the money, but since you guys are paying, I wanna fly 1st Class."

Mike grinned, obviously relieved. "Only the best for you, Julius." Then he brought up the Voice Changer. "Is that outfit (that sells it) bogus?"

"You guys should know better than me. Think it works?"

"Probably, the Israelis can do anything." Then he surprised me by adding, "Actually, it isn't the device they (the Soviets) want. It's a chip that's inside it." When I asked what circuit, all he'd say, "You'll have to ask the People Down South." Then he made an off-the-cuff remark that really sent my wheels spinning: "Michael will take his rightful place in history."

Mike drove us back to the parking garage on Amsterdam Avenue and 183rd where I kept the Dodge. "Did you bring the money with you," he asked.

"No, I left it in my apartment."

"Give it to John before he leaves."

"Yeah, OK," I growled, getting out of the car.

***

On Friday, April 4th, I attended a conference sponsored by *The Library Association of the City University of New York* (LACUNY): Shrinking World/Exploding Information: Developments in International Librarianship. The theme of the conference was: "The free flow of information across national boundaries."

The keynote speaker the day I attended was a Soviet named L.F. Kitrov. He served as director of the Dag Hammerskold Library, the U.N. library. Ever since the library's founding Soviets have held that position. It was one of their perks; many believed that the U.N. Library was also a hub of Soviet industrial espionage in this country.[1]

I sat among a group of U.N. librarians (non-Soviets). When Kitrov swam off to the deep end of the pool and began talking about Chairman Gorbachev peace initiative the U.N. librarians smirked and rolled their eyes.

1 Nyren, Karl "National and International Tensions Surface at LACUNY Institute" p.14, *Library Journal* 6/15/86.

The conference had been kind enough to supply attendees with a list of names and affiliations of all other attendees. One of the names on the list, Anatoly Sidorenko of the U.N. Library, drew my attention. I spotted him during the first intermission. Tall, nice-looking with sandy hair and about the same age as Katkov, he did not look like a librarian to me. I observed him from a discreet distance. He prowled the periphery like one of those guys at a club looking for hot chicks. Guess he either struck out or scored because that was the last I saw of Anatoly for the rest of the day.

My name on the attendee list read: "John Pansini, *Computerized Information Retrieval*." On my name tag I'd written: "John Pansini, CIR."

Near the end of the conference a guy came up to me and said, "Are you with the CIA?"

Confused, I looked down at the tag still pinned to the lapel of my new sharkskin suit paid for with money I gouged out of Berns & Katkov. "Oh, no, that's an R not an A."

No wonder none of the Soviets approached me.

Chapter 25

Nowhere Man

I feel like a knife that has been stabbed into a guy's back. I drip blood.

***

Monday, April 14, 1986

I called Mike and told him about the LACUNY conference. He asked me to send him the list of all attendees.

An eager, "*Sure*," I replied. I felt like a true red, white and blue American patriot.

Two days later, on April 16th, I smartened up. A real American patriot would never turn over a list of innocents to the federal government.

That's not how it works in this country, asshole, I reminded myself.

I put in a quick call to FBI agent Mike Berns. My final word on the matter was: "I'm not bringing the list."

(Aud 25.1) 1:56

Minutes after I hung up and detached my recording device, Mike called back. He sounded a lot more conciliatory. He said he just spoke with the other FBI agent. He asked me to repeat the name of the two Soviets (Kitrov and Sidorenko), the name of the conference, and the date and where it was held.

"That's all I want," he said.

"That's all you'll get," I replied.

Thursday, May Day, 5 p.m., and I had to get a move on because I was late for my appointment with Mike at the Star Diner. I still had my work clothes on: tar splattered jeans with holes in the knees and butt, long johns, a ripped, blue flannel shirt cut at the elbows and worn over a thermal, long sleeved undershirt. I hadn't shaved in four days which added to the *Derelict Chic Look* I had hoped to capture. When I turned the corner of 181st Street, I saw Mike walking towards me on Broadway. We were about ten feet apart when he smiled and offered his hand. I hesitated. He was impeccably dressed as always in a tan sports jacket, white shirt and tie. I made like I didn't know him, pausing only long enough to say: "No good, the odd couple, like cop and informer. Up here in the Heights that might get me killed."

"Yeah, OK," he murmured. "Walk on ahead."

I went into the diner. A short time later, he entered.

After we ordered, Mike said the FBI had to have a tape of my next meeting with Michael. "For your own protection," he added, "we need documentation. And when he calls, none of this I'll see you in five minutes bull. We need time to get the recorder to you first."

"Why don't you just give me the damn thing and let me hold it?"

"Can't, they're in heavy demand. We just don't have enough of 'em to go around."

The waitress served the food. When she was out of earshot, Mike said, "We wanna know why he's sending you 3,000 miles away. Is it just to say, 'Yeah, I went out there, shook the guy's hand and said, 'Hi, my name is John.' Make him be more explicit. Maybe he'll give you a name. Play dumb, like you do with me."

Before digging into another salmon steak — I'd slipped back into a tasty old habit — I said, "I'll do my best. How much does the L.A. field office know about this case?"

"At this point, very little. We've only asked them to run a check on NAS."

"I'm a little concerned about something. (Richard) Miller" — the FBI agent arrested for espionage worked out of the L.A. field office — "is back in the news again. Is it even remotely possible that the L.A. office is further penetrated?"

"Anything's possible. There's a lot we just don't know. They have a small (GRU) residency out there. Why not let them check NAS out?"

I figured there was more to this NAS thing than he, the Bureau, or those who dwelt in D.C. let on; therefore, if a tape was so important to the American intelligence community, then I needed one too.

For... my... own... protection.

A coffee table — nicked, knocked and footless — sat on the floor in the back room. Strategically located just inside the doorway in front of a decrepit white bookcase that ran along the wall, it served as a junk table, a thing to dump other things onto. Since it was in direct line with the sofa, I placed my own tape recorder there. I hid it under a bundle of clothes, blankets and a sleeping bag. Maybe these heaps of fabric would muffle the sound if the recorder clicked off. A thin black wire ran from the recorder through a mesh laundry basket to a mike secreted among some dirty roof clothes waiting to be washed. I ran a few sound checks and everything worked fine. I'd hidden the FBI's recorder in its usual place, in one of the speakers behind the blue chair. Michael would be bugged in stereo.

I left everything in place and went to bed, but I could not sleep. I always tossed and turned the night before one of Michael's visits; especially when he was being bugged. What if he found out? The consequences for him, and me, too, were too awful to even think about. What if I had to defend myself with a hammer? I liked Michael. Could I really bash his skull in even to save my own ass? Especially since I couldn't help feeling like the bad guy.

John Pansini, American patriot, but also the guy who betrayed another man's trust.

The next day, Friday, May 30th, was a hot one, too hot to roof. I stayed home and spent the afternoon jumping in and out of the tub to stay cool. At 5:58 p.m. Michael called; judging from the background noise, he made the call from a subway station. He said he would be over in forty minutes, plenty of time for me to run one more sound check: *nada*! Then another: static and broken parts of speech. I took the system apart and immediately discovered the problem: tiny teeth marks on the wire that ran from the mike to the recorder. Stinky was too dumb to find the wire, so it had to be *her*, the little gray beast.

In March, I found a gray kitten crying under a mailbox outside the Post Office. I figured she wouldn't last long on this particular mean street. She'd either end up under a car, or eaten by some crack-head. I also took her home with me because Stinky needed a friend. I saved her life, and how did she repay me? By using my chord as a teething ring!

In March I loved her. Now I charged through the apartment kicking boxes, yelling, and threatening to throw her out the window. She had the good sense to stay hidden. So did Stinky; sometimes he wasn't so dumb.

I turned on the FBI's recorder and waited for Michael. I sat on the sofa, arms crossed at my chest, with *harrumph!* burned onto my face.

Michael arrived at 6:21 dressed in a light brown summer suit. He asked for a drink of water. I went into the kitchen and filled a glass. When I turned around his tall, smiling self stood right behind me. I gave him the water, brushed passed him, and headed back to the living room.

After drinking the water he deposited the glass in the sink. "So what you've got for me?" he asked, following me back into the living room.

I continued walking, heading for the front room to get the stuff. Instead of parking his ass on the sofa and waiting, Michael followed me. He paused in the hallway between the living and front rooms and opened the bathroom door. The floor had been torn up leaving nothing but dirt, and walls had been removed exposing heavy wooden beams.

"How primitive," he casually remarked.

Bet it reminded him of the Fatherland.

"Hey, Michael, what do you expect? They're renovating, remember?" According to my neighbor, the Jamaican landlords who owned the building had won money in the lottery. They decided to invest some of it in fixing the place up. It sure needed it.

Michael closed the door. "It seems to me work is progressing quite slowly." He turned, headed back into the living room and sat down on the sofa. I gave him what few documents I had. He looked both surprised and annoyed. “Is this all? What about the synthesizer?”

In no mood for another one of his *I’m Disappointed In You, John* lectures: “Oh, yeah, the fucking Voice Changer.” I went back to the front room, got the original clipping, and gave it back to him. “You still want it, you call this motherfucker. His name’s Cohen. He’s been giving me the run around for months.” I stood in an aggressive posture: arms folded against chest, legs spread apart. “Every time I call, he’s outta stock. Keeps telling me he expects a new shipment in real soon. Yeah, right. By the way Michael, where’d you clip that from, *Screw Magazine*?”

He raised his hand as if to say, *Enough already.* Then he put the clipping in his pocket.

I never did get that Voice Changer, and I never refunded the money the FBI had paid me in advance. The way I figured it: fuck ‘em.

I handed him the tire manual that had come in the mail from NAS. It was not the tire and rim data book that he had asked for. I never did get that thing, either.

“You mean it took you four months to come up with this, pardon me, shit?”

“It wasn’t my fault,” I whined.

“Yes it is. You have not been paying proper attention to your duties. Quite frankly, I think you have some beautiful girlfriend and have been neglecting your business.”

Yeah, I wished.

“And why is it so old?” he added. The publication was dated 1975. “You told me that he (Bob of NAS) has interesting material.” His voice grew progressively louder. “This is not interesting,” he said, waving the booklet in my face. "This is shit." Before I could come to my own defense, he cut me short: "The dictionary (of army terms), and why don't you've got it?"

I made a B-line for the front room to get the letter from NAS that said the dictionary was in reprint. I hadn't intended to show him it, but I was in a panic, a panic to please. He read the letter, then removed the attached carbon copy and put it in his pocket.

He'd been knocking me around all evening; now it was my turn to counter punch: "You know, Michael, my association with you is dangerous."

He bobbed and weaved: "John, I am not your enemy." The sincerity in his voice almost flattened me.

"I didn't say that," I stammered. "That's not what I mean. Look, Michael, you tell me you're a little annoyed at me—"

"I did not say 'a little.'"

"OK — well I'm a lot annoyed with you too."

He ignored me again, flipping through the pages of the tire manual.

"You told me I'd be getting big orders. So where are they, huh? All you keep giving me is these scrappy little bullshit little shits!"

He looked up. "You are annoyed with *me*?" His finger pointed to his chest. Then two more *You Are Annoyed With Me*'s, and with each one, his face grew more incredulous, his voice more shrill.

Time to throw in the towel: "OK, Michael. Forget it."

He removed a small white envelope, fat with ten dollar bills, from his inside breast pocket. He counted out only $250 before putting the envelope back in his pocket. The damn thing was still stuffed!

"I was planning to pay you quite a lot of money tonight, John, but frankly I am quite disappointed in you."

"Oh, yeah, then why is the envelope filled with tens instead of hundreds?"

A wiseacre he chose to ignore. He said that he would be taking his "holiday" soon and that after that he would be making another trip. "You should not expect to see me again until October or November." Then he gave me a new order: seven journal articles, three of which seemed to be pertinent to the Chernobyl disaster.

After ten minutes of bashing my brains in, all of a sudden he wanted to get chummy again. He patted the sofa and motioned for me to sit down next to him. Since he wanted to chat, I figured now was the right time to bring up Chernobyl. The People Down South wanted his thoughts on the matter.

"I was thinking about going to Russia this summer on vacation," I said casually, "but now I'm not so sure. All that radiation, you know."

The wrong button to push with Michael: "You really shouldn't believe all those terrible things about us in the American press." With each point he made, his voice rose one decibel: "How many did they said died? 20,000? Do you know how many really died? Twenty."

I tried to agree with him hoping that would shut him up. It didn't.

"My sister lives in the area. I will visit her and her family this summer. I will take my family. I am unconcerned with the so-called danger."

"Just don't drink the water, Michael." I laughed.

He didn't. He stared at me, grim-faced. Finally he calmed down and began to remove the NTIS documents from their wrappers.

The crinkling sound of the cellophane drew unwanted attention. The little gray princess pranced into the living room. (The big orange dumb-dumb preferred to stay hidden.) She sniffed at the wrappers lying on the floor in front of Michael. Then she sniffed up at him. She jumped into his lap. He laughed, genuinely delighted.

I smiled. "She likes you, Michael; must be because you're both Russian. The vet tells me she's got some Russian Blue in her. Her name is Bookie."

"So you like me," he cooed to the kitten. Those hands, trained by Spetsnaz to choke or bash the life out of a man, now gently stroked my little cat.

"So tell me, John, have you taken a trip recently?" He smiled.

"Not yet. I wanna go over a few things first." I leaned forward, taking up a more relaxed position: hands clasped together and arms dangling between my knees. "How's this for a cover story: I'm an engineering consultant trying to land a government contract."

"Yah, is OK." His face showed no clues from which I could gauge his level of dissatisfaction.

"So what am I supposed to do when I get there?"

"You will go to him with your, as you call it, *cover story*." His intonation of "cover story" indicated that Michael might be a tad miffed. "Tell him you don't have necessary security clearances and you would like his assistance in obtaining certain classified material."

A fatal faux pas: *classified material* instead of asking for *something interesting*; those two words rendered Michael a dead man talking. Set up, knocked down, game over. I felt like a knife that had been slipped out of its sheath to stab a guy in the back. I dripped blood.

The corpse continued to speak: "Remind him that he said he can cut through red tape. Find out what information he's got, classified or not. But you must be careful not to be specific. Speak only in most general terms, so not to draw attention to yourself."

After Michael left I went into the kitchen and plopped down at the table. This was the same chair, at the head near the entrance, where I always ate solo. I laid my right forearm on the table's white, vinyl surface; the other arm rested across my right knee, left hand hanging between my legs. I closed my eyes, took in a deep breath, held, and then let out a long, slow sigh.

***

My mind feels like contested property.

Guilt moves in first, dragging all its shit in with it. Guilt puts a curve in my back, cricks my neck, presses my head down, and puts a slump in my shoulders. I feel like a statute made of flesh and bone.

"Do they've got classified material?"

He trusts me! Wants to protect me from the FBI! Pays me money, gives me bonuses. Shit, that's what I feel like, a piece of shit! I've betrayed him!

"Do they've got classified material?"

Game over, Michael, you lost.

Cooperative farm in the Ukraine. Army; wonder if he served in Afghanistan? Selected by GRU. Graduated from the Academy. Posted to London and now New York — only the best of the best. On the fast-track.

"Do they've got classified material?"

I can't feel good about any of this.

But am I wrong for wanting to get the hell out of here? To make a better life for myself? But then, making a better life for me by wrecking the life of another person, that's some bad shit.

I whine and bitch about Berns and the People Down South being manipulators — ha! I'm every bit the manipulator they are. I see it every morning when I look in the mirror and shave. Maybe this is why I don't shave every day. "Loser," it's written all over me. I'm a Nowhere Man. No wonder I can't keep a woman.

THUMP! THUMP! THUMP!... Like a horde of Vikings with a battering ram, something outside my head wants to get inside. And then a *CRASH*! The fortress that protects my humanity is finally breached. A full-pitched battle begins: Self-interest attacks, Conscience defends. Who will win?

Yet-to-be-decided.

GRAYARC™
P.O. BOX 2944, HARTFORD, CT 06104
CALL TOLL FREE: 1-800-243-6250

REPLY MESSAGE

REORDER ITEM #F270

TO
CIR INC.
515 W. 183 ST. APT 6C
N.Y. N.Y. 10033
ATTN: JHON PANSINI

FROM
NEWPORT AERONAUTICAL SALES
P. O. Box 1845
NEWPORT BEACH, CA 92660
(714) 631-8250 Telex 69-2493

SUBJECT: YOUR REQUEST DATE: 4-18-86

FOLD

THE AR 310-25 YOU ORDERED FROM US IS IN REPRINT AND WILL HAVE TO BE REORDERED AT A LATER DATE.

SORRY FOR ANY INCONVENEINCE

PLEASE REPLY TO → SIGNED Annette Everett

(Fig 25.1) NAS note: dictionary of army terms in reprint

0072 **FAST Computer Model to Predict Smoke, Toxic Gas Spread**

National Bureau of Standards, Gaithersburg, MD.; Department of Commerce, Washington, DC
May 85 *(A, D)*

Researchers have completed an initial version of a fast, re liable computer model which can predict the spread of fire smoke, and toxic gases throughout a structure. Smoke and toxic gases that are produced when materials burn are o particular concern since 80 to 90 percent of the people who die in fires succumb to smoke and gas rather than to flames or heat. The model incorporates the same chemistry and physics as other models, but it is considerably faster. It can complete calculations where some programs would run and not come up with an answer. Computer modeling of fire phenomena has been almost solely a research tool, but this model--called FAST--is designed for use by building and product designers, fire safety experts, and regulatory officials in state and local governments. Written in ANSI Fortran, FAST can run on mainframe and minicomputers, and the NBS researchers are experimenting with it on a microcomputer. Anyone who is moderately knowledgeable about computer modeling can use FAST. Initially it will probably be used by some of the larger fire protection engineering firms and architectural firms which now use modeling to solve problems.

FOR ADDITIONAL INFORMATION: Contact: Both an NBS publication on the model and a computer tape of FAST are available through the National Technical Information Service, Springfield, VA 22161. A Model for the Transport of Fire, Smoke and Toxic Gases (FAST) can be ordered by PB85-109130+NAC for $10 prepaid. The tape, which includes a sample data file, can be ordered by PB85-150555+NAC. Contact: NTIS Computer Products Center, NTIS, Springfield, VA 22161; (203) 487-4763.

0226 **EVENT, Explosive Transients in Flow Networks: The rapid addition of energy and mass at specified ventilation system locations simulates accident conditions**

Department of Energy, Washington, DC
Apr 85 *(A, D, J)*

#1,400
#1,100

A major concern of the chemical, nuclear, and mining industries is the occurrence of an explosion in one part of a facility and the subsequent transmission of explosive effects through the ventilation system. An explosive event can cause performance degradation of the ventilation system or even structural failures. A more serious consequence is the release of hazardous materials to the environment if vital protective devices, such as air filters, are damaged. The computer program EVENT was developed at the Los Alamos National Laboratory to investigate the effects of explosive transients through such fluid-flow networks.

FOR ADDITIONAL INFORMATION: EVENT is written in FORTRAN programing language for the CDC 7600 computer. To order documentation including a User's Manual and the EVENT FORTRAN source and sample problem on magnetic tape (NESC No. 9952), contact: National Energy Software Center, Argonne National Laboratory, 9700 South Cass Avenue, Argonne, IL 60439; (312) 972-7250.

(Fig 25.2) Two citations from 'Michael's list 5/30/86

Chapter 26
An Odd Couple

"Our tax dollars at work... Still think they're FBI?"

"The Bureau would never condone that sort of behavior. Maybe I am losing it."

Again she arched a brow at me. "Maybe?"

***

Saturday, May 31, 1986

I called Mike Berns to debrief him about yesterday's meeting with Michael.

(Audio 26.1) 2:10

***

On September 10th, Mike Berns called to tell me that Michael would be back in New York soon. Then he asked if I'd made reservations to fly out to L.A.

"I will as soon as I know how much money I'll be getting from you guys. I have to know so I can decide how long I can stay out there."

"Well, you know the money situation over here —

Sure did. Those guys were so tight they squeaked in high octaves when they farted.

"…I can probably justify two nights in a hotel and two days car rental, plus a couple of hundred for you." He added that I'd be getting at least seven hundred dollars.

In my mind "at least" meant more: seven hundred plus some spending money.

On September 11th, I made the reservations. I'd be leaving Friday morning, September 26th; I'd stay until Tuesday night, September 30th. I'd just started a job at Columbia University's engineering library and had Fridays off. I'd miss only two days of work without pay. That would give me the weekend to enjoy L.A. and visit with an old friend.

On Friday, the 19th, Mike called again. "Have you made the reservations yet?"

"Not yet," I lied. "Why haven't I gotten my money yet?"

"You'll get it."

Sharply, "When?"

An equally pointed, "When you make the reservations."

On Sunday night, the 21st, at 10:30 p.m., I got a phone call from Mr. Berns. "I'll be putting the check in the mail tomorrow," he said.

"OK, I've already made the reservations. I'll be leaving this coming Friday, so the check better get here soon. I had to put everything on my charge card. I have no, and let me repeat, *no*, pocket money. If that check doesn't come before I leave, then I'm gonna hit up your L.A. office for some cash. I'm gonna say, 'Those guys in New York are a bunch of cheap bastards.'"

“Don’t worry you’ll have the money before Friday.” He sounded relieved.

Two days before departure, Wednesday the 24th, I went to the Post Office after work and found that the check still wasn’t in my box. When I got home, “Where’s the damn check?” I barked into the phone.

“Mailed it yesterday, you should have it by tomorrow,” said Mike.

“I better have it tomorrow, or I’m gonna kick down the L.A. field office’s door!”

He chuckled. “Don’t do that, Julius. They’ll slap the cuffs on you.”

Thursday I finally got a check from the FBI for seven hundred dollars. Apparently *at least* meant *the least* possible.

Three o’clock in Columbia’s engineering library, I had my hand cupped over the mouthpiece so not to be overheard. I’d made the call from the reference desk. “Mike, this is Julius. We have a problem. Got the check this morning, couldn’t cash it.”

“What do you mean you couldn’t cash it?” On the day before my departure, it sounded like he didn’t appreciate a last minute glitch. “It’s a money order. You can cash it anywhere.”

“It’s from a Jersey bank. My bank wouldn’t cash it; they said it’ll take three days to clear.”

“That’s bull. Go back and have them call the bank in New Jersey. It’ll clear.”

“Too late, I already deposited it into my checking account.”

An audible groan on his end of the line.

“I have exactly $11.43 in my pocket. The banks will be closed by the time I get home from work. I’m leaving early in the morning before they open. I need some cash, pronto."

Poor Mike had no choice. "Be at the Star Diner tonight at six," he said, suddenly sounding either very tired or very disgusted. I didn't give a rat's ass which. "I'll have some money for you then."

It never ceased to amaze me how quickly Agent Berns adjusted to adversity. When we met in front of the diner, he was all smiles again. I was in a hurry to get home and pack, but, for some reason, Mike wanted to hang around and chat. While talking, he kept moving closer, advancing into my space like he wanted to kiss me good-bye or something. Native New Yorkers like me are born with fixed boundaries; we don't like being crowded. The closer he inched towards me, the further away I inched from him. We were headed west, so had this conversation continued for any extended length of time, we'd both end up in the Hudson River.

"If for some reason I have to contact the L.A. field office," I asked, "should I use my code name, Julius?"

"No. They don't know who Julius is. Use your real name."

"Is that wise?"

"No need to be overly concerned. These guys (Soviet intelligence) aren't *that* good. If they were, they'd be winning. And I can assure you, they're not." He put his hand on my shoulder and smiled. "Relax. Enjoy the trip."

Up to now the only physical contact between the Bureau and me had been limited to handshakes; and sometimes not even that. This new intimacy disturbed me. I felt like I was being set up for something.

"You'll love it out there. It's a lot better than here." Mike looked around, disgusted. Guess the Big Apple had lost some of its polish.

"He won't show it, but he's gonna be elated when you tell him you have a job at Columbia." Mike turned away for a second and began nodding in the direction of the Hudson. "Yeah, he's gonna be real happy."

"Good. I have some plans of my own in regards to our friend. I'm gonna start putting more pressure on him for more money and bigger orders."

"Don't put too much pressure on him yet. Give him a chance to act. We'll be applying some pressure ourselves soon enough in conjunction with a few other things."

Mike seemed unusually full of bravado tonight. Time for me to do some probing: "Read in the papers that you guys expelled 25 Russians."

The Reagan administration had expelled a shit-load of Soviets from the U.N. in September, 1986.

"Yep," Mike said, standing with his hands on his hips, feet spread apart like he owned the sidewalk. The way he acted, someone might get the impression that he'd personally put the boot to their butts. Never seen him so puffed up and full of himself like this before. Then he discreetly passed me a small white envelope. "Here's some spending money."

The envelope contained $200 from the Bureau to go along with the seven hundred that already sat in my checking account. God, in His infinite wisdom, had righted a wrong.

"One more thing, Mike, of those twenty-five Russians who were expelled, was one of 'em named Vladimir Bolochine?"

Mike grinned. "No, he's still around."

My eyes widened. "You gotta be kidding."

***

A breeze gently blew against the side of my head like a soft whisper. It was telling me, *She's beautiful, John, and she's with you.*

What could be better than this, being in L.A. with Christine, an old friend from New York. She had moved out here a long time ago and never looked back. After we spent last night together I wondered if maybe New York was a doormat where I should wipe the dust off my sneakers.

We stood facing each other far apart from the rest of our tour group. The Santa Anas blew hot that afternoon. They tossed long, tawny strands of hair across her face, giving her a wild, untamed look. Not much hidden by cutoffs and a pink halter top she wore, either; her golden skin glistened, reflecting the sun. My eyes traced every curve and explored every ripple of subtle muscle in her well-toned body. California living agreed with Christine; she looked like a sleek, sexy, green-eyed cat.

She spoke in an endless loop of words about how much she loved L.A. and hated Brooklyn. Her New York accent long gone, she not only looked like a typical Southern California girl, she sounded like one too —*furr sure*. I couldn't wait for this stupid tour of Universal Studios to begin and be done with so we could grab dinner and go back to her place.

"Ooh! It looks like they're getting ready to open the doors," she said, sliding her right arm inside the crook of my left elbow. "Let's go."

Christine was a wisp, no more than 110 pounds. If I'd really wanted to I could have become an immovable object. Instead I went into my whiny persuasion mode: "Christine, it's really no big deal.

I've seen the movie about a hundred times." I always hated that big ape, anyway; no tears from me when they blew his fat ass off the Empire State Building.

And speaking of blowing off, "Don't be silly. I take all my friends from New York here."

Subtlety hadn't worked, perhaps a direct approach would: "He's just a big metal monkey. Let's go back to your place."

"He's an ape, John, not a monkey. Even I know that." She smiled and nuzzled up against me. Her body language said, *I know exactly what you're thinking, John. Be patient. You'll get what you want, but only when I'm ready to give it.*

We walked over and joined the rest of the tourists. Christine was so excited that we were finally going to see the King that she didn't notice when two bookends, one male and one female, took up positions on either side, and just behind, her. Forget that going back to her place shit. Now I had a new focus. Those lusty Santa Ana that once blew in my sails and drove me forward suddenly went dead.

The male bookend, in his mid to late-twenties, had dark hair cut short, military style, and a stocky body draped in light colored, loose-fitting athletic clothing. Something in the way he carried himself grunted, *Me cop!* The female bookend looked ten years older than him. She had dark, wavy hair and looked just as tough, just as athletic, and just as sturdy as he did. Her body language chimed in, *Me cop, too!*

Neither spoke to the other nor gave any sign of mutual recognition, but Instinct, another resident in that happy home inside my head, told me: *They're together. And they're here for you.*

Why would the FBI put a tail on me?

When we got inside the sound stage I grabbed Christine's hand and led her to the rear of our tour group. From there I could keep a better eye on the odd couple, who were now walking and talking together. Eventually, me and the odd couple began to jockey for position as the tour group moved from set to set. I tried to keep them in front of me, while they tried to keep me in front of them. As for Christine, she had absolutely no idea what was going on.

"Isn't this fun," she said, beaming. "Aren't you glad we came?"

"Yeah," I said yanking her by the arm, "let's sit over here."

"Ow! Pan-Zini, why are you so weird?"

"Sorry. Thought I already explained." I lowered my voice, "I'm a spy. I'm on a secret mission. Don't look directly at them, but you see those two over there," I said with a quick nod in the odd couple's direction.

"You mean the man and woman standing over there," she said, pointing.

I groaned, "I said don't do that… They're following us."

She arched an eyebrow, her expression for skepticism. "Furr sure."

If the FBI really went looking for me, then they did a pretty good job finding me. I hadn't been to my motel back in Newport Beach — where I was supposed to be — since dropping off my backpack and suit yesterday afternoon. I never told Mike that I'd be staying with a friend because he had no need to know. So if I had grown a tail, then it must have sprouted when I drove from Newport Beach to Christine's apartment in North Hollywood.

The tour ended. Out in the real world again, I saw the odd couple put their arms around each other's waist and walk away snuggling.

Christine smirked. "Our tax dollars at work. Still think they're FBI?"

"The Bureau would never condone that sort of behavior," I said, sounding more confused than convinced. "Maybe I am losing it."

Again she arched a brow at me. "Maybe?"

The following Monday, I stood in my motel room admiring my reflection in a full-length mirror: shoes polished, white form-fitted shirt, yellow silk power tie, chocolate brown suit, attaché case at my side, horn-rimmed glasses. The perfect disguise: I looked like a Reagan Republican. Inside, though, because of the weekend I'd spent with Christine, I felt like James Bond: shaken & stirred.

Ready to make a call on the office of Newport Aeronautical Sales (NAS), I assembled some of CIR's promotional literature and neatly folded them inside a business envelope. The motel manager had given me a map — no Google Earth in those days. Good with maps, I easily found my way to NAS, a small storefront in an industrial mall. I parked directly in front and walked in. A woman in her late 40s sat at the reception desk. The office, small and very plain, looked like a waiting room at the free clinic. To the left of the reception desk a door led into another room. How big an outfit was NAS? Couldn't say for sure, but my guess: probably not very. I asked if either Bob or his brother George were in, and the receptionist said, "I'm sorry, they're both out."

We exchanged promotional literature. NAS' 10 x 12 manila envelope dwarfed my little 8½ x 11 white job. Mission accomplished, I said good-bye and left.

Back at the motel, an empty manila envelope and papers lay scattered all over the bed. It didn't take me long to sift through the bullshit and rake out a gem the fat bovine had swallowed: an article from the *Wall Street Journal* entitled, "Obtaining Data to Bid on Military Jobs" (10/15/85). It summarized a lawsuit NAS had been involved in. They successfully sued the Department of the Navy to release certain technical data to them. NAS then sold this information to small companies bidding on defense contracts. This was not the only time NAS had made its way into the public record. Later, I did a computer search and found another article, "The Never Ending Controversy: Why the Pentagon Will Keep Spending $7,600 for a Coffee Maker". It had appeared in *Inc. Magazine*, March 1985. Both articles said that the Pentagon wanted to restrict certain proprietary technical documents to large defense contractors such as Boeing, General Dynamics, Grummans, etc. The Pentagon feared that if this information was disseminated too freely it might fall into the wrong hands, i.e., the USSR or its satellites. NAS had successfully argued in court that making the information available to all defense contractors would allow more competitive bidding and reduce costs.

Since all this was public record, for sure the GRU knew about NAS long before I stumbled onto them. When I reported my contact with the company to Michael, Moscow was notified, indices were checked and these articles pulled. Word was then sent from the GRU Center that I should visit L.A. That made me feel kind of important, like I was making a worthwhile contribution after all.

These articles and the attendant interest of the Soviet Union in NAS might have been just cause for the Bureau to put a couple of snuggle bunnies on me. I began to rethink my earlier dismissal of the odd couple.

Armed and dangerous, that be me, a man with new intelligence. The big ole jet airliner that carried me back to New York couldn't get there fast enough. I couldn't wait to see the expressions on the two Michaels' faces when I showed them that now I knew what they'd known all along.

THE WALL STREET

SMALL BUSINESS

Obtaining Data to Bid on Military Jobs

Newport Aeronautical Sales is a military-equipment data broker. It obtains technical information—engineering drawings, operating manuals, specification sheets—and sells it to companies that bid on military contracts. It exists because getting this information isn't so easy, even though it is supposed to be available to the public.

"We make thousands of requests a year," says George M. Posey III, owner and vice president of the Newport Beach, Calif., company. "Most of our requests are from small business."

Small companies need the data to bid, usually on spare parts contracts, against big military suppliers such as General Electric Co., United Technologies' Pratt & Whitney division or McDonnell Douglas Corp. The big companies, of course, already have the data because they are the original suppliers of the equipment. Their advantage in supplying spare parts has been documented in government studies that found that original equipment suppliers sell the military about 90% of the spare parts it buys. (The prices they charge for some of these parts have become a national scandal.)

LAST APRIL, Newport successfully sued the Navy to release data. That court victory, however, may not mean much if the Defense Department adopts new rules controlling the release of technical data.

The rules permit the military to refuse to divulge nonsecret data if it relates to anything requiring a federal export license. That's to prevent unclassified but sensitive data from going to the Soviet Union and its allies.

A Defense Department lawyer who has worked on the regulation, says, "Much of our unclassified but critical information has proven to be of immense value to the Soviet Union. . . . You have to take that on faith."

The proposed regulations are designed, the official says, to "delay transmission of this technical data and help reserve the technological lead this country enjoys."

However, Newport objects that the proposed rules give procurement officers too much unchallenged authority. These "low level bureaucrats," the company says in a written criticism of the rules, have a "proven bent for withholding" data. Mr. Posey says he fears the rules will be detrimental to his business.

CONGRESS AUTHORIZED the Defense Department to draft the rules last year, after testimony about the ease with which unclassified data can be obtained by foreign companies.

General Electric Co. has lobbied to restrict data from going to overseas users. Donald Zarin, an attorney with Blum, Nash & Railsback, a Washington law firm, and GE's lobbyist, says the company is concerned because foreign competitors obtain data about products GE develops for the military and use the information to compete successfully against the company for military contracts overseas. Some European countries use the same planes and weapons as the U.S., and overseas manufacturers have become tough competitors of U.S. companies that used to have foreign markets for replacement parts to themselves.

Mr. Zarin says the restrictions "are not at all directed to small business or U.S. companies."

But William Glennon, an official of the National Small Business Government Contractors of America, says this is just another ploy by the big suppliers to eliminate competition. They'll do almost anything, he says, to keep themselves a sole source for supplying military goods.

(Fig 26.1) Full text of WSJ article

Chapter 27
Russian Royalty

"Told you governments are bullshit. Your government is bullshit, too. And they're cheap.*"*

***

October 20, 1986

When I entered the Star Diner on 178th Street, Mike was already seated at a table in the back at the last booth. As soon as he spotted me, he jumped up and ushered me to another table up front.

"We're we going?" I said. "That table was perfect. Quiet, away from everyone."

Mike didn't say anything. With his right hand on the small of my back, he gently but firmly aimed me towards the front of the diner.

"Why were you sitting there when I came in?"

He mumbled that given my paranoia about meeting him in this neighborhood, he was trying to stay inconspicuous.

"If you wanna be inconspicuous, why not stay where you were?"

No response.

Almost a month had passed since my return from L.A. NAS' lawsuit against the Department of Defense was like a hammer slung on my belt hook. I couldn't wait to pull it out and whack somebody with it. Today, Special Agent Mike Berns would take the first hit.

In the new booth I scanned the menu; then I happened to look up for a second. The table that Mike had recently vacated was now occupied by a man in a business suit. He was about Mike's age and with dark features. He could pass for either Hispanic or Americano. Better dressed and better groomed by far than the regular clientele, he sat facing me. As the conversation with Mike grew more complex, the next time I happened to look up, the guy was gone. He'd slipped past without my noticing. Shit!

Was Mike occupying me here while Mr. GQ went back at my place rummaging through my papers? One way to find out would be to suddenly tell Mike, "Geez! Think I left a pot on the stove! Be right back." If his mustache twitched and he shot me one of his cop stares or if he tried to talk me out of it, then I'd know. Instead I remembered a far more subtle way: if a stranger did invade the premises, then all I had to do was read my cat, Stinky. When I got home, if he was hiding, then I'd know. But if both cats greeted me at the door when I got back, I'd also know: no unwanted visitors. Since there was nothing in my apartment I didn't want the Bureau to see anyway — except the mess — I decided to stay here and enjoy another free lunch.

After placing our orders — I had a salmon steak — I slid a large manila envelope across the table to Mike. Tap, tap, Roofman's silver hammer was ready to come down upon his head: "Here's what I picked up in California. It's promotional literature from NAS. I have two copies. There's another one waiting at home for our friend." I leaned back in my seat and waited while Mike sifted through the packet. When he picked up the WSJ article, I said, "Interesting, isn't it?"

"Yeah," he mumbled, reading as if he saw it for the first time. When he finished, he put the NAS material into his briefcase. He took out a notepad. "So how was your trip?"

Geez, what a letdown!

"I visited their offices on Monday, September 29th, but Bob wasn't there." Pointing, "The secretary gave me that stuff. Found out that Bob isn't the big man at NAS. He just works there. His brother George owns the place. Went back the next day, this time he was there."

"Who? George or Bob?"

"Bob. You should've seen me. Dressed like a real slob: flannel shirt, open, blue T-shirt underneath and jeans—"

"You mean you were dressed like normal."

"Yeah, anyway, I told Bob that I was on my way to the airport and had stopped by because I'd lost the papers his secretary had given me."

"So what kind of guy is he?"

"Can't say for sure, only spoke with him for a couple of minutes. Another guy — short, fat, crew cut, fascist-military-Republican type — came in while we were speaking. Bob had a girl show me around upstairs where they keep the documents while he spoke with the Republican. They seemed to know each other pretty well. I noticed the Republican giving me the hairy eyeball—"

"I'm not interested in his customers. What about Bob?"

"Forties, about my height, black hair, greased back, trim, fit, commercial pilot." I hunched my shoulders — "Polite, friendly," — because I didn't have much of a read on the guy.

"What about George?"

Sometimes Mike could be denser than a pile of petrified dung — or was he trying to trip me up? Sharply, "I told you. I never met George. Never spoke to him either. So why you keep asking about

George?"

"Are they a big outfit? Does he want your business?"

"He doesn't seem nearly as hungry as the first time I spoke with him. Really don't think he gives a shit about getting my business."

Mike closed his notepad, an indication that the debriefing was over. But it was only half over, his half.

"I'm gonna start playing harder to get with Michael. I'd like him to cover my relocation to Southern California. You were right, it's a lot nicer than here. That's the direction I want to take him."

Mike shook his head. "Unless that's what the Soviets have in mind, you're not gonna lead him anywhere. You may think you're in control — you're not."

Once again, Mike got up to leave, but once again, I made him sit.

"What's the Soviet interest in NAS?"

"At this point, we don't know," Mike replied.

"Can we safely assume that they knew about NAS long before I stumbled onto them?"

"Yeah, you can assume that."

"So who's getting the positive intelligence we've been gathering, CIA or DIA?"

I'd read that both intelligence organizations were giving completely different estimates of the Soviet military threat.[1] As an instrument of the Pentagon, the DIA's (Defense Intelligence Agency) estimates were said to be overstated. Also, there was a paragraph from the *WSJ* article that I found particularly disturbing:

1 Bulletin of the Atomic Scientists, May 1987, p. 6.

"(NAS' court victory) may not mean much if the Defense Department adopts new rules controlling the release of technical data. The rules permit the military to refuse to divulge…unclassified but sensitive data."

The basis of this new classification was document *NSDD-145,* which the government had hidden under a shade tree, a tree soon to be exposed to the sunshine when *NSDD-145* came under public scrutiny; more on that later. For the moment, I was concerned that the information I had helped gather on NAS might be used as a justification for closing them down — WRONG! Other plots were being hatched, and, for now, Soviet interest in NAS was the only thing that kept that company in operation.

In answer to my original question about who got the positive intelligence I generated on NAS, Mike said, "Can't get into that with you. You have no need to know."

No Need To Know. I really think he *enjoyed* using that catch-all phrase on me.

Mike changed the subject. He said that the Soviet Union spent 15% of its GNP on the military whereas we spend about 4%. "Gorbachev would love to take 10% of that and put it in other areas so the people could live better. That'll increase his popularity. The more technology they can steal, the more R&D costs they can save. I really feel for the Russian people because their standard of living is so low. Until there's a major change on the part of their government, the prospects are bleak."

Mike took out his notepad again. Guess he suddenly remembered he needed to know more about the materials I had for Michael, including where I got each document. I began reading them off, item by item. Everything went fine until I came to the *Dictionary of Army*

Terms.

I smiled. "Michael will be real happy with this one. I got it from a friend of mine in the National Guard."

"What's his name," Mike asked casually, his head down.

"I can't get into that with you, Mike; you have no need to know."

A pause, a cop's stare, and then, "I thought we were through playing games? You have to trust me, and I have to trust you."

Silence from my side of the table.

"It's really no big deal," he said, flipping his notepad shut. "Just need it for my report."

"So where's your report going? DIA or CIA?"

Mike mustache twitched. "Really, Julius, it's nothing to worry about."

"You're right. The guy checked with his superior officer. It isn't classified; even the public library has it."

"The UN library has it too. Michael can get it there if he wants."

I slapped the table. A few heads turned in our direction. "I was right! A test! And I'm gonna score some big points!"

"Don't get carried away, Julius. It's not a big deal."

"Good, then you won't feel bad when I don't tell you."

On that sweet note — for me not him — the debriefing ended. When I got back to my apartment, both cats greeted me at the door. They behaved like they usually did; like they hadn't eaten in months. Six o'clock was their dinner time.

***

On Monday, November 3rd, Michael called. He said he'd been

recovering from a "long illness", and that was why he hadn't gotten in touch with me sooner. I told him to bring a lot of money with him because I had a new job.

(Audio 27.1) 0:32

On Monday, November 10th, the burnt orange rug still lay rolled up against the far wall opposite the sofa; although the renovation on my apartment had been completed, I'd been slow putting things back together. I didn't like the way the cats eyeballed that rug. Tucked neatly inside a fold was my recorder, its built-in mike aimed at the sofa. Bookie, the kitten, began poking her nose into the fold. Even Stinky, the stupid one, acted curious. The problem: what if one of these felines decided that *my* recorder was *their* toy and dragged it out while Michael was here?

Using my higher intelligence, I formulated a plan: from past experience I knew that whenever I opened the hall closet, the cats would run in to investigate. Perfect! I opened the door and waited. They just sat on their haunches and stared at me. I tried shooing them in; that didn't work. I tried throwing them in; that didn't work either. As soon as I tossed one in, the other jumped out. Finally they ran into the back room to hide.

"And stay there!"

***

Michael entered the foyer and handed me his coat and hat. I deposited them on top of the laundry full of dirty clothes waiting to be washed. He took his customary seat on the sofa. I babbled about my new job at Columbia, only to stop in mid-sentence and blast off the sofa to get the documents I had for him.

"How was your dealing with that company? Uh…" he called after me, pretending to forget the name of NAS.

"It went very well," I yelled back.

I crossed into the back room, and a little gray blur whizzed past me. She jumped onto the sofa and began sniffing at Michael. He smiled and scratched her head. I picked her up and gently deposited her on the floor. She jumped back on the sofa. Despite a cool facade, I sensed that Michael was anxious to hear about my trip. I was anxious too, to see his reaction to the *WSJ* article.

I handed him his copy of the literature packet describing NAS. "He had one of the girls take me upstairs." While I described the document room in detail, his eyes blinked like semaphores. I hadn't seen him do that in a while. "It's a small outfit, but they seem to have a lotta stuff there."

"What kind of stuff?"

I pointed to the manila envelope he was holding. "It's all in there. Have a look."

Michael would not turn a page. "Technical manuals?"

"Yeah. Told him I was from Columbia University. He didn't—"

"Told who?"

"You know, Bob. He didn't seem very impressed. He told me that he sells airplane parts. All of a sudden, he's not too interested in my scrappy little orders."

"But did you make some kind of technical arrangement with him?"

"What kind of technical arrangement, Michael? You didn't give me anything to go on."

"There wasn't any unnecessary attention to yourself?"

"No, no. As far as he knows, I work at Columbia." Enough already! I dug out the *WSJ* article and practically shoved it under his nose. "Read this very closely."

While Michael read and blinked, he stroked the little gray pain-in-the-ass who sat in his lap. Cats have supersensitive hearing. I was terrified that she might get bored with Michael, hear the recording mechanisms chugging away in the rug, and go over to investigate.

"She's gonna get hairs all over you, Michael." I picked the kitten up — she meowed, annoyed at being disturbed — and carried her to the bathroom. I shut her in. "And stay there!"

"Very interesting article," I said, sitting down on the sofa again.

"Did they give you this?"

"Yeah, it was in with the brochures."

Michael had seen enough. He put the article aside. "I will study it. John—"

I cut him off at the pass. "Did you see the part about the Soviet Union?"

"John, but if you ask them about ordering documents, is it possible for you to obtain them without drawing attention?"

"As long as I'm not a Russian, they'll sell me anything."

He laughed. "You are not?"

I laughed back. "No, you are."

"But if they ask you for which purposes you are buying them, what you will do?"

"I'll have to think of something in connection with Columbia. In other words, that's my cover story."

"If they telephone to Columbia, what you will do?"

"What do you mean what will I do? I'm at Columbia. That's where I work."

Something about Columbia had Michael spooked. "But you should be careful with this Columbia University, because is not good place. They are looking out for bad people there."

What the hell was he talking about?

"In this place, it is possible that someone will come to you and pretend to be Russian. Don't believe it."

I thought that Michael was afraid of another Val incident — wrong again. Later I found out he feared something far more serious.

Meanwhile — "Meeeoow! Meeeoow!" — the little princess was pissed at being held prisoner in the bathroom. She scratched at the door. The bathroom door had multi-layers of paint on it, so it did not close all the way. Finally she broke through and trotted back into the living room. She sat down on her haunches in the middle of the floor with her tail swishing back and forth. She stared up at me. Easy enough to read her thoughts:

Animal! How dare you treat me like this in front of company!

I continued to waltz around the *WSJ* article, but Michael refused to hear the music. All he would say regarding my trip to California was, "John, I am quite pleased with your performance."

Not pleased enough. I grabbed the article and located the incriminating paragraph with my finger. "What does it say here, Michael?"

"Yes, John, I understand everything completely," he said, turning his head away as if I had shoved something foul in his face.

Right to the point: "You're not a spy, are you, Michael?"

He reacted as if he'd been asked, *Was that you who farted?* "Of course not."

"Too bad, because if you were, I'd be making a lot more money."

He laughed. "I like to hear you talk."

Another manila envelope, this one containing 200 photocopied pages of the army dictionary, lay on the sofa between us. Another point of contention, around and around we went, haggling over its price. I wanted the $300 he promised.

"I went to a lotta trouble for this shit. It's outta print. NAS couldn't get it. Nobody could. Know how I got it?"

"How?"

"From a friend of mine in the National Guard. It came out of the Army's own library." I sat back and clasped my hands behind my head and smiled. "Very resourceful, aren't I?"

"Ya, you are very resourceful. I am quite pleased with your performance. I will give you two-hundred bucks for it, not more."

I dropped my arms and shot forward. "Michael, I went through a lot of trouble for this. I got it from the U.S. Army." My voice lowered into a more conspiratorial tone: "I got this from the U.S. Army, and I'm giving it to a Russian who *says* he's no spy, but I'm not so sure."

Then a detour: "Let me ask you this: you once told me that if I got a good job, you'd give me a $1,000. So how about it?"

"John, we spoke with you about Grummans or EDO Corporation and you up ended at Columbia University."

Obviously Michael was not impressed, but it's my nature to question even the obvious. "You don't like Columbia?"

"What's so good about it?" he replied, his tone stained with disdain.

"Yeah, but Columbia is a good jumping point, it looks good on a resume."

"Ya! I tell you, you're shooting an up."

"So you should be *happy.* You should give me a nice big bonus. You paid me $900 for that fucking bullshit job at the Power Authority."

He slapped his knee and began rocking back and forth, laughing. "John, if you remember at the moment when I gave you that money you were already out of that place." More laughter. "It is simply too funny."

"What can I say? OK, I'll take the $200, but I'm pissed off. And you're not gonna gimme anything for Columbia?"

"This is it," he said, holding up an empty envelope. Then Michael instructed me to get a pen and paper because he was going to dictate my next order. When I returned from the front room, I noticed his briefcase open. Its contents: a plastic shopping bag and a copy of the *New York Post.* The shopping bag indicated that he had expected to receive a lot more material than I provided tonight.

I decided to tease the big Russian bear: "Got a gun in there,

Michael?"

"No." He held up the case for inspection. "See."

"Thought all spies carry guns."

"I am not spy, I told you," he said, putting what little material I had for him into the case.

"Guess that's why you're so cheap."

"Cheap? What do you expect, John?" He pointed to the contents of the case. "You give me such a shit." (I assumed he was referring to documents not bowel movements.) "I always try to help you, John, so you will make a lot of money. But you will make a lot of money in a safe way."

"This stuff with NAS is risky business, Michael. Read the article very carefully."

Michael got serious: "John, it seems to me that if you think is too risky with them, maybe we shouldn't do it. Do they've got classified stuff or not?"

He used the C word again. I winced inside.

"The stuff's not classified, but it probably should be."

"How do you mean? You say they've got interesting material?"

"Yes. According to the article, the stuff is very interesting. The government is afraid you guys will get hold of it."

"Your government," he waved off the mighty U.S. of A. with a limp wrist. "Your government deals with Iran." The Iran half of the Iran-Contra scandal just broke. Michael must have read about it in the *Post.*

"Told you governments are bullshit. Your government is bullshit, too. And they're cheap."

Michael got a big laugh out of that one.

He said he'd see me again at the end of December or early January. We walked to the front door. He put on his coat and pointed down at the kitten. She followed us into the foyer. "Is he or she?"

"A...bad...little...girl!" I said, wagging a finger at her.

"Oh, that is why she likes you so much."

"Think she likes you better, Michael."

(Aud 27.2) 5:08

Please listen carefully to hear kitten meowing to be let out of bathroom. There's a gap near end of tape but don't worry, audio continues.

Chapter 28
The Women in the Window

Grinning, "We're probably the best things they've seen all day, just a couple of students sitting in a car, huh?"

"What are you talking about? You don't look like a student. You don't even look Jewish."

***

Tuesday, November 11, 1986

Today, the day after my meeting with Michael, I was on the phone with FBI Special Agent Mike Berns. He asked me about Michael's health. Never before had the guy shown such concern for "our friend's" well being. Was it concern for Michael or something else? My guess: something else, even though Michael himself had made reference to a health problem.

(Audio 28.1) 0:20

Not that I needed it, but this was further confirmation that the People Down South had another fang in Michael's neck. When the time came, it would be that much easier to rip his throat out. But why tell me? I had no need to know.

(Audio 28.2) 1:42

In this same conversation Mike and I also discussed the latest computer search Michael wanted me to do: neodymium powder technology and General Motors. Finally, we discussed the possibility of Michael becoming a mole inside Soviet intelligence. I mentioned a former KGB officer who had defected and was code named Fedora by the Bureau. They believed the intelligence Fedora fed them was true. The CIA's counterintelligence chief at the time, James Angleton, had his doubts. Angleton was convinced that Fedora was really a KGB provocateur who fed the FBI disinformation. As it turned out, Angleton was right.

(Audio 28.3) 2:49

***

It didn't take an Einstein to grasp the implications: the Soviet Union was interested in a specific technology. Using the keywords Michael had given me — neodymium, powder technology and

General Motors — my computer spit out eighteen citations. Then I noticed a recurrent theme ran through all of these papers: magnets.

Neodymium (Nd) is a rare earth metal that when compounded with iron (Fe) increases the magnetic strength of the alloy. One article entitled, "Neodymium promises low-cost high strength magnets" gave an excellent overview of the technology. According to the article, rare earths began a revolution in the design of motors, controls, sensors, etc. Neo-iron-boron magnets (Nd-Fe-B) were the strongest of these rare earth based magnets. So strong, in fact, that they required careful handling. The attractive force between two 6" cubes was measured in tons, enough to crush a human hand. The strongest Nd magnet is called *Crumex 35*. Powder technology was used to form these magnets into various shapes.

I changed my search strategy to: "magnets" *AND* "Nd *OR* neodymium". This time the computer spit out hundreds of citations. Obviously, magnet was a critical keyword. So why had Michael deliberately left it out? Like I told Mike on the phone, based on past experience, my guess was that the Soviets were deliberately trying to camouflage their primary interest in neodymium powder technology as it relates to fabricating magnets. One more critical fact: the Raytheon Corp. had an experimental plant, the only one of its kind, in Ohio where these Nd magnets were being fabricated.

Although it might not take an Einstein, even Einstein had to put his theories to the test. Just how hot were Michael and the GRU for this experimental technology? I figured a way to find out: he'd only get the eighteen citations I retrieved using the information he provided; if he wanted more, he'd have to tell more.

On Tuesday, December 8th, another unsolicited report addressed Michael W. Berns, of Somewhere, New Jersey, went down the mail chute. The report, which took about 20 minutes to intellectualize (I think fast) and one hour to type (I type slow), included all eighteen Nd citations, an article on the Raytheon plant, plus my theories about Soviet intentions and how I intended to test those intentions. I could've told Mike most of this on the phone, but why should I? I was not an FBI informant, I was an FBI consultant. Washington D.C., in fact, was, and still is, filled with consultants who do nothing but feed the government's voracious appetite for bullshit. And the gods Down South loved to pay top dollar for all that crap. So I charged the government $659.98: $150/hr consulting fee for 4 hours work (modest by Beltway standards), plus on-line costs and $2.98 in postage.

On Monday, December 29th, at 7 p.m., once again, I chose convenience over safety. But if I did have to sit in a car with an FBI agent in Washington Heights, this was the best place: double parked on 187th Street between Amsterdam and Audubon Avenues, next to one of Yeshiva University's buildings.

The buildings of Yeshiva were like sleek cruise ships floating in a sea of urban flotsam: tenements, abandoned buildings, crack houses, etc. The poverty and despair that made up the rest of the Heights was always pressing in, making for turbulence that threatened to swamp or capsize YU. But YU's security, as well as NYPD, patrolled the area regularly, making it one of the few safe harbors in Washington Heights.

That was why I told Mike to turn up this block and park. I felt secure. Not so my *campañero*. I heard the simultaneous click of four automatic door locks slam shut.

"Power locks, eh." I laughed. "Does this rental also come with bulletproof glass?"

"Relax," Mike said, slightly annoyed. "I'd like to go over the stuff you sent me."

"I am relaxed," I snapped back. "You're the one who locked the doors."

A smirk, then he reached into his briefcase and pulled out the Nd report I'd mailed the Bureau. Mike turned on the interior lights and shuffled through the papers.

"There're a few things I found confusing," he said, "and I'm hoping you can clear 'em up for me."

"Sure. Did you see the diagrams I drew?"

Mike grinned. "Yeah, neat little lines and arrows pointing every which way; very impressive."

"Thanks. I used a ruler."

With papers spread out on the front seat and in my lap, and looking at the material for a second time, even I was confused. The diagrams were no help. It took a few minutes for me to sort things out in my head so I could upload them into his. Then I began reading the report aloud.

Certain species of worm can be cut in half yet still continue to live. One organism, two parts, and apparently Mike Berns was one such worm. A piece of him was calm, absorbed in taking notes, interrupting only when something required clarification. But the other half — the eyes gave it away. They were constantly shifting, from his notepad to the rear view mirror to the front or side windows. Any car or person that passed drew his immediate attention.

"Where are we?" he said, interrupting my detailed dissertation.

Annoyed, "Where're in the middle of the Yeshiva campus. See that building over there." I pointed to my right. "It's one of theirs.

We're very safe, Mike, I promise. I wouldn't let anything happen to you. You owe me too much money."

"What about over there?" He pointed to a building across the street and to our left. "See those two in the window?"

Two women cloaked in shadow stared at us from the second story of a tenement. I shrugged. "I dunno. Just an apartment building not connected with Yeshiva."

Grinning, "We're probably the best things they've seen all day, just a couple of students sitting in a car, huh?"

"What are you talking about? You don't look like a student. You don't even look Jewish."

I went back to debriefing, while Mike's eyes continued to be drawn to the women in the window. Must have been the best things he'd seen all day.

I finished reading and asked, "By the way, did you find the bill enclosed with the report?"

"Sure did." His mouth spiraled into a large, obnoxious grin. "Needless to say, you know what you can do with this," he said, handing the bill back to me. "You can paper the walls with it." Ever polite, I think what he really preferred was that I stuff a particular cavity on my body with the bill.

"Are you saying that I'm not gonna get paid?" I asked.

"Exactly."

"What!" I began to bounce up and down in my seat. "Hey, how about diverting some of that Iran money this way?"

Mike grinned. "Yeah, me and Ollie North have it all stashed away in a Swiss bank." He shook his head, then, "And what's this about

$150 an hour? You went from fifty to one-fifty."

"Inflation."

"That's more than we pay the Contras."

"That's because I'm better than the Contras." I handed the invoice back to him. "You keep this. We'll settle up at a later date."

He asked how I liked working at Columbia, and I said, "I like it just fine."

"Glad to hear that. I was wondering if you could tell me a little more about the library. What's your boss's name?"

Sensing where this line of questioning was headed, and with no intention of driving my choo-choo down that track, I fed Mike some disinformation. I gave him the name of a higher life form, the University Librarian. She was about as far removed from me as William Webster (then FBI director) was from him.

He jotted the name into his notepad. "Is there a directory of library personnel?"

Yes; it sat on the reference desk. "Why do you ask?"

"There're a few names we'd like to check out. Maybe there are people like you who have had contact with the Soviets. We'd like to find out. Can you get me a copy?"

"You know how I feel about that."

He paused, twitched his mustache, and looked away. "I'm not out to get anyone, John."

From me a silence found only in tombs. I was getting good at ignoring questions I didn't want to answer, a technique I'd picked up from both these Michaels.

Finally, Mike let out a puff of air, smirked and snapped his pad shut.

First Michael Katkov's skittishness about me being at Columbia and now Mike asking about library personnel: what was going on? Were libraries in general and/or Columbia in particular hotbeds of intrigue?

Mike was not happy to hear that Michael was still being vague in regards to NAS.

"It's sloppy," he said to himself out loud. "He's not doing his homework. Tasking you to make a trip to L.A. to see a guy, he doesn't say who, to find out about a company and to establish a business relationship based on only the most general of terms. It's screwy. Doesn't match what they've done before. None of this makes sense, sending you all the way out there for what amounts to a vacation. It's a waste of your time and theirs."

"Not mine. I loved it. I'll make a hundred trips out there if he wants." Then my turn to think out loud: "What puzzles me is Michael suddenly being so jumpy about NAS. He told me that if I thought dealing with them was too risky, drop them. What's he afraid of?"

Mike would not, or could not, answer.

I continued, "Bob had mentioned a large shipment of airplane parts that NAS was selling to some Near Eastern country. Is NAS selling embargoed parts to Iran? Do the Russians suspect this?"

Rather than answer, Mike offered to drive me home. Since I lived only a few blocks away, I refused, but he insisted. I told him to drop me off at St. Nicholas Avenue & 183rd Street. I didn't want him pulling up in front of my building because of the Watch Committee. We headed southbound on St. Nicholas Avenue when suddenly another sedan cut us off from the left. It screeched to a halt in front of a bodega. Mike jammed on the brakes.

"PD," Mike mumbled as two uniformed police officers got out of the unmarked car. They swaggered into the bodega, one with his hands at his belt, the other with a hand on his holster. We were stopped right behind the cruiser. I looked to see if he had a gun hidden in his crotch. It was empty. I tensed, excited by the possibility of some action. Then an image flashed on that big screen in my head; it was the front page of tomorrow's *New York Post*: *Hero FBI Agent, Michael W. Berns, Rescues Cops in Blazing Shoot Out — bystander, John Pansini, killed in crossfire; story page 2.*

Shit, after Michael Katkov read all about it at breakfast, I bet he'd say, "I trusted him! Good! I'm glad the *moodak* is dead."

Satisfied that everything was OK, "Must be getting sandwiches," Mike drove around the cruiser.

I got out at the corner of 183rd. Mike's attention was once again drawn to the street scene. I suppose to someone like him, with his white ass planted safely in the shrubbery of suburban New Jersey, the fauna of Washington Heights must have seemed like a jungle. He leaned across the front seat. "Don't know how you do it," he said, rolling up the passenger-side window. Then four automatic door locks went, *Click!*

Chapter 29
A Dignified Death

"Yah, we celebrate New Year. On New Year's night, I went to bed at five in the morning... I put towels on my face, but without pretty girl's mas-sage."

***

Friday, January 9, 1987

Hurtling along multiple lanes of traffic on a Friday afternoon, I was being driven across the George Washington Bridge by a nut job with jet-propelled hemorrhoids.

FBI Special Agent Mike Berns shot me a grin. "My driving makes you nervous?"

"Yeah," I replied, pressing a foot down hard on the imaginary brake pedal because it looked like we were going to run right up the ass of a car in front of us.

He aimed a grin out the windshield, "Relax. You're in good hands."

If he meant with the Lord, I wasn't ready to rest in peace yet.

Like tiny corpuscles slogging through a main artery, everyday hundreds of thousands of vehicles surge between two massive gray towers and a lattice of steel and roadway we in the Heights called, "The G-Dubbs."

Mike had picked me up in Manhattan near an on ramp to drived us to the Red Oak Diner in Fort Lee, New Jersey for a debriefing. I'd ridden with him many times before but never had I felt like crapping my pants. He weaved the Monte Carlo in and out of lanes like a needle shooting through fabric on a loom. For whatever reason, the guy was in a big hurry.

"Hey, see that article in the papers about Sheer?" he said, referring to FBI Assistant Director Thomas Sheer, the Bureau's head honcho in New York at the time. "Says FSCI (Foreign Service Counterintelligence) is a top priority here. Even tops organized crime."

Thinking back to the old lady murdered in her apartment, I didn't share his pride in the importance of what we were doing. "Nothing worse in this town than crime — little old ladies get murdered for their TV sets."

Mike's mustache twitched. "They're both important. Besides, making the streets safe for little old ladies, PD handles that."

Suddenly Mike jerked the car hard in a three-lane swerve that moved us into the far left. He pressed down on the accelerator. The engine roared; we zoomed past a long string of cars to my right.

"Reading this book," I said. Buckled in, I leaned back in my seat trying to tip all thoughts of a fiery crash out of my eminent domain. "*FBI* by Ungar. Good book. Says you guys log an hour and nine minutes overtime every morning.[1] That true?"

"Yep. Hit it right on the head." Another quick grin. "See you're learning all our little secrets."

"So tell me about you?"

A wry smile, "Why? Writing a book?"

Pat McKinney had once used the same line on me. Instead of telling Mike more than he needed to know, I said that I'd known him

1 Ungar, Sanford J., *FBI*, Little, Brown, c1976, p. 362

for three years and he knew (almost) everything about me, but I knew nothing about him.

Mike said he was from Philadelphia, graduated Drexel, did not have a law degree, and had been an FBI agent since 1974.

"You came after Hoover. You're lucky. Read the guy was a hard ass."

"Don't believe everything you read. Knew a guy who worked under Hoover. Knew him personally. Said if you were a worker and had problems, there was nothing the guy wouldn't do for you. But if you were a screw up, he couldn't care less." Then he grinned and added, "Of course, Hoover decided who the screw ups were."

"Read in Hoover's day, CI (counter-intelligence) was not a priority, that—"

"You're right," he broke in before I could shine more of my bright lights on him. "It was car thefts. Boosted the stats and—"

I would not be denied: "And helped you guys get larger appropriations from Congress."

Then I noticed the road ahead had opened up. Mike gunned the engine, and white lines whizzed by faster and faster until they became one long stripe; the lane in front of us narrowed into a tunnel as the distance between us and the preceding car decreased. This was as close to a near death experience I ever wanted to get. Just when I thought we were about to ram through the car's trunk and come out its grill, Mike suddenly veered right, cutting across all five lanes of traffic and moving us into the far right. He squeezed us in between two tractor-trailers. The trucks had us sandwiched. Mike sat with his right arm resting on top of the back rest, his left index finger wrapped around the bottom of the steering wheel. I imagined how embarrassing it would be to be pulled out of the wreckage with a big, brown stain in my underpants.

I sought dignity, even in death.

Then smoothly, gently and slowly, Mike headed onto the Route 1-9 exit ramp. A few minutes later he deposited us in the parking lot of the Red Oak. Now I knew how a butterfly felt after having its wings tugged out by a sadist. I vowed to never let this loony drive me anywhere ever again.

***

When I'd gotten up yesterday morning, Thursday the 8th, my body felt like a bag of rocks my will had to drag across the living room floor to get to the bathroom. I hurt all over; hockey at midnight will do that to a person. I didn't get home until two a.m. I tossed and turned all night, replaying the game in my head. By the time I finally wound down, it was time to get up for work. I washed myself, and then fed the cats. I'd clean their litter box after work. Seven torturous hours awaited me at the reference desk in Columbia's engineering library. Coffee would keep the eyelids propped open while the brain buzzed *Zzzzzzs*.

At 6:02 p.m., I got home, fed the animals, put off cleaning their litter box once again, and put off feeding me. I was about to lay me down to sleep when the spy phone in the front room rang.

"Do you mind, I will drop by your flat in thirty minutes." No inflection in Michael's tone, so even if I minded, he was coming anyway.

At 6:30 the doorbell went *Ding-Dong!* (Renovation: new door, new doorbell.) Michael breezed into my flat. He lay an expensive looking light gray topcoat and flap-cap (or whatever it's called) on top of the laundry wagon. Dressed in a dark blue pin striped suit and red tie, he looked like a young IBM executive. We sat down on the sofa. Bookie jumped up on the backrest, trotted right past me, and perched herself just behind Michael, sniffing at his hair and neck. What was her fascination with this guy?

Michael blinked as he read the neodymium printout I handed him. When he had finished going through all 18 citations, he handed the search back to me. "John, you will get all these documents. You will look in all the bbibliomfmdfkie-"

"In the bibliographies."

"Ya, in the bbibliomfmdfkies to find other articles and maybe pay-tents (patents)."

Although he couldn't say the word, Michael sure knew the concept. He wanted me to use the bibliographies of these papers to find other papers, the underlying assumption being that authors cite other authors who write on the same topic. It's called *citation indexing.*

I'll bet Google uses a variation of this technique for its web crawlers.

"I want to give you several thousand dollars when you have all the documents for me," he said, opening his hands wide as if he expected a whole universe of literature on Nd magnets. "But not for this search. For more comprehensive search you will do later."

A surge of adrenalin: "Several thousand dollars!" That sure woke me up. Leaning closer, "Michael, my heart's going like this," I said, sticking a fist under my white T-shirt and thumping my chest. "I'll do anything for several thousand dollars. *Anything.*"

"OK, I understand everything completely, but today I will pay you

$700."

(Audio 29.1) 0:27

$350 was the previously agreed upon figure for the Nd search. Naturally, I assumed the additional $350 would be a gift from Christmas Past.

"OK, that was—" before I could add, *"for Christmas, what about my birthday?"* he cut me off with: "That is more than enough."

***

Mike safely landed us in New Jersey; we entered the Red Oak Diner. He told me, "Grab a table while I make a phone call."

A short call: he returned, sat down and opened his notepad. Then his beeper went off. His eyes rolled in their sockets. "Excuse me, gotta make another call. Be right back."

His notepad lay opened on the table. Absorbed trying to decipher his scribble, I didn't notice his immediate return.

"Know how you librarians are, always trying to read things upside down," he said.

"Not librarians, spies."

Mike grinned, snapped his pad shut and took it with him. When he returned, he looked even more harried than before. After the waitress took our orders, he promised me his complete, undivided attention.

I said, "Michael used thc word classified again. He seems to think NAS has access to classified information. Do they?"

A wide smile, "Sure thinks so, doesn't he? So what did he have to say about NAS?"

Yesterday Michael had dropped NAS into the conversation like a worm on a hook: "One more thing, do you expect some communication from that bloody firm?"

After I snapped at it, he instructed me to find out more about what they had to offer and to develop a business relationship with either of the brothers, Bob or George, who ran the company. "Tell him you might place an order worth several thousand dollars with him."

"Makes me sound like a bullshit artist, Michael. Give me something I can order from him."

"Do they've got only unclassified or also classified information?"

"I don't think they have any classified information."

"At this time." His tone was hopeful, so were his eyes.

"Did you read that (WSJ) article I gave you?"

"But last time you told me they've got classified material."

"What I said was they have stuff the government wants to classify. I read the article. Did *you* read the article?"

More insistent, "But you told me you saw classified material. Upstairs."

I never said any such thing. Why was he pushing it? What did he tell his boss? "I didn't say that. You misunderstood me, Michael. What I said was—"

Out of nowhere Stinky, the shy one, decided to make an entrance.

He ran into the room. The kitten saw him and jumped off the sofa. The cats began wrestling on the floor.

"Look! The other one's out," I said, rocking back and forth, clapping my hands. This was the first time Stinky had come out in front of Michael.

Michael made some *meow* noises; then he asked, "Which one is your better?"

I said I loved them both. We chatted about the cats, completely forgetting about whether or not NAS had any classified documents. Stinky had screwed everything up. I didn't realize what had happened until I played back my own tape recording (I'd hidden my recorder in the laundry wagon where the cats couldn't get at it). Then I smacked myself on the head for being so easily sidetracked.

When I relayed this to Mike Berns — except the part about my tape recorder — he said, "Hate to think of us losing the Cold War because of your darn cats." Then he shook his head and grinned.

Again I asked Mike why Michael thought NAS had classified information.

"Well," he paused to make a few notations in his pad, then, "the Soviets know that at times the government has to release certain classified data to enable contractors to bid on government contracts. And since NAS supplies defense contractors with information, the Soviets believe they have some."

"Do they?"

Instead of an answer, I got another lecture on pinning Michael down.

"I'm trying," I whined. "Think it's easy? Like this guy is just gonna tell me?"

"Did he say anything about Stealth?"

A stealthy question that my radar failed to see coming: "He made a joke about me stealing a B1 for him. Why?"

"B1 is the bomber, Stealth is the technology. In what context did it come up?"

"It came up in the context of specifics. Michael said he wouldn't be specific until I was specific. And I can't be specific until you guys let me get a job with access."

"That," Mike replied, "is something we have no intention of doing. Not yet, anyway."

It hurt banging my head, over and over, into the same damn wall!

In regards to stealth technology, Mikhail Katkov had asked me, "And how is your search for a position at Grummans progressing?"

"I told you where all the interesting positions are, Michael, in Southern California. I wanna move out there."

"What-Are-The-Interesting-Positions, John?" he said with special emphasis on each word, like he was annoyed with me.

"All the aerospace jobs."

"Where, John? What kind of positions? If you've got something specific, then we will discuss it. But if you don't, then what will we discuss with you? When you speak only in general, I give you only general answers. But next time I come to your flat and you tell me, 'Michael, I've got Stealth Bomber,' and I will say, 'Ya that is quite interesting.' "

I grinned. "How much would you gimme?"

"How much do you want?'

"Well, it's a big plane. Have to hide it in the basement." (If the rats didn't eat it first.) Then a dramatic pause followed by: "Millions."

"OK, is no problem."

"I'll start sending out résumés again, but it's much easier to get a job there if I already am there. Know what I mean, Michael?"

"I understand, John," he said in a singsong voice. "But when you've got specific results, I will be specific."

(Aud 29.2) 1:05

Two Michaels + two walls = one sore head.

Something about Columbia still spooked Michael. When I told him that I was going to use my position as reference librarian as a cover in dealing with NAS, he said, "And if they offer themselves to Columbia University library, what you will do?"

"No, no. I'll give my name. It'll come to my mailbox."

He pointed to the floor. "Here?"

"No, at Columbia."

"And somebody will look through your mailbox."

I laughed in his face. "Michael, this is America. Not Russia. People don't open other peoples' mail here."

"John, don't tell me about Columbia University. I tell you don't do it."

"OK. Whatever you think is best, Michael. After all—" I put my hand to my mouth and whispered — "you're the spy."

"Yes of course, John. If you want to think it, think it."

(Aud 29.3) 0:15

I told Agent Berns, "He gets annoyed when I call him a spy." I chuckled. Mike just shrugged.

The very best little tidbit I had saved for last: "Again I told Michael about my suspicions regarding NAS' ethics. Given recent events, I said that I thought that they might already be involved in something illegal, like selling airplane parts to Iran."

Mike stared back at me from a blank, cop's face. Was I onto something? Only one way to find out, so I added, "Michael said that if they are, I am to break contact immediately."

"He said the same thing last time."

"Last time he sounded iffy. This time he was a lot more certain."

Mike's eyebrows raised and his mustache twitched ever so slightly.

Something personal between Michael and me that I decided Mike had no need to know. It occurred at the end of our meeting when Michael had asked about my family's health. I did likewise. Then I asked him if the Soviets celebrate New Year's.

"Yah, we celebrate New Year. On New Year's night, I went to bed at five in the morning." He told me about drinking too much. Then he leaned his head back and laid a forearm across both eyes. All I could see was teeth. He was smiling. "I put towels on my face, but without pretty girl's mas-sage."

Being a good librarian, I was proud of the extensive research I'd done. I'd learned that the real world of mirrors was not at all like the World of 007. I'd been one of the few allowed a peek behind the glass; so I knew that operations like the Katkov Affair rarely lasted more than two years. January 1987 marked the beginning of Year Four. This was the beginning of the end for Michael. I doubted there would be much for him to celebrate in 1988.

Maybe me, too.

Chapter 30
A Night at the Oscars

Spies, spy catchers, and those in between, we all have a special talent: we're excellent actors

***

Tuesday, March 24

From my research I knew that operations like the Katkov Affair rarely lasted more than two years. 1987 marked the beginning of year four. I sensed The Katkov Affair had already past its expiration date.

And then — *WOW! JACKPOT!* — a totally unexpected event occurred on the West Coast that, like the hot Santa Anas, blew new life into the whole damn thing.

Tuesday night at 8:30 p.m., I was working in Columbia's engineering library. As what usually happens when I sit on my ass at a desk instead of up on a roof, Time, while not completely stopped, was crawling on all fours. In thirty more minutes I'd be free. With no students and no faculty around I decided to run another computer search on NAS. Ever since I first suspected that something might not be quite right with that outfit I'd been running an occasional search; and each time I came up with the same two articles from 1985. But tonight, when I keyed "newport aeronautical sales" into the news wires AP and UPI, I hit the jackpot. Thirteen citations, all within the last two months: NAS made the news again, big time. The full text of what had happened flashed across the screen: Bob's brother George, the proprietor of NAS, was in jail. Needless to say, both sides in the Cold War knew what had happened long before me.

Now I knew something they didn't know I knew.

The next day Mike phoned, opening with his usual greeting, "Hey, guy, how you doing?"

My reply was not as friendly: "So where's my money?"

The latest contention between me and the People Down South involved $659.98 they still owed me for the Raytheon/neodymium report; the one with all the neat little arrows and diagrams; the one I'd given Mike the night we'd been parked on Yeshiva's campus; and the one he'd tried to hand back to me. Every single bill I'd ever submitted to the Bureau had been paid — eventually. They always kept me waiting, but never this long.

The way Mike now explained it, or tried to, the People Down South had balked at paying such a ridiculously high figure for such bullshit, his subtext if not exact text.

"Well, Mike, that's why we have courts of law in this country. Hope I won't have to sue you people."

Let him and the People Down South wrestle with that for awhile.

***

1987 marked my 21st year as a roofer. That meant a lot of energy spent banging new layers of shingles onto roof decks. In all that time I never gave much thought as to what lay beneath the plywood: intricate lattices of beams and crossbeams with every member in support of every other member. Yank one out and the whole thing might collapse. I never cared about the drama that went on inside those homes either. None of my business what people did or how they lived. My job was to keep them dry.

I now found myself on top of a house that had been under construction for four years. Its architectural drawings had been carefully planned and laid out. I was the roofer hammering on a protective layer. That put me on the outside, not inside. Beneath me, below the deck and the beams where the People Down South lived, were rooms holding secrets that I would never be privy to. The entire structure of the Katkov Affair rested on a foundation of secrecy. Like one of those California mini-mansions built into a hillside and supported by stilts, yank out one of those secrets and the best laid plans of the American intelligence community would slide into the sea. And it didn't take a weatherman to know which way the heavy rains blew, either. I could demolish the whole damn thing and without using a wrecking ball. All I had to do was file a lawsuit in small claims court to collect the $659.98 the government owed me. Let that stain the public record for awhile:

Roofman sues Federal Bureau of Investigation, the Central Intelligence Agency and the White House.

I'd be going after the deepest pockets.

Would the Russians find out? Maybe, maybe not, but just like with a roof, even a tiny hole meant a leak drip, drip, dripping into one of their secret rooms. Something like that could not be good. The way I figured it, they had to either pay me or kill me. The latter (the nuclear option) involved too many secret papers with too many secret signatures.

My guess: sooner or later I'd get what was owed me.

***

When Michael strolled into my living room on Thursday evening, April 9th, his eyes focused on a large red welt on my upper right arm.

I wore a white T-shirt. Two nights ago some asshole had whacked me instead of the puck.

Noticing him noticing, "Hockey," I mumbled, showing him my arm.

Michael misunderstood. He pointed at the bruise and grinned. "So who is this nice girl who did that to you?"

It took me a few seconds to catch his drift: "No, no, Michael. I said hockey not hickey."

Michael planted himself in his usual spot on the sofa. Across from him, two piles sat side-by-side on the blue chair. One pile contained the neodymium documents ordered from the first computer search; the other contained a printout of the new, expanded Nd search and a few other documents. When I sat down next to him, he handed me an envelope containing eleven one hundred dollar bills.

"Have you had any further communication with that bloody man in California?" he asked, flipping through the pages of the printout.

Grinning, "No, and I won't be either. Not anymore," I snickered.

"And why not?"

The punch line: "Because George, the owner, is in jail."

Michael looked up. "How do you know this?"

"Because that's what you pay me for, Michael, to find out interesting things that will keep us out of trouble. And I'm good at it too. Damn good." I leaned back and rested an arm on top the sofa, expecting a well earned pat on the back. Instead he repeated the question.

I said, "I've been suspicious of those people for a long time, so periodically I've been running computer searches on them."

That was how I knew that on February 6, 1987, Edward James Bush, 51, a former vice president with Litton Industries, was arrested at Los Angeles International Airport. He was about to board a flight to Buenos Aires, Argentina. At the time of his arrest, UPI reported that Bush had been carrying boxes of technical manuals dealing with the generator for General Electric's J-79 engine used on the F-4, F-104 and F-16 fighters. Also in his possession were airline tickets for Johannesburg, South Africa. Because the State Department had banned the exportation of published material with military applications to South Africa, Bush was charged with violating the Arms Export Control Act: a law with considerably more teeth than FARA. In addition, the government charged that two-hundred manuals seized from Bush contained some classified information.

Maybe more was hidden in a basement at Mar-a-Lago.

The People Down South had taken a big bite out of Bush's ass, and as reported in the press, he made a full confession. Bush said that he'd been working as a private consultant to Newport Aeronautical Sales. The day after Bush's arrest, special agents from U.S. Customs and the FBI raided the same NAS office I'd visited back in September 1986. On Friday, February 20th, George MacArthur Posey was arrested and charged with aiding and abetting violation of The Arms Export Control Act and The Anti-Apartheid Act, which prohibited trading in munitions to South Africa. Prosecutors said that George MacArthur took orders from various people, including a naval attaché (most likely an intelligence officer) in the South African Embassy in Washington D.C.

That put Mr. Posey's name in the history books: his indictment marked the first time anyone had ever been charged with violating the Anti-Apartheid Act; and later, in July, 1987, he would become the first person ever convicted under this statute. George MacArthur was not only the first but also the last person. As far as I know, no one else was ever charged.

My embers glowed. I felt like giving myself a warm hug. But Michael went back to reading the printout. What did he really think of his Roofman the Spy? I searched his face for clues: Was that a shine in his eyes, a faint grin on his face?

Yes!

Out of nowhere the phone sitting on the end table right next to Michael rang. It was 6:30, prime Michael time. I knew who it was even before picking up the receiver. Instinct had warned me to be prepared for an intrusion of some kind.

"Hey, guy, how you—" said the caller.

"Mike," I said, pretending to be happy to hear from him. "How you doing?" Before he could respond, I quickly added, "You get the tickets for the game Saturday night?" I was referring to fictional tickets to a very real Ranger hockey playoff game.

Michael sat quietly reading the printout, but I sensed his antenna was up, his radar tracking nuances in my voice. As for what was going on inside my head:

For best performance while under considerable duress — and the winner is! John Pansini!

Thank you members of the Academy. I would especially like to thank that asshole Mike Berns for calling me when he knew that Michael would be here.

A pause on his end of the line while Mike sorted it out. Then, "You mean he's there?"

For best performance pretending to be grossly incompetent and stupid — and the winner is! Michael W. Berns!

"Yep. Where we sitting, the reds?" The red-backed seats were the most expensive in Madison Square Garden at the time.

"I just wanted to call to let you know that Michael was up and around and you might be hearing from him soon."

Like no shit! My voice took on a disappointed tone: "Oh, the blues, huh." The blue-backs were the cheap seats. If the Bureau really did spring for playoff tickets, undoubtedly we'd be sitting way up in nose-bleed country behind a pillar. "Oh, well. Hey, Mike, I really appreciate it, but I gotta go. I'm on the computer. Can't talk now, bye."

I hung up, and Michael casually asked, "And who was that?"

Some asshole. "Some guy I know."

Finally, for the best performance pretending he wasn't listening when he really was. And the winner is! Mikhail L. Katkov!

Ladies and gentlemen of the Academy, three Oscar winning performances.

After four years of dealing with Katkov, Berns, et al, I wondered if my true calling might be acting.

Michael got up, lifted the pile of documents off the blue chair and sat down. He laid the material on the floor in front of him. He separated each document from its wrapper and matched each title against a list he'd taken out of his pocket. Documents, papers and cellophane lay scattered all around him. The crinkling of cellophane wrappers drew unwanted attention from the usual suspect.

She sat on her haunches with her tail swishing back and forth in the archway between the living and front rooms. A year old, Bookie was now a feline teenager (fifteen in our time). The little gray terror crouched. Then she sprang and dove into the papers. That these documents were important to the future economic and technological development of the Soviet Union, that they represented big bucks to my bank account and food for her and Stinky, that a Cold War raged all around us, meant nothing to this stupid beast. To her the mess Michael made was like a patch of catnip, something to jump into, roll around in, hide under, and chew on.

Michael scratched her head, gave her a couple of friendly "meows" and simply worked around her. His briefcase lay open next to him on the floor. Bookie jumped into it.

"Michael. Now she's in your case."

"Is OK," he mumbled still busy matching titles.

"But you got all your secret spy shit in there. What if she accidentally sets off the nuclear destruct device? What if she blows up the whole building?"

A smirk, "It seems to me no one will miss it. You have even said yourself that you want to go somewhere else."

"Not the moon, Michael."

He gently picked the cat out of his case and scratched her head again. "You want to go home with me, ya?"

Then she jumped right back in. He slapped his knees and laughed.

"Take her, please, Michael. She's a pain-in-the-ass."

"Let her be your pain-in-the-ass," he said, jabbing an index finger in my direction.

"Look at the mess you made, Michael."

He looked at me, then around, and then back at me. His face said,

You Gotta Be Kidding! After packing everything into his briefcase — everything except Bookie — he gathered up all the excess wrappers and papers and bundled them into a neat little pile. "Nice and tidy, so you don't accuse me of leaving your flat in disarray."

He took out an appointment book to study a calendar page. Then he snapped the book shut. "If I am ill in July, you will be visited by one of my colleagues. He will have quite a lot of money for you."

Michael's words past by me like a slow-roller going foul. Only later did I find out their true significance. Right now the only thing that shifted through my neural filters was that I might be seeing him for the last time. Like I said, this was the fourth year of his tour, and most GRU officers were reassigned after four years.

"Uh, Michael… This isn't, uh, permanent, is it?" A question a perfect spy should not have asked.

Michael replied with a shrug and a poker face.

Waves of powerful emotions began to pound my shorelines, feelings that might easily swamp my surface and wash away the cool facade. I'd shared a great adventure with this guy. I liked him. Should I warn him? But this unexpected stream of conscience that rushed towards my mouth could not surge passed a high levy:

You don't really know this guy. He's not your friend. This is what he does. This is what you do: a job, nothing more, a means to an end and all that.

But there was some spill over*: He likes cats! He trusts me. He's shown a lot more concern about me than the other Michael and his pals ever did.*

Two such fine actors, Michael and me, stuck for words. Finally, "So, John, tell me: and how is your business?" The equivalent of asking, *So, John, how's the weather?* Since he brought it up, I decided to give him a gift, one he could do with it as he pleased: "I'm having a little problem."

He leaned forward on the blue chair. "What kind of problem?"

"A client who owes me money."

"Is too bad. Who is this person?"

The asshole who just called on the phone. "Sorry, Michael. Confidential. Remember?"

"Ya, I remember. So what you will do about your money?"

"Sue him in Small Claims Court."

"Be very careful, John. Do not draw attention to yourself."

"Don't worry, Michael, I think he's gonna pay."

What was left unsaid: *Because they don't want to draw attention to themselves.*

Chapter 31
Silent Screams

Four attendants in jumpsuits hoist a stretcher onto a pair of guardrails. They begin pushing a man, feet-first, towards the open mouth of a roaring furnace.

***

Friday April 10, 1987

The day after my meeting with Michael, I called Mike Berns. Pissed-off about his ill-timed phone call, I insisted on a face-to-face sit down with one of his bosses. I could afford to take an attitude with these guys because a new GRU officer might be entering stage right.

Michael's six weird words cast a light deep in my mind. I convinced myself they held a hidden message, so I climbed down a ladder. No, not a ladder from roof back to the ground, rather one that led down into twisting catacombs of memory where obscure facts were stored. *If I am sick in July* were like torches that hung on the walls to light the way.

Ill/sick, ill/sick, ill/sick — remains I knew I'd tripped over once before. I felt fairly certain that Michael was not speaking of a pre-existing condition; therefore, I skipped the blind alley marked, "Health Care." In addition to Russian, the GRU and KGB spoke another common language, the language of intelligence; so I turned into a passageway marked, "KGB." There, in one of my earliest, primary sources, I found what I'd been looking for. In the jargon of Soviet Intelligence to "swim" meant to travel, a "wet affair" was an assassination, a "legend" was a cover story, and a "shoe" a false passport. "Illness" or "To be sick" meant to be arrested.[1]

No doubt in my mind that this was Mr. Katkov's hidden message — but Michael being arrested by the FBI? Possible but not plausible; I'd know for sure when I ran *If I am sick in July* by Special Agent Mike Berns. As for Michael being arrested by his own people: plausible and far more likely. Again, Mike Berns' reaction would tell all.

Why would Soviet intelligence go after one of their own? At the bottom of the scale *How to Best Screw Up Your Life* the reasons were pure soap opera. For example, maybe Michael got caught fooling around with the wrong person's wife. Given Mike and Tom Black's unflattering remarks about Mrs. Katkov, comparing her to a plough horse, did Michael find himself a Philly in another man's pasture? I'd read enough case studies to know that when it came to foreign embassies — both ours, theirs and everyone else's — on a human level it was *As the Diplomatic World Turns*.

At the very top of the *How to Best Screw Up Your Life* scale is the red zone: high treason. If his needle moved into that territory Michael would make the ultimate penance: if caught and convicted by the KGB, he would be given a bullet in back of the head. But if the GRU got to him first, he would end up a burnt offering.

Closets are more than useful, they're necessities. No home or apartment would be livable without them; and the more closet space a person has the happier he or she will be. Like with closets, people also need space in their minds to stash unpleasant things they'd rather not think about.

Back in the days of the Katkov Affair I had so many bad thoughts

1 Barron, John, KGB, c1973

stuffed away that I had to build a new addition onto the rear wing of my mind. One closet in particular was marked off with yellow "Do Not Cross" tape and three big red signs that said, "Stay Out!" "Beware!" and "Open at Your Own Risk!" I'd been there only once before, when I told Anne about the consequences if Michael betrayed his country. Now Michael's *If I am sick in July* brought me back there for another look. And when I opened the door, this was what I saw:

A silent film flickers its grainy black and white images on a small screen. Two men in silhouette, seated side by side, watch. From behind them a thin beam of light cuts the darkness. One of the men, a short, broad-shouldered box of a man, holds a cigarette; a smoky plume snakes upwards from an orange ember. Cut to the screen: a man in a dark suit, white shirt and dark tie has been tied to a stretcher with steel wire. Four attendants in jumpsuits hoist the stretcher onto a pair of guardrails. They begin pushing the man, feet-first, towards the open mouth of a roaring furnace. The stretcher and its human cargo pause just short of the furnace doors. Flames lick at the man's patent leather shoes; the heat is so intense the soles smoke.

A close-up on the man's face: he's screaming, but the only sound the two men watching hear is the clicking of film sliding through the projector. Pullback: the attendants lift one end and the stretcher slides off the rails and into the furnace. The flames eat the man alive.

The doors close, the film ends, and the lights come back on. The audience of two is a chain-smoking senior colonel in the GRU and a recruit. The recruit's face is clear to me: it's Mikhail Katkov.[2]

The burnt offering in the film had been a senior colonel in the GRU. His name was Oleg Penkovsky.[3] In the early 1960s Penkovsky had defected-in-place for Western intelligence. If he had betrayed the

2 Suvorov, Inside the Aquarium
3 Penkovskiy, The Penkovskiy Papers

KGB, he would have been humanely dispatched. The GRU was not so gentle. For those who betrayed Soviet military intelligence, their fate was biblical: ashes to ashes, and dust into the dust bin.

After peeking inside this closet for a second time I had to avert my mind's eye. I told myself that whatever mess Michael had gotten into had nothing to do with me. There'd be no soot on my hands.

***

(Audio 31.1) 3:09

#26 Federal Plaza is an imposing structure of glass and steel. Located in Lower Manhattan, it is the mighty United States of America's footprint of power in New York City. It towers above the streets, the traffic, and the little people.

At 9:15 a.m., on Tuesday, April 14th, a long, thin tongue snaked from the glass beast's mouth. The tongue grew longer and longer almost dipping into the street.

"Who are those people?" I said, pointing to a line that stretched from the main entrance and wound its way around the plaza.

"Illegal aliens registering for amnesty," Mike Berns replied as he tried to lead me in that direction.

I stopped and caught hold of his arm. "Wait a minute. What if the Russians are taking pictures of people entering and leaving the building?"

"You worry too much, John. Thousands of people come in and out of there every day."

"Humor me."

So he did. We entered at a side entrance that led into a basement garage. Mike smiled at the guard and flashed a gold-plated shield that looked like it came right out of a box of Cracker Jacks. Then we took an elevator up to the reception area on the 28th Floor, the same place I'd been to back in December 1983, when I met with agents Dan Pierce and David Nelson.

After signing us in, he led me to another bank of elevators. I noticed his attire: a well tailored, dark gray, pin striped suit, a white shirt and red tie. I'd never seen him so well creased before. Bread could be sliced off his pants leg.

"You look really sharp today. What's up?"

"So do you," was his casual reply.

True. No blue jeans and sweatshirts today. I wore a charcoal gray blazer, sports shirt and slacks. "I gotta go to work this afternoon (at Columbia's engineering library). Where are we going?"

"Down to the 25th Floor where our division (the Intelligence Division) is headquartered."

Mike and I stood in the corridor with our eyes focused on the Up/ Down triangles above the elevator doors. Swirling elements of young men in white shirts rolled up at the sleeves bustled in and out of doorways. It looked to me like they all shopped at the same clothing store; so much for variation. Two or three of these eager beavers stepped in behind us to wait for the lift. Mike acknowledged no one and no one acknowledged him.

Just as the red Down light pinged, a bunch of chatty secretary types holding coffee mugs rushed through a set of glass double doors, their high heels clattering across the vinyl tiled floor. Inside the elevator a pleasant scent of perfume easily overpowered that of aftershave.

On the way down, the elevator stopped at every floor between twenty-eight and twenty-five. People got on; people got off. But at twenty-five, no one got on and only Mike and I got off. I felt special.

At the cream-colored double doors, Mike shoved a card into a slot and keyed in a code.

I joked, "So where does the money come out?" Then I remembered, "Speaking of money, what about the $659.98 you guys still owe me?" I referred to the neodymium magnet search I'd given the FBI back in November.

Mike gave me a tired look. "I put you in for $650. You'll have to trust me for the other nine."

"And ninety-eight cents."

A buzzer went off and we entered a very long corridor with doors on each side, some open, some closed. I felt like I was back in school strolling past classrooms. Mike made small talk. I ignored him, slowing down at each door to look inside. I saw people busy at desks, but no one bothered to look up. Mike touched my arm whenever he felt the need to get me moving. At the end of the corridor we made a right. A tall, young guy stood in front of a closed door. He looked anxious. When I saw that was where we were headed, I felt like an old file that had been hanging around RAM for too long. A sense of immediate deletion overwhelmed me.

"This is Jim Knapp," Mike said.

Jim smiled. We shook hands. Then Mike opened the door marked Counterintelligence Library. We sat down at a long, rectangular reading table. Jim sat at the head of the table to my immediate right, his back to the door. Mike sat across from me, one seat over and to the left. We weren't so much occupying our chairs as spread out in them. I had the urge to put my feet up, but I checked that impulse.

Mike didn't say much at first, allowing me to get acquainted with Special Agent Knapp. I guessed Jim to be no more than thirty. He had short, neat, dark hair, and dark eyes set in a round, boyish face. Jim was tall — almost tall enough to go eyeball to eyeball with Mr. Katkov. "I majored in poly sci and Russian studies as an undergrad," he said in an accent straight out of the heartland. "I have a law degree from Ohio State."

Impressive credentials.

I said, "Mike tells me you're a computer expert."

"Ah, shucks, hardly. I've had no formal training. Most of what I've learned I've picked up on my own."

Back in the 1980s, guys without formal training who became computer experts were known as "hackers."

He sounded and looked like a bright guy, but then again, except for Richard Miller, I doubted there were any dummies in the FBI's Intelligence Division.

"So Jim, lemme ask you: why are you here all of a sudden?"

"I'd rather let Mike fill you in. This is still his case."

Mike sent a *What Did I Tell Ya* grin at Jim'. Then to me, "How 'bout telling us what happened beginning with the new guy Michael wants to introduce to you. In what context did it come up?"

"Michael didn't say he was going to introduce me to anybody. He said that if he is sick in July, I will be visited by one of his colleagues. He also said the guy will have quite a lot of money for me."

Mike sat back in his chair with hands clasped behind his head while Jim scribbled notes. Then Mike said, "This is very important: did he say anything about leaving the country?"

An *Ah-Ha!* moment for me. Why Mike's sudden concern about Michael leaving the country? Because when the GRU or KGB intended to arrest one of their own officers, the first step was a sudden recall back home.

"He didn't say. I just assumed that he'd be going home for the summer. He always does."

After some probing on my part, Mike finally admitted, "We think he might be in some kind of trouble back home, but we don't know what. Anything you can tell us, any little detail, no matter how trivial it might seem, might be helpful. Think hard."

I retreated back into those catacombs of memory searching for a stone I might have overlooked. "I can't remember. Honestly. That's all he said."

Mike asked me about Michael's psychology. I replied that I couldn't really say without being speculative. Then he asked, "How about his English?"

"Seems to have deteriorated; maybe he feels totally relaxed with me, but I can't be sure. Tell you one thing: he hardly blinks anymore. That's a fact."

Mike shot Jim a look, and then Jim noted something in his pad.

Mike said to Jim, "He's (meaning me) has already given us his permission, and the Attorney General his approval, for us to *Nagra* (plant a recorder) in his apartment several times before." Then they discussed between themselves the possibility of taping July's meeting with Michael or whomever. Mike asked if I could send him the envelope that Michael had given me, the one the Soviets had stuffed with ten $100 bills. "It's a long shot, but we want to see if there are fingerprints on it other than yours and Michael's. Next time he gives you an envelope, hold it by the tips."

"Yeah, sure, and when our friend asks me what I'm doing, I'll say, 'I'm trying not to get my fingerprints on it.'"

Smirking, "Just try and handle it as little as possible."

"Yeah, OK. This new guy, if he shows, what do you think it means?"

"Could mean something," Mike said. "Or nothing. We'll just have to wait and see."

Jim furiously scribbled on a yellow legal pad, tearing off pages, and then laying them next to him. I took a peek. There must be a special course at the FBI Academy: *How To Make Your Handwriting Unreadable to Some Asshole Looking Over Your Shoulder 101.* Bet both Mike and Jim passed that class with honors.

While Jim continued to write, Mike asked to see my copy of the *New York Times* that I'd laid on the table when I'd sat down. He said he wanted to check the hockey scores. I handed him the sports section. Then, without lifting his eyes off the page, he casually asked, "Is there anything bothering you? Anything you'd like to talk about?" He must have sensed my curtness on the phone the last time we spoke; but that wasn't what bothered me.

Had the time come to lay it on the line with them? To tell them that I was feeling guilty about betraying Michael? For Mikhail

Katkov, no matter what he chooses, he loses. If he stepped through door #1 and refused to cooperate with the FBI/CIA, he would get expelled. There would be no pat on the back from the GRU Centre in Moscow despite him doing the right thing. To them, Mikhail would be a failure. The KGB rewarded mediocrity. Its officer corps was filled with Moscow Boys (scions of the well-connected), and the elite always takes care of their own. But because its officer corps were taken mostly from the proletariat, failures in the GRU were given one-way tickets to the Elephant's Graveyard; i.e. a teaching position at the Military Diplomatic Academy of the General Staff. At the Academy GRU recruits were trained by GRU officers who had each suffered a cataclysm in their careers; like being expelled from a foreign country. Thus, instructors at the Academy were called "elephants," and a teaching position there was called the "Elephants Graveyard" because that was where careers went to die.

If Michael stepped through door #2 and defected-in-place, he could expect to be doused with lots of money and early retirement in the West. But if the GRU ever found out, that meant a passionate embrace by hot flames. Did I really want to discuss any of this?

"No," I told Mike. "There's nothing bothering me."

With that, Mike and Jim seemed to be in a hurry to conclude this meeting and get rid of me. But I had one more card to play on Michael Berns before I folded. "Aren't you gonna ask me if Michael said anything about NAS?"

Mike still sat with his hands clasped behind his head; he looked a bit grayer than the last time I saw him. "OK, what about NAS?" His tone gave every indication the company was a dead issue.

I intended to resuscitate it: "Not like that. First you say, 'Did he ask about NAS?' and I say, 'Yes.' Then you ask me, 'What did you tell him?' and I say…" I motioned for him to recite the correct lines in the little scene I was about to direct.

He chuckled, then, "OK, if it'll make you happy: what did you tell him about NAS?"

"That George is in jail."

That sure flipped Mike's switch; his bright, cheery smile went out. Hands still clasped behind his head, he tried to stare holes in my face with his cop's eyes. "How do you know?"

I turned to Jim, who looked confused, and said, "Hey, that's what the other Michael said." I chuckled.

Jim did too. Then he saw how truly, madly and deeply pissed Mike was, so he shut up. Mike repeated the question.

My lead in, "Because I'm an informed citizen," only heightened the man's irritation. Too fucking bad. This informed citizen was fed up with all the, "I can't get into that with you, Julius," crap he'd been giving me for four years. I grinned and told him that I'd done a computer search and read it off the news wires. Then to Jim, "Aren't computers wonderful tools. We live in an information age."

Mike rubbed his eyes and temples hard. "You never cease to amaze me, Julius." The non-issue of NAS temporarily became an issue again, so Mike began filling Jim in on all he needed to know.

An over aggrandized sense of self now flooded the empty plain that often existed between my ears: *Nailed his ass! I never cease to amaze me either... Wait!!! What's that??? He said something! He said something!*

"… sent him (meaning me) out to LA to make contact with another information broker. A guy named George Posey…" were the only words of Mike's that I caught. The one that began the above phrase is the keyword I missed.

Wait... What?... CoCon?... ConCon?... ComCon?... John, you dumb fuck!

"Wait a minute, Mike. You said Co-something or other. How come you didn't say GRU? I thought Michael worked for the GRU?"

Mike ignored me. When he finished filling Jim in, he said to me, "We and some other people in Washington had our eyes on NAS for a long time." The knife plunged deep; then Berns gave it a twist: "Long before you stumbled on to them."

"Before December '85?"

"Yeah, that's why Michael sending you out there had us mystified. We thought they might want to make you a courier like Bush (the guy arrested along with the owner of NAS)."

"Who *they*?"

No response.

"OK, I'll just have to figure it out myself." Then I remembered, "No wonder I had people following me all over the place."

"Yeah, you walked right into the middle of the whole damn thing. I'd like to see a copy of your news wire printouts."

"Sure. There'll be a charge, though."

"I'm not paying $600 for it!"

I grinned. "Don't worry about it. For you a special rate."

He waved me off. "Forget it."

"I did good by telling Michael, huh?"

"Yeah," Mike admitted, begrudgingly. "You shared a valuable piece of intelligence with him. You're a good spy, Julius."

"Why did the government move against NAS?" I said. "We never did find out what the Soviets had in mind. Clearly they were a major target."

"That decision was made at a higher level."

I sensed something from his tone. "You guys didn't agree with it?"

"Let's just say we expressed our opinions, but the ultimate decision was made somewhere else." Then Mike excused himself and left the room.

I got up to browse the collection and saw many of the same books I'd been reading. On the wall I noticed aerial photos of the Soviet compound in Riverdale. To the immediate left of the photos was a bulletin board with an organizational chart of the KGB here in New York. The board had mug shots and photos of KGB officers that branched off according to line: political intelligence, counterintelligence, Line X, etc. I noticed a small section under the heading "GRU" but that chart went straight down and had only a few photos. None of the men looked familiar. Jim hovered over me like I was snooping in areas where I had no need to know; which I probably was, but like I gave a rat's ass. He insisted that the photos were all out of date.

"So why are they still up here?" I said, pointing.

I continued to browse; Jim continued to try and distract me with inane conversation. Then he took me over to a display case and showed me a crushed milk carton. "That was used in one of their dead-drops. Are you familiar with the writing papers they use?"

I chuckled. "Only white tracing paper. I'm really not into that type of tradecraft anyway. I'm more into the psychology of how agents are recruited and used — also intelligence as in The Games of Nations."[4] (Grabbed that from the title of a book I'd just read.) I finished spying and sat back down. Mike had been gone an awfully long time, fifteen minutes at least. I casually remarked, "That must be some big shit he's taking."

When Mike returned, he was all smiles again. His capacity for recovery never ceased to amaze me. "Come on, I'll drive you to work," he said.

The three of us were standing in the hallway outside the library shaking hands. Out of the corner of my eye I noticed an older guy standing at a door some thirty feet away. He was tall, balding, wore glasses and a light suit. His arms were folded across his chest. He stared straight at me, and it wasn't a friendly look either. It was a *So That's The Asshole* look. Before I could ask to be properly introduced, he disappeared back inside.

Mike led me back down to the parking garage. He headed straight for a late model white Monte Carlo with a maroon roof and red pile interior. Inside I noticed an AM-FM radio. I nestled into the front seat and took a deep breath. It even smelled new, a far cry from that jalopy he'd been driving back in '84.

"You're moving up in the world, Michael."

"Jim's taking over. I'm still on the case, but you'll be dealing directly with him from now on," he said, maneuvering us out of the garage. Then he turned on the A/C.

"Get a promotion or what?"

"Something like that."

4 Spanier, John W. *Games Nations Play: analyzing international politics*, c1981.

We headed cross-town towards the Westside Highway.

There was a loose nail in my apron that I *did* want to talk about. If Michael was in some kind of trouble back home, then why did he tell me?

I thought I had the answer: "Have you guys ever considered the possibility that Michael suspects that one of his assets is controlled? You even said that he may be in some kind of trouble."

"That's not the kind of trouble we were talking about. Besides, if that were true" — Mike shot me one of those *We're the Professionals* look — "then all the information you've been delivering would be suspect."

Mike, The Pro, just exposed a crack in the *Wall of Secret Knowledge of the Chosen Few*. Time to put a chisel to it: "That would be true, if the information I delivered was classified. But it's not, so how can it be suspect?"

"Classified, unclassified — doesn't matter. We once had a case we wanted to terminate, so we doctored an unclassified report. When the Soviets found out, they broke contact." To Mike, that meant end of discussion.

Fuck no! A large chunk of that wall came off when I smacked that chisel with a hammer: "Was this done with both the knowledge and consent of your controlled asset?"

Silence and a mustache twitch answered my question: proof positive that when it suited their needs, the FBI would expend one of their assets.[5]

From the very beginning, I'd never let the FBI get hold of

5 "My Dinners With Andrey: a true story of the cold war" by Carl Oglesby, Playboy Magazine, Nov. 1983. See p. 215-216 for an example of the FBI deliberately exposing a controlled asset.

anything I was going to give Michael. I'd always ordered them a separate copy. That meant if they now wanted to zero me out of the Katkov Affair they'd have to work a little harder.

Mike tried to steer me back onto a safer trail: "I wouldn't really be giving anything away," he said, tentatively. "I'm sure you've read it somewhere: because the GRU is so much smaller than the KGB, they have neither the resources nor the manpower to launch a penetration. They're only interested in collecting positive intelligence. If we were dealing with the KGB, then everything you've said would be within the realm of possibility. Defectors have told us about cases when the KGB knew they were dealing with a controlled agent, but played along in the hopes of turning the penetration by using it as a source of disinformation."

"What you're saying might be true," I said, "except for one thing. Ever hear of Wennerstrom?"

A snarky, "You're no Wennerstrom, Julius."

Stig Wennerstrom was a colonel in the Swedish Air Force recruited by both the GRU and CIA. Secrets about the Soviet Union he sold to the United States; secrets about the United States he sold to the Soviet Union; a resourceful guy. The GRU was the first to catch on to Wennerstrom's duplicity, but instead of terminating him, they used him to feed disinformation to both American and Swedish intelligence. The Wennerstrom Affair was proof-positive that the GRU did occasionally run counterespionage operations; therefore, it was within the realm of possibilities that the Katkov Affair was such an operation.[6]

When I asked if the FBI and CIA thought that Michael would

---

6 Whiteside, Thomas, *An Agent in Place: the Wennerstrom Affair*, Viking Press, c1966.

betray his country, Mike replied, "Everyone has a price." It was as if his matter-of-fact tone made it true. Mike added that he didn't know exactly when the FBI/CIA would move against Katkov, but he hinted that it might be soon, as soon as July.

"When you interdict, can you make it look like I wasn't the one who betrayed him?"

Mike turned to me, and in a tone that made me feel like a whimpy, whiny schoolgirl, he said, "Don't get emotionally involved, John."

Way too late for that. I *was* emotionally involved in what I'd done to Michael.

The Monte Carlo pulled up to the main gate outside Columbia. I reached over and shook Mike's hand. "Congratulations on the promotion. You deserve it. You had a tough job, and you did it well."

"Take care of yourself, John."

"You too, Mike."

It occurred to me as I watched him drive off: He never offered to show me a picture of his baby daughter. But then, I never asked. Guess it was better that way. Like the man just said, Don't get involved.

Chapter 32
A Spy in the Stacks?

"You've seen the best. It'll be interesting to see how the new guy measures up."

***

At Columbia's engineering library I searched in a dictionary of abbreviations for the acronym Berns had used:"CO-something".

I let my right index finger do the walking, scanning down a column beginning with "COMA". The finger stopped at COMECON, and I poked the page twice: *That's it!*

COMECON was an acronym for The Council for Mutual Economic Assistance. A starting point; then I went to the stacks to check another source. I found that COMECON (also known as CMEA) was an international trade organization created in 1949. Its member states consisted of the USSR, Poland, Czechoslovakia, Hungary, Romania, East Germany, Mongolia, Cuba, and Bulgaria. Its headquarters was in the USSR. (COMECON was later disbanded in February, 1991.) COMECON's purpose was to extend Soviet power on an economic basis both at home and abroad. Most interesting of all, I discovered that in the mid-1980s COMECON began work on a comprehensive program in science and technology meant to overcome the West's lead in high tech. Thus COMECON's plans to overcome the West's lead must have involved sending me to California. I felt like a cold warrior again, someone who made a small but vital contribution. Then I thought back to the summer of '84 when the People Down South were frantic that Michael's and Val's reports would cross in Moscow. My guess had been the VPK — wrong! The Katkov Affair soared even higher, into the cloud called COMECON.

My appreciation for libraries as a resource grew tenfold.

***

Tuesday, May 5th, 6:30 p.m.: I had the late shift all to myself in Columbia's engineering library. A man — tall, slim, dark like an Indian or Pakistani, mid 40s, in a light gray suit and dark tie — stood by an index table. I sat at the reference desk. He motioned for me to join him. His sharp facial features and stealthy demeanor reminded me of a weasel.

"I am looking for a particular book," he said in accented English. "Can you help me?" His tone: master to servant. I sensed that he came from a country where class distinctions were strictly observed, but this wasn't his fucking country. Here in New York City, Brahmans and Untouchables pushed and shoved for seats on the subway.

He said the book was by a man named Boyd and titled, Electronic Countermeasures. Then he mentioned something about the book being classified.

"Then forget it, it's not here," I said gruffly and turned to walk back to my desk.

"No, no. It is merely based on classified material. The book itself is not classified."

I silently motioned with cupped right hand for the weasel to follow me to a nearby computer terminal. There I keyed in the information. The book wasn't in our online catalog.

"Never mind," he said. "It is not that important."

Michael's English, though excellent, was spoken with a Boris

Badenov accent. Val's English was more refined, spoken like the highly educated professor. The weasel's accent was even more refined than Val's. This guy definitely sounded upper crust.

I went back to the reference desk to finish reading a magazine. I looked up and saw him standing in front of me, grinning. His superior attitude pushed up the mercury on my *Pissed Off Scale*. Whoever taught this asshole English apparently forgot the words "please" and "thank you." Taking a more aggressive posture, I leaned forward in my seat. Then in a challenging tone: "You affiliated with Columbia or what?" He looked like he might be a professor, but I knew all the engineering professors by sight, and I'd never seen this guy before.

The only response I got to my question was a pause and then a smirk. Then he placed the reference book he'd been holding on the desk in front of me. He turned it around so I could read it. "I have not been able to find anything here. Perhaps you can find something interesting for me."

How many times had I heard those words before?

By now I had finally figured out his game and desperately wanted to play. But a rope tied around my neck held me back: Michael's explicit instruction not to have anything to do with anyone at Columbia. Still, I had a few options to play.

In a strictly bureaucratic tone, "Would you like to fill out an interlibrary loan request for the countermeasures book?" I hoped to get his name and affiliation on paper, not to mention a sample of his handwriting. My freebee to the FeeBees.

"I am not interested in that."

"Would you like me to do a database search for you? Perhaps we can find other, related material." If he said, yes, then he'd have to fill out a request form.

Instead, the tricky bastard said, "That will not be necessary. Do you work here full time?"

"No, part-time," I replied.

"Where do you work full time?"

"I have a business—" I pulled up short because he had no need to know. "I work here."

He pounced. "But you said just part-time. So which is it?"

Annoyed, "You looking for a book or what? If you are, then I'll help you. If not" — *then go fuck yourself* — "then you'll have to excuse me."

He smiled. "If you find something interesting, leave it here for me. Now I will take my evening meal. I will be back later."

After he left I searched RLIN, a bibliographic database of library holdings nationwide, looking for more information on the electronic countermeasures book. According to RLIN, it was originally published as a secret textbook for U.S. personnel involved in electronic warfare work. Declassified in 1973, there was nothing unusual about his request. Anyone working in the field would be familiar with this source.

He did not return again that night. The next day I called Jim. "He looked Pakistani. I know they do a lot of industrial spying in this country. But do you think he might be a Soviet from one of their Asian Republics?"

"I dunno. Anything's possible. Wish you could've gotten more out of him."

"I tried, but the guy was real cagey. Maybe I should've been friendlier. Sorry if I blew it."

"Don't worry, if this guy's somebody important, he'll be back. Your instincts were right. You followed Michael's instructions. At this point, that's what matters most."

(Audio 32.1) 2:41

***

A victory for me! On Thursday, May 14th, payment for the neodymium search, a money order for $660, finally arrived at my PO Box. Also in the envelope was a handwritten note from Mike instructing me to sign the receipt "Julius" and mail it in an enclosed SASE. A signed receipt and two pennies went into the envelope because $659.98 was what they owed me.

On Thursday, June 4th, three of us, two other engineering librarians and myself, were clustered by the reference desk. Mary, Head of Reference for the Science Division, charged into the engineering library. She was breathless, like she had run all the way. "The FBI was just in the math library! I came in and found two female agents talking to Richard (the circulation clerk in Columbia's math library). You should've seen him, sitting with his feet up on my desk blabbing away with these women!"

Hard to tell what annoyed her more, Richard blabbing to the FBI or Richard with his feet on her desk. In the library world, there's a strict pecking order: professionals and nonprofessionals. Both get paid shit, so as far as I was concerned, that fine line was more imaginary than Maginot.

I asked Mary a very important question: "Were they good looking?"

Mary, a motor-mouth when excited, fluttered her eyes and slowed down long enough to inform me, "I hadn't noticed." Then full speed ahead: "They asked a lot of questions about the collection. Who has access? Do people from the Eastern Bloc use the library? I told them to go see Paula (the acting University Librarian). Then I asked them to please leave."

Later, I visited the math library myself. "Heard you had some excitement this morning," I said to Richard, comfortably nestled in Mary's chair with his feet up on her desk.

Exasperated, "The only excitement was the reaction of some of the people around here." Richard, an army veteran, had absolutely no qualms about talking to the FBI. "I don't understand what the fuss is," he said, throwing up his hands. "They asked me a few questions about the collection, like who has access to it and can someone from the U.N. use the library?"

Columbia has many libraries and library divisions on campus. The Science Division consists of the engineering, math, physics, psychology, geology and chemistry libraries. Nothing in any of these collections is classified, although the basement of the engineering library holds some uncataloged Manhattan Project papers. A fellow librarian once told me that she had received an interlibrary loan request for a particular Manhattan project paper from a scientist working for the Iranian government. "I threw the damn thing away," she said.

Only the Engineering Library was open to the public, including people from the U.N., because it housed the NTIS (National Technical Information Service) collection. That made the engineering library a government repository library. None of the other libraries in the division had that same ease of access; however, if someone looked like a student or faculty member, they got in no questions asked.

The FBI agents told Richard that they were visiting a few local libraries to make some routine inquiries. “Then Mary walked in and all hell broke loose. She sent them to Butler.” (Butler was the main library and the location of the office of the acting director.) Later I found out that their reception in the acting director’s office had been even more hostile.

“So tell me, Richard, were they good looking or what?”

Richard arched his eyebrows. “I’ll say.”

“Wish they came to me. I would’ve told ‘em everything.”

Richard laughed. I left him where I’d found him, still seated at Mary’s desk, his hands behind his head, and his feet up.

The next day I called Jim to tell him about the FBI’s visit. He said, “I didn’t know anything about it. I’ll check into it and get back to you. Hate to tell you how many agents the Soviets have recruited right off that campus.”

Jim assured me that the storm the FBI’s visit had caused would soon blow over. He was wrong. A week later an email from the acting director was sent to all Columbia librarians and staff. It said, “Columbia’s policy is that the FBI is not welcome here. If they want information they can subpoena it. We will move to quash the subpoena.”

Things were just beginning to heat up.

Then I asked Jim, “What’s with Michael? Is he still around? Why haven’t I heard from him?”

“He’s still around. We think his head is elsewhere, and frankly, we don’t know why.” He added that the People Down South were convinced that I’d be getting a new GRU officer in July. “What we’re really concerned with right now is who this new person will be.”

I wanted to know, too. If I got a new GRU case officer, this thing might go on for another four years. Wouldn’t that be great!

On Thursday, June 25th, I got another look at minimalism as practiced by the Bureau. A conference room on the 28th Floor had two long tables that looked like they belonged in a cafeteria. The wood paneled walls were bare, not even a sign that dared to warn me that everything discussed in this room was secret. The room had one door, no windows, and the lighting was fluorescent. Jim and I sat at the very end of a table across from each other. He smiled at me and said, “Go ahead. Shoot.”

This special meeting had been at my request. I told Jim that I wanted to speak with “one of the chess masters.” Maybe even the tall guy who’d given me the hairy eyeball last time I was here. No such luck, though. The old gator must have slipped back into the muck. The Bureau would only provide FBI Special Agent Jim Knapp.

I tossed a line into the water anyway: “Why are the Soviets giving me a new guy?”

“They’re probably trying to limit Michael’s activities to some extent because he’s been a very busy guy. We think he might have over extended himself. And the Soviets don’t like to tie too many assets to one officer. In the event the officer has to suddenly leave the country, it would leave too many loose ends. It makes no sense from their point of view to have one guy running his tail off with several agents while other guys with no agents sit around doing nothing."

That made sense. So did the possibility that Michael was going to be made ill by his Soviet colleagues and have his assets divvied up.

I noted, "Michael must be very good. I didn't always think he was."

Jim nodded. "You've seen the best. It'll be interesting to see how this new guy measures up. He's near the end of his tour. Normally it can take as long as six months for a new case officer to be briefed and ready to take over. Apparently they think enough of you to bring in a new guy even before Michael leaves."

All the while Jim had been looking at his watch as if he had another pressing engagement. But I wasn't finished with him yet. "What about COMECON?"

"I'm not sure." He paused as if trying to recall something, then, "There's a Western counterpart… An alliance of Western nations who have some kind of trade agreement… COCOM! Yeah, that's it. It's called COCOM."

"Yeah, I know what COCOM is." (Bet he did too.) "It's a trade group that has made a series of bilateral agreements limiting technology transfer to the eastern Bloc. And I know what COMECON is. So what's Michael's connection?"

"All I know about COMECON is that they're a trade group roughly equivalent to the EEC (European Economic Community). And I don't know what Michael's connection might be. Or even if he has a connection."

"When Mike mentioned COMECON you didn't ask him any questions. You seemed to know then, why not now?"

Jim suddenly got that constipated look a guy gets when he's straining. "I'm really not sure. I can't even recall the conversation. I'll ask Mike about it when he gets back." Then he changed the subject. "Know what really surprised us about NAS: that the Sovs would send you out there to talk to a guy under federal indictment."

"That's not true. That guy wasn't indicted until February, 1987. I went to L.A. at the end of September, 1986." A pause, then, "Last time I saw Michael, on April 9th, we were talking and suddenly the phone rang. It was Mike. He said he was calling to warn me that Michael was out and about. No shit! Like the guy was sitting right next to me. Mike had called at 6:30, Prime Michael Time, so I don't think the phone call was an accident."

"I remember that call very well. I was with him when he made it. He even said to me, 'Jesus! I think Katkov is with Julius.' We were as surprised as you were."

"Know what I think? I think you guys were deliberately trying to blow my cover."

Scoffing, "Why would we do a thing like that?"

My explanation came in the form of a hypothetical question, complete with diagrams and pointing arrows (no charge this time): "Given Comrade Boris has four assets: A, B, C and D. Two of these assets, A and B, are controlled by the FBI. The Soviets know that one of Boris' assets is controlled, but don't know which one. My question is: if A is more valuable to the FBI than B, would the FBI deliberately point suspicion at B to save A?"

Jim smirked. "Theoretically, there could be hundreds of cases where this could occur, but in real life it just doesn't."

Strange that Jim would equate the World of Mirrors with Real

Life.

I continued: "OK, let's try this: suppose you guys have some big plans for Boris, like getting him to defect-in-place, but B is in the way. Asking a lot of questions, maybe a little too independent—"

"I can assure you," Jim cut in, "if an asset is not under our complete control, he's not going to be an asset for very long."

"My point; so you dump him. The best way to do that is show Boris that B is compromised. There are hundreds of ways you can do this, not just ill timed phone calls. Like every time Boris comes into B's neighborhood, you let him see that he's being followed. Pretty soon he catches on and then it's good-bye B."

"Enough with this hypothetical bull, if you think any of this applies to you, you couldn't be more mistaken. Why would we do something like that? It serves no purpose. We still don't know who the new guy's gonna be."

"Mike's phone call came before you guys knew I was being passed off."

"It still doesn't serve our purpose. It's hard enough to get people to cooperate with us as it is, we're not about to go around expending them."

Bullshit! I remembered Mike Berns' exact words to me on Tuesday, April 14th: "We once had a case we wanted to terminate, so we doctored an unclassified report. When the Soviets found out, they broke contact."

Proof positive: the FBI will deliberately blow one of their assets when it suits their purpose. No need to argue the point, though. I was growing sick of the whole Katkov Affair.

One final question for Agent Knapp while he was in such a

talkative mood: “Is it possible that the Pakistani-looking guy I saw at Columbia will be the new case officer I get in July?”

Jim arched his brows. “That… would be very interesting.”

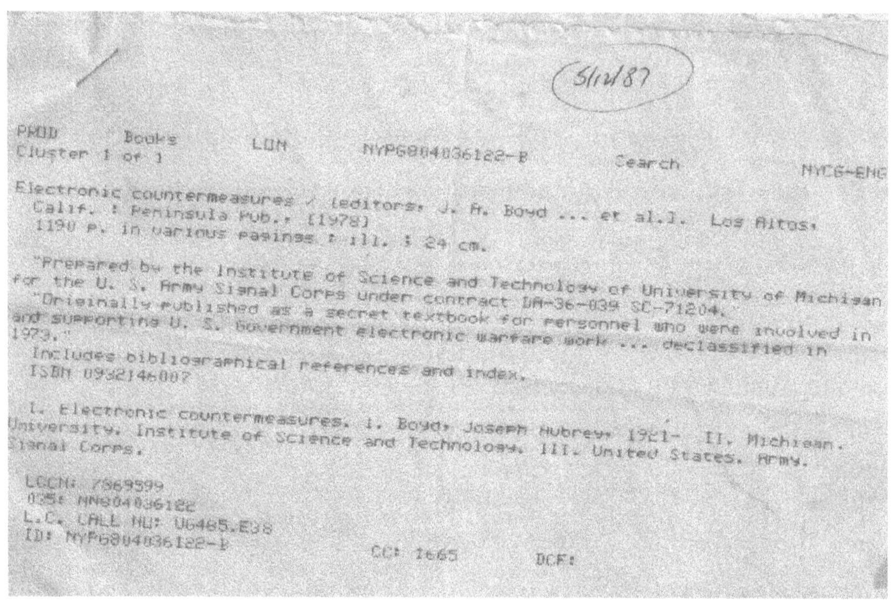

5/12/87

PROD Books LCM NYPG804036122-B
Cluster 1 of 1 Search NYCG-ENG

Electronic countermeasures / [editors, J. A. Boyd ... et al.]. Los Altos, Calif. : Peninsula Pub., [1978]
1190 p. in various pagings : ill. ; 24 cm.

"Prepared by the Institute of Science and Technology of University of Michigan for the U. S. Army Signal Corps under contract DA-36-039 SC-71204."
"Originally published as a secret textbook for personnel who were involved in and supporting U. S. Government electronic warfare work ... declassified in 1973."
Includes bibliographical references and index.
ISBN 0932146007

1. Electronic countermeasures. I. Boyd, Joseph Aubrey, 1921- II. Michigan. University. Institute of Science and Technology. III. United States. Army. Signal Corps.

LCCN: 7869599
035: NN804036122
L.C. CALL NO: UG485.E38
ID: NYPG804036122-B CC: 1665 DCF:

(Fig 32.1) RLIN record

Chapter 33
Ronald McDonald

"Hey, Jim... How about coming up here and bailing me out?"

"Golly, gee whiz, officer. Pan-Zini who? Never heard of him."

***

Wednesday July 15, 1987

July blew in with the same scorching heat it always did. With my ass safely planted in the cool environs of Columbia's air-conditioned engineering library, I could care less. I eagerly awaited either Michael or a new GRU officer.

A funny thing happened at work today, the chance for me to play the good guy for a change. A golden leaf blew in an opened window, a window of opportunity to do the right thing. It landed right in front of me. Naturally, I picked it up. The leaf was an interlibrary loan request (ILL) from a staff member at the United Nations library. The name on the ILL was L. Kolesnikov, like the rifle.

I did the math in my head: *UN library + Soviet staff member + NASA documents* (related to the space shuttle program) = *positive intelligence.*

I'd been watching the Iran/Contra hearings all week and was very impressed with the joint committees. I especially liked the way they stuck it to Oliver North and John Poindexter. I wrote the following in my journal that day:

"The patriotism exhibited by these committees is beyond reproach. By contrast, some of my own motives (as they relate to the Katkov Affair) seem venial, self-serving and small. I am not feeling so good about myself lately."

So instead of cashing in on this small piece of positive intelligence, I photocopied the ILL and called Jim Knapp the next morning. I wanted this to be my free-be to the fee-bees. We also briefly discussed the Iran/Contra hearings.

(Audio 33.1) 2:46

July 1987, finally passed into history. No Michael, no new guy, no nothing. As for the Katkov Affair, and my participation in it, how soon would that also pass into history?

***

Sometimes breaking a habit is like trying to crawl up a steep-pitched roof on a rainy day. Wet and slick, you keep slipping back down to the base scaffold. It might be safer to stay there, but then you say to yourself, *Let's try again.*

Thursday was my late night at the library, and every Thursday at around 10 a.m., I ate breakfast at McDonalds on 181st & Broadway. And since Friday was my day off, every Friday about the same time, I'd be inside McDonalds eating breakfast. And every breakfast always the same: an *EggMac* with sausage, cheese and ketchup, and a coffee.

On Thursday, August 13th, at 9:30 a.m., for no reason at all, I decided to crawl up a steep-pitched slope again, but not so far as to upset the delicate balance of my planking: the bright lights of the breakfast menu shined on high. With my head tilted backwards and lower jaw slightly ajar, I strained to make a decision. Then to the girl behind the counter at the Burger King on 181st & St. Nicholas Avenue, I said, "May I have a bagel with egg, sausage and cheese, and a small coffee, please."

Eager to enjoy yet another breakfast high in cholesterol and poly-saturated fats — so what if it slowly killed me, it tasted good — I found a table and took out a copy of the *New York Times.*

The breakfast crowd at both Burger King and McDonalds was mostly as brown as a hash patty: people of color (Hispanics), some off-whites (like me and the Greeks), and a sprinkling of salt (pale faces that hung on the junkies who habituated Broadway). That was why this particular individual stood out like a cornstalk sprouted in a city sidewalk. A lily-white, clean-cut, Middle-American type sat a few tables away from me. Must be a cop, I thought, since the Three-Four Precinct was only a few blocks away.

The next morning I returned once again to the safe harbor of McDonalds. After I finished eating I got up to dump my tray. Then I saw the same guy I saw in Burger King yesterday sitting a few tables behind me near the trash bin. He was reading the *Times;* a lone coffee container rested on his tray. Twice in two days at two separate locations — coincidence? I didn't think so. I took a closer look. Damn this guy had a big head. Not round like a Slav but narrow like a Goth. He had dirty blond hair cut short, military style and light eyes. I guessed him to be in his mid-thirties. He wore a light gray suit, a print sports shirt and hush puppy-type shoes, an odd coordination, part business, part leisure, part asshole (the shoes). He had a look about him that said: *I'm not from here. Not this neighborhood. Not this city.*

My guess: this particular Ronald McDonald was an FBI agent disguised as a normal person. Why would the Bureau bother to follow me? Because I strongly suspected that the Bureau wanted to cut a certain polyp named John Pansini out of the Katkov Affair's asshole.

When I walked passed Ronald to the trash bin, he didn't look up. Damn the FBI for thinking they could intimidate me! If the Bureau wanted to play tag — instead of leaving, I returned to my booth and sat facing *him*. I took out my own copy of the *Times.* When he left, I'd follow him, all the way up to the 25th Floor of #26 Federal Plaza if necessary.

At 10:45, Ronald gathered up his newspaper, dumped his cup in the trash, and neatly placed his tray on the rack. He walked down my aisle at a brisk pace towards the front door that let out onto Broadway. He glanced down at me as he passed. Watching through the glass front door, I saw him stop at the corner, throw his newspaper in a trash can and put on sunglasses. Then he turned his head and looked back into the restaurant — right at me! Definitely a No-No, because intelligence officers are taught that if they suspect they're being followed, to act natural, go about their normal business and abort the mission. And never under any circumstances turn around to look for a pursuer. That was tantamount to acknowledging that, *Yes, I'm on a mission, and, yes, I know you're following me.* No intelligence officer, even one as dumb as Val Bolochine, would do something like that; unless, of course, Ronald wanted me to know I'd grown a tail.

He paused to adjust his sunglasses, and then began walking south on Broadway. I got out of the restaurant just in time to see him duck into the Citibank in the middle of the block. Since that was my bank too, I went inside. I deposited myself at the end of a line at one of the two ATMs in the vestibule. With my peripheral vision I noticed a guy in a gray suit inside the bank on the far left partially hidden by a pillar. Gray Suit looked to be filling out a bank form at a shelf table that ran against the wall.

Those damn cash machines always had long lines, but not today. In no time I was at the keyboard. While I withdrew some cash, Gray Suit moved behind me. He stood on a line to my immediate right. When I finished my business and turned around, I saw that Gray Suit was an old man! Frantic, I searched the bank. Even went downstairs to customer service — no Ronald anywhere. I ran back out into the street — *nada*. The first person I ever attempt to tail, I lose. Shit!

I went back home and phoned Jim to convey my annoyance. But for every reason I offered that the FBI had tailed me, Jim countered with a denial. And his denials were a lot more plausible than my suspicions.

"But the guy slipped into the bank and ditched me," I said. "Like a real pro. He can't be some Joe Schmoe off the street."

Jim agreed that the way the guy had eluded me had showed good tradecraft. "There's a remote possibility," he added, "I'd say a 10% chance that he could be from the other side."

"You mean the new guy who was supposed to show up in July?"

"It's possible. Sometimes a Soviet who is going to take over a new asset will follow that person around just to see what he looks like and to get to know that person's habits. It also gives them something to do."

Jim also mentioned that the Soviet who had requested the inter-library loan I'd sent him, L. Kolesnikov, was "very dirty."

I said I was happy to be of help.

***

When I arrived at the McDonalds on Friday morning, August 21st, Ronald was already there. He was dressed more business-like this time in a tan suit, light shirt and brown tie. He sat in a booth by the far wall reading the *Times*. Guess Ronald didn't share my passion for *EggMacs*, because all he had on his tray was a cup of coffee. I took a seat in a booth across the room and behind him. Not once did he turn around or acknowledge my presence. Nevertheless, while my belly filled with food that would choke my heart in another thirty years, my mind filled with doubts: *Losing it, John. Guy's just a businessman that's all. Call Jim. Tell him to forget it, that I'm an asshole. Don't bother. He already knows.*

Ronald left at about eleven. Despite a certain skepticism regarding my own sanity, I followed him anyway. Once again Ronald entered the Citibank at mid-block. Did he work there? Had he disappeared into a back office last week? Instead of waiting outside, I just walked on by. As I passed the bank, I shot a quick glance at the shaded window. Ronald was coming out! What can someone do that quickly in a bank? Not a damn thing.

I continued south on Broadway, Ronald following a short distance behind me. At the corner of 180th a ***DON'T WALK*** signal flashed. I could easily dash across the street, but this was no time to take risks. I stepped off the curb to wait for permission to walk. Ronald stopped too — right behind me! The bastard could push me into oncoming traffic if he wanted to. I stepped back onto the curb, turned my head and looked at him. Ronald stared straight ahead. We stood side-by-side, and then he unexpectedly crossed to the other side of 180th to wait. The light changed, and we both crossed to the east side of Broadway. I faked going down 180th, and he continued heading south. I peeked around the corner and waited until Ronald was at least a block ahead before following.

The main entrance to the Port Authority Bus Terminal is located on the west side of Broadway between 178th and 179th Streets. Directly across the street from the terminal a large steel abutment spans the entire block. A canopy extends from the abutment to the bus terminal. Below the abutment and terminal a multi-lane underpass feeds into the George Washington Bridge. Ronald took up position at the far end of the block, at 178th. He stood with one foot up against the wall like one of those gangsta teenagers from the 50s. He lit a cigarette. The guy had a flair for drama. No way for me to continue without being spotted, so I hid around the corner at the other end of the abutment.

Every so often I peeked. Ronald did not move. An old man vending hot-dogs right next to me offered good cover. The hot-dog guy motioned to sell me a frank. I smiled and waved him off. When I peeked again Ronald was still there, still enjoying a smoke. Again a persistent hot-dog guy tried to sell me one. I waved him off. I thought I heard him mumble, "*Maniatico*," as he packed up and left. Fuck him and his ptomaine franks. (I eat only *Hebrew Nationals*.)

The next time I peeked, Ronald was gone. Did he duck around the corner? Was he waiting for me to make the next move? What if he called a cop and said, "Officer, there's a nut following me."

Then I'd have to call Jim and say, "Hey, Jim you know that guy in McDonalds? Well he wasn't. How about coming up here and explaining and bailing me out?"

Easy enough to guess Jim's response: "Golly, gee whiz, shucks, officer. Pan-Zini who? Never heard of him."

Not even the risk of extreme embarrassment deterred me, though. I made the long walk to the far side and turned the corner. No Ronald.

I noticed a bus parked across the street on 179th. It faced east. This was the last stop on the M5 that ran south on Broadway. Was Ronald sitting behind one of those shaded bus windows watching? And laughing? Without exact change or a token to board the bus I had to leave.

The score: Him two, me nothing.

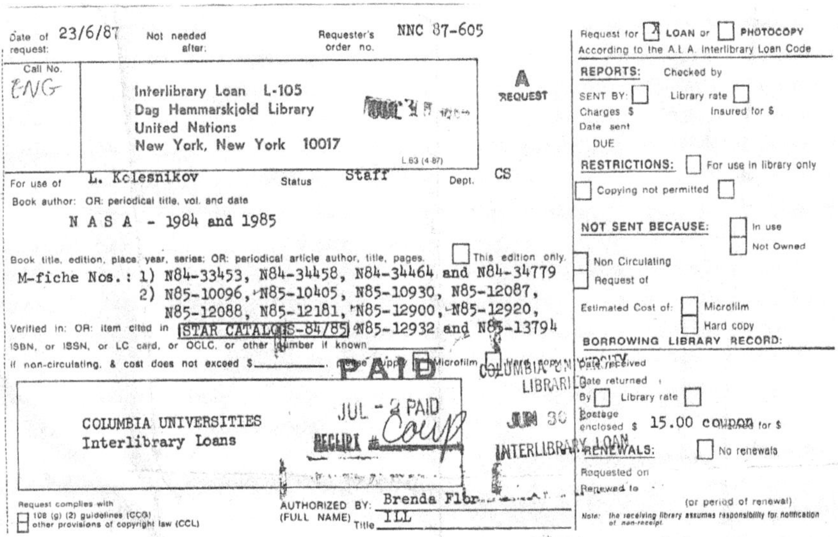

Date of request: 23/6/87 Not needed after: Requester's order no. NNC 87-605

Call No. ENG

Interlibrary Loan L-105
Dag Hammarskjold Library
United Nations
New York, New York 10017

L 63 (4-87)

A REQUEST

For use of L. Kolesnikov Status Staff Dept. CS

Book author: OR: periodical title, vol. and date

N A S A - 1984 and 1985

Book title, edition, place, year, series: OR: periodical article author, title, pages. ☐ This edition only.

M-fiche Nos.: 1) N84-33453, N84-34458, N84-34464 and N84-34779
2) N85-10096, N85-10405, N85-10930, N85-12087,
N85-12088, N85-12181, N85-12900, N85-12920,
N85-12932 and N85-13794

Verified in: OR: item cited in STAR CATALOGS-84/85

ISBN, or ISSN, or LC card, or OCLC, or other number if known

If non-circulating, & cost does not exceed $, please supply ☐ Microfilm ☐ Hard copy

PAID

COLUMBIA UNIVERSITIES
Interlibrary Loans

JUL - 2 PAID
RECEIPT # Coup

COLUMBIA UNIVERSITY LIBRARIES
JUN 30
INTERLIBRARY LOAN

Request complies with
☐ 108 (g) (2) guidelines (CCG)
☐ other provisions of copyright law (CCL)

AUTHORIZED BY: (FULL NAME) Brenda Flor
Title ILL

Request for ☒ LOAN or ☐ PHOTOCOPY
According to the A.L.A. Interlibrary Loan Code

REPORTS: Checked by

SENT BY: ☐ Library rate ☐
Charges $ Insured for $
Date sent
DUE

RESTRICTIONS: ☐ For use in library only
☐ Copying not permitted ☐

NOT SENT BECAUSE: ☐ In use ☐ Not Owned
☐ Non Circulating
☐ Request of

Estimated Cost of: ☐ Microfilm ☐ Hard copy

BORROWING LIBRARY RECORD:
Date received
Date returned
By ☐ Library rate ☐
Postage enclosed $ 15.00 coupon for $

RENEWALS: ☐ No renewals
Requested on
Renewed to
(or period of renewal)

Note: the receiving library assumes responsibility for notification of non-receipt

(Fig 33.1) Kolesnikov ILL request

Chapter 34
Bad Company

It was all on me now. When it came to my future, had the time come to be more proactive?

Only one thing stood in the way: instead of walnuts I had peanuts hanging between my legs.

***

Thursday August 27, 1987

My contract with Columbia was set to expire in a few days, on Tuesday, September 1. I'd never given much thought to my future. I figured it would always take care of itself — and ever the optimist, I assumed, in the end, things would always go my way.

A book and movie deal, millions of dollars did not seem like real possibilities; especially since the final scene as directed by the People Down South would not include me. Where was the tension, high drama, the emotion? Somewhere else, but not with me.

Despite Anne's warning running in an endless loop in my head — *"It's dangerous for a writer to create his own fiction by manipulating real people and real events."* — I had to add a new plot point. The fact that what I was planning might get me in a lot of trouble with the mighty United States government — might even land my ass in jail —it would be worth the risk.

Last week I made inquiries to Jim in regards to the Bureau setting me up in a dummy corporation to sell Katkov embargoed computer hardware and software. He phoned me back today.

"Isn't gonna wash, running a business, I mean."

I didn't think it would. The idea seemed ridiculous even to me, but at least I gave them the courtesy of a heads up. I told Jim, "If you guys aren't interested, then maybe I'll run it by people who are."

"That might not be such a bad idea," he'd replied. I could almost hear a shrug in his tone.

OK, so the People Down South wouldn't go for it, but there was another organ of government, just as powerful as the FBI/CIA, who might.

It was all on me now. When it came to my future, had the time come to be more proactive?

Only one thing stood in the way: instead of walnuts I had peanuts hanging between my legs.

***

The next day, Friday morning at 9:50 a.m., squinting and grinding my teeth, I leaned into a gusting headwind that blew down 181st Street. A stinging rain pelted my umbrella like hailstones smacking a roof. Cold and dreary, it felt like November had come early this year. The storm that raged outside darkened my mood inside. Jim Knapp called yesterday. He said he had to see me today. "There's something we need to discuss."

Memories of a much hotter day back in July, 1984, when Mike Berns said he needed to see me piled into the empty space between my ears like rowdy kids onto a school bus.

Inside the Star Diner on Broadway, I sat down in a booth with Jim. The tempest that pelted Washington Heights did not affect him at all. Jim seemed to be filled with sunshine and flowers that gently blew in a cool summer breeze. "We think it's about time we had a little chat with Mr. K." A dramatic pause, then, "We think it's time we told Michael about you."

His words stunned me, and I'm sure it shown on my face.

By now the kids on my bus were screaming, ripping seats out of the floor and throwing them out the windows like this was the last day of class. I felt like driving the whole bus load of bad Karma off a cliff.

Jim continued, "Our friend has been a very successful guy, but most of his success is due to us," a snicker, "only he doesn't know it... yet."

"So why are you telling me," I replied, the subtext of my tone: *Pardon me for being less than thrilled.* "I know about Michael's success because I know about your other controlled asset."

"It would be against the law for me to discuss that person with you."

"Then tell me this: why me?"

Snow in August: "Because you've been one of his biggest successes."

"Come on, Jim. Don't give me that crap. I never got him anything classified."

"But you were his first. For us to tell him that you've been under our control from the beginning it will be lights out for him."

True. When an intelligence service grabs an officer from a hostile service, the first step in breaking that officer down is the appearance of omnipotence. The psychological assault begins with, "We know all about you" and ends with, "We're so powerful that you would do well to throw in with us. We can guarantee your personal safety, and you will be well compensated."

I smirked. "Guess the little scenario I laid out regarding our hypothetical friend Boris wasn't too far off, huh?"

Jim looked strained, like a guy sitting on a turd (that be me) that would not pass. "It has to be you for reasons which, unfortunately, I can't go into." Then he asked if I'd be willing to sign a waiver authorizing the FBI to tell Michael about me. That surprised me because when it came to things that involved national security, I'd always figured the Bureau did what it pleased.

Confused, I fell back on an old trick: stall. "Sure, but first I want to show it to a lawyer."

"We'd rather you didn't do that because then the lawyer would know about Michael."

I smiled. "Jim, a lot of people know about Michael."

"You mean besides your father?"

"My father, my uncle — some close friends."

Jim looked at me as if I had violated a trust. But I'd just presented him with my life assurance policy.

"I want you and your friends down south to be aware that should something happen to me, there'll be some people asking questions, know what I mean?"

Guess I insulted him, because, "You've been reading too many spy novels, Julius." That was about as close to a snarl as Mr. Midwest Polite ever gave me. "Nothing is going to happen to you. We don't operate that way. This is America. Things like that just don't happen here."

I shrugged. "You're probably right. Still, if I were you guys, I'd be lighting candles for the health and safety of one John Pansini. You never know what my friends will think if I suddenly cease to exist. You know how paranoid the general public can be about you guys. One of my uncles is convinced that CIA gave Casey that brain tumor."

The smirk slid off my face. I rested my right elbow on the table and held up my chin with the palm of my right hand; melancholy returned. "So when's this gonna happen?"

"I don't know for sure. It might be in two weeks—"

I shot back in my seat as if he'd kicked me in the chest. "Two weeks!"

"Or six months. There are a lotta things coming up: Shevardnadze's visit, and then Gorbachev's."

That would be Eduard Shevardnadze, then the Soviet Foreign Minister, scheduled to begin preliminary talks with Secretary of State George Shultz in the fall. These talks were a prelude to the Reagan-Gorbachev summit later in the winter of 1987.

"We wouldn't want to do anything that might embarrass the Sovs," Jim continued, "so this will have to be handled very discreetly." He added that the final decision on when to move against Michael had to first be approved by the State Department at the very highest levels. "Remember the Zacharov-Daniloff thing?[1] It almost started WW III. We wouldn't want a repeat of that."

We prepared to leave (separately), Jim asked if I'd seen Ronald today.

1 After the FBI arrested KGB officer Gennadi Zakharov for spying, the KGB roughed up *U.S. News & World Report* reporter Nicholas Daniloff in Moscow. For further details see *The Economist*, September 13, 1986, p. 21.

"No, I didn't stop in McDonalds today. Don't know about this guy. He looks like a duck, walks like a duck. Bet the guy even quacks. You think he's an intelligence officer or what?"

"Maybe I'll head on over there and have a look myself."

"Got a better idea, I know what he looks like, you only have a description. I'll go in first. If I spot him, I'll come out and open my umbrella."

Jim nodded. "Yeah, sure, we do things like that all the time."

I left the Star Diner first and headed straight for McDonalds.

When I came out of the McDonalds I saw Jim staring at me from the other side of Broadway. A head taller than the Hispanics who surged passed him, Jim stood hunched against the driving rain under a black umbrella. Wearing a light gray suit, he reminded me of a dead tree sticking up from a fast flowing stream.

No Ronald inside meant a wet head for me outside. I waited for the light on the corner to change. Then I continued down 181st. When Jim was out of sight I opened my own umbrella.

Dogged by wind and rain, step after soggy step — there were holes in the tips of my sneakers — I made my way back home. The finale as scripted by the People Down South would have a dramatic climax, but, unfortunately, I wouldn't be in that last scene!

Like The Incredible Hulk, a colossal pair of hulking balls began to grow between my legs.

I can't let this happen. I'm the writer, director and star in this drama, not those assholes down south! It's my obligation to keep the plot moving.

I knew exactly what I had to do next to stop the FBI/CIA's plan to interdict with Mikhail L. Katkov.

The lie I told myself to justify such a selfish act: No way would Michael betray his country. But maybe he and his GRU buddies would want to give that impression; i.e. pretend to mole for U.S. intelligence. (The technical term is agent provocateur. The Hollywood term is triple agent.) Add to this a hard truth that also flung a few boxes around in one of the back closets in my mind: *Once the Katkov Affair ends, then it's back to the moronic masses for me.*

All the above were more than enough to finally convince me to do what I had to do. As soon as I got back from that long walk in the rain I made a phone call.

I dialed the offices of U.S. Customs, headquartered at #6 WTC. (Fourteen years and twelve days later, on 9/11/01, that building also came down along with Twin Towers #1 and #2. Fortunately, no one was killed in #6.) I spoke with Customs Special Agent Bob Del Toro. I told him that I was currently in contact with a Soviet intelligence officer — I did not name Katkov because at this point Customs had no need to know — and that I'd been an FBI controlled asset for the past four years. I asked Agent Del Toro if Customs might be interested in using me to sting Mr. Katkov.

"How about coming down Monday (August 31st) at two?" he said in a heavy Brooklyn accent.

An excited, "I'll be there," I replied in a heavy Queen's accent. (There *is* a difference.)

After hanging up Customs, I immediately called Jim and informed him, "I wanna give it (the signed waiver) some further thought." I did not mention my conversation with U.S. Customs.

Jim informed me that the decision to approach Michael might be made as early as next week, and interdiction would likely occur soon regardless of whether I gave the Bureau permission to tell Katkov about me or not.

(Audio 34.1) 2:09

Once geared up, the machinery of the intelligence community could move quickly, but not as quick as me. No way was the FBI going to snatch Katkov before Monday at two; especially since there was a weekend in between. Satisfied that I'd had the guts to meet the People Down South head on, I settled in for a long, hot bath.

Suddenly my conscience burst into the bathroom.

Hey, I'm naked here!

You're always naked to me, John," the better part of me said. "You just pulled an Ollie North!"

No getting around that; yes I did.

Me and Ollie, bad company.

Chapter 35
It's the Intrigue, Stupid!

"And we're not talking hundreds of dollars here, we're talking thousands."

***

Monday August 31, 1987

No sooner had my ass touched down in a seat at the offices of U.S. Customs than Special Agent Ed Tomeo (the boss) said to Special Agent Bob Del Toro, "Get his pedigree."

None of this, *"Do you own a car, John?"* crap. That sure impressed the hell out of me.

I eagerly told them everything they needed to know about John Daniel Pansini, including information about my car even though they didn't ask. I also gave them the names of my last two FBI case officers, Michael Berns and Jim Knapp.

Bob looked tough: about 28, with light hair and light eyes, my height but stockier. Ed, somewhere in his 40s, was tall, slim, without a speck of gray in his jet-black hair. Both wore white shirts and ties. Bob's long-sleeves were rolled up at his forearms like Popeye, and his tie was loosened at the collar. I wore a short-sleeved shirt and tie; my last good first impression for U.S. Customs.

I also told them all they needed to know about my Russian friend, too, except his name. When I mentioned my idea about how to entrap *my friend*, Ed made it clear that any future involvement between me and Customs depended on a continued relationship between me and the Soviet Union. Outwardly, they played it cool, but inside their hungry tummies must have been gurgling because they repeatedly asked, “Are you sure he’s gonna contact you again?”

And each time I had to feed them the same anti-acid: “No, I’m not sure. It’s all up to the FBI. They think he’s gonna defect-in-place. And they’ve hinted that they’re going interdict soon. And I mean *real soon*. If they do, then there will be no more meetings with him or anyone.”

Then the two cops from Customs began playing head games with me: “So why don’t you give us his name. You told us everything else, his height, that he works at the Mission—”

“Yeah, the U.N. Mission.” My mistake; up to this point the only thing I’d told them was that I had a GRU officer on the hook. I did not tell them that he worked at the U.N. He could’ve been from the U.N., the Soviet Consulate or a trade delegation.

Ed pounced quickly. He pointed to Bob and said, “Make a note of that.”

Then I learned that the telephone line Bob and I had spoken on Friday was not nearly as secure as I had been led to believe. My turn to jump on their mistake: “You told me I could say anything I wanted. What if the Soviets monitor that line?”

They exchanged apprehensive glances, and then Bob said, “Don’t worry about it. You were a lot more circumspect than you think. There’s nothing they could deduce from what you said.”

Alarmed: “What about my name; I told you my name.”

A pause; then Ed said to Bob, “We’ll have to be a little more careful with this case.” To me, “This is not an area we specialize in.”

Like, no shit!

“Our mission is different from the Bureau’s,” Ed continued.

"We're more concerned with proscecution than they are. Remember that."

"And none of this defect-in-place crap," Bob added. "We wanna pop this guy, then PNG his ass." (Declare Katkov persona non grata and expel him.)

I mentioned in passing that the FBI had recorded some of my meetings with Katkov.

"They wired you?" Ed asked.

My reply was matter-of-fact: "No, we hid it in my apartment."

"You've been meeting him in your apartment?" Ed said. He shot a quick look at Bob, who arched his eyebrows and jotted something in his pad.

Then I told them about Ronald McDonald, that he might be a Soviet, and that he might be following me. They agreed that the professional manner in which he had given me the slip each time was not something you would expect from Joe Q. Public.

"No meetings in his neighborhood," Ed told Bob. They both expressed concern that I might have been followed down here.

"Don't worry." I waved off their fears. "If my Soviet friend ever asks me what I was doing down here, I can say that I was checking on export licenses for computers. Then I can tell him about a high tech connection I have with my uncle. He works for Radio Shack." A wry smile, "It all fits together nicely, doesn't it?"

"Yeah," Bob said nodding at Ed. "We could come up with some stuff you could show him."

Then came a point of confusion: on the phone I'd told Bob all I knew about the NAS case and of my peripheral involvement. But Ed and Bob were under the impression that I had additional information.

"No, no, I'm sorry. I didn't mean to imply that. I was just trying to establish my bona fides. What do you guys know about that case?"

"Not much," Ed said. "Our West Coast office handled that one."

"I know that it was a joint FBI/Customs operation," I said. "Do you guys cooperate often?"

"When necessary," Bob said. "It was mostly our case." I thought I detected a hint of inter-agency rivalry in Bob's tone; exactly what I had hoped for.

The aggressiveness these guys showed, especially Bob, grabbed hold of me too. When they asked if I ever contacted my Soviet, I replied, "Yeah, we've worked something out where I can contact him in an emergency. I'm supposed to place an ad in the Computer Services section of the *New York Times.* But I'd better have a damn good reason."

"We'll see," Bob said. "We might ask you to make contact. But first we gotta speak to the FeeBees." Bob gave me a long look, then, "You gotta problem with that?"

I shrugged. "Be my guest, I have nothing to hide."

On Wednesday, September 2nd, the day after laying down a pencil, I picked up a hammer again. As much as I liked working at Columbia, it was good to be outdoors roofing. I called Bob as soon as I got home from work. He said he went to see the "FeeBees" today and everything was fine, whatever *fine* meant.

On Labor Day, September 7th, Bob called at 10 p.m. He hinted that should Customs and I hook up with the Soviets again, I could expect a considerably larger compensation package than the Bureau had been paying me. Not terribly interested in the money — it was the intrigue that had me hooked — until he added, "And we're not talking hundreds of dollars here, we're talking thousands."

Bingo! Jackpot! A gale of thousand dollar bills began swirling in that empty space behind my eyeballs. Whatever guilt I should've felt by banging another nail (Customs) into Katkov's deck blew out my ears. Yes, I betrayed him, but wasn't that what spies do? And besides, his career had ended in December 1983, when I reported my contact with him to the FBI.

Bob added that not only was I through with the FeeBees, but they were through with me. "For the time being," he added, "talking with Katkov is off."

My mind pumped a fist, *Yes!* Then, "How'd you know his name? Did they tell you?"

Bob laughed. "No they didn't. We figured it out based on the information you provided."

"Not much of a closed-mouth spy, am I?"

"Don't worry about it. They're still interested in him, but they have another source they can use."

"So let 'em." Even I could hear the jealousy in my own voice; another source meant despite all the hard work I'd done I'd still be on the outside looking in when the Katkov Affair ended. He or she would be a part of that scene and I would not.

"Thanks for telling me, Bob. By the way, I picked out a code name I'll use on the phone with you guys: Vito."

Bob chuckled. "OK, Vito, I'll be talking to you."

I called Bob on Thursday night, September 10th. He said I could meet his partner as soon as the guy got back from vacation. No sooner had the phone touched down, than it rang again. It was Jim. He said he wanted to meet me tomorrow morning at the Star Diner to discuss a few things. What few things? Thought they were through with me?

The next morning, at 10:30, out of the corner of my eye I watched a keyed-up Jim practically gulp down his eggs. Ever polite, though, he waited until I finished an order of ketchup with a western omelet on the side before he slid me a copy of the waiver the Bureau wanted me to sign.

“We’re still considering telling Michael about you; if we do, we’ll ask you to sign something like this.”

After glancing at the paper, “So you’re still gonna talk to Katkov, huh?”

“That’s one of many options. Both sides are looking for an arms control agreement. No one wants to rock the boat.” Then he rubbed the back of his neck and grimaced. “This Katkov thing has gone on much too long.”

While I read the waiver, Jim shifted nervously in his seat, probably thinking: *How much money is this asshole gonna try to shake out of us?*

I had a surprise for him and the People Down South: “OK, I’ll sign your paper. But first I want two things.” I held up two fingers in a spread V: “First, I want a copy of what I sign. Second,” I said, removing a digit from the spread, “I want a letter of commendation signed by the DCI.” That would be the Director of Central Intelligence, the newly appointed William Webster. Since Webster was the FBI Director for most of the Katkov Affair, I figured he knew all about me.

“Oh, sure! I don’t think the Bureau will have any objections.” Jim smiled looking like a load had been lifted off him. When I asked him about Bob and Ed from Customs, he replied, "They're good guys. I've worked with them before. If you wanna continue your association with Customs, that's fine with us." Then he added a warning: "Keep in mind those guys have no security clearance. Nor are they trained in this area."

Remembering the secure line business, "Yeah, I know."

"They're mainly concerned with the movement of millions of dollars of equipment out of the country. You'll also find they're real cops," he said, arching his brows. "They're gonna be a lot tougher on you than we've been." Then he asked, "Should the Soviets contact you again, will you notify us?"

"Of course," I said, surprised that he thought I wouldn't. "It's still your case. I understand that, and so does Bob."

I asked if Michael was still in town. Jim said, yes, that sometimes so much went on at the U.N. that even guys like Katkov had to put in time at their cover jobs. Then he snickered, "Someone's gonna have to show him a map so he can find the place."

"What about Ronald McDonald? I'm still running into him every so often on Fridays. Is it possible that Michael has somehow fallen under suspicion? Think Ronald is KGB? Think the KGB is checking out Michael by checking out his assets?"

"John, don't spend the rest of your life looking over your shoulder for phantoms."

A week later I was back at McDonalds for my habitual Friday breakfast; so was Ronald, but my attention was sharply focused on the New York Times. On page A21, staring me right in the face was Jim's fib. Back in June, regarding the FBI's visit to Columbia, he had said,

"It was an aberration. Some gung-ho types screwing around in areas where they don't belong."

Not quite. According to the Times, the FBI's visits to New York libraries were not aberrations but part of a large-scale counterintelligence effort. They even had a name for it: "The Library Awareness Program." I remembered a government report I'd read once entitled, "The KGB and the Library Target." It had been prepared by the Intelligence Division, FBI Headquarters, in Washington D.C. According to the report, the utilization of libraries and efforts to recruit librarians and students has been an integral part of Soviet intelligence gathering since 1962.

When asked why librarians were being contacted by the Bureau, James Fox, then director of the New York field office, said, "Most libraries have computer links to sophisticated research and information banks that could provide sensitive information, even if it's not classified."1

I'd told Jim that I fully supported the program, so why did he dis-inform me? Guess they trusted me about as much as I trusted them. Back in June when I told Jim about the stir the FBI's visit had caused among some of my library colleagues, he said, "It'll blow over."

Not so. A cyclone of charges — Intellectual freedom! The First Amendment! — and countercharges — Patriotic duty! National security! — blew in gales through the stacks and even the halls of Congress. A hearing was called and both sides testified before the House Judiciary Subcommittee on Civil and Constitutional Rights chaired by Rep. Don Edwards (D-Calif.), a former FBI agent himself.

"The purpose of the program," according to James H. Geer,

1 Library Journal, 10/15/87, p. 12.

Assistant Director, Intelligence Division, "is to sensitize librarians to unusual occurrences that might indicate espionage, such as when an agricultural attaché seeks information on pulse power, a form of energy used in radar… Such information becomes parts of bits and pieces that we put together that tell us that he might not be an agricultural attaché but a KGB (officer)… No records or reading lists of American citizens have ever been sought or obtained."2

Those who argued against the program said that libraries should not be extensions of the "long arm of the law" or "the gaze of Big Brother."3

After the hearing, Rep. Edwards concluded that the program went too far. It turned librarians into informants. Edwards was "chilled" by efforts of the federal government to convert library circulation records into suspect lists. Further, "The unconscionable and unconstitutional invasion of the right of privacy of library patrons," wrote Edwards, would do irreparable damage to the educational and social values of American libraries. Regardless of reservations held by Rep. Edwards and the civil libertarians, the program was an FBI counterintelligence success. Why? Publicity.

Take for example the woman who was the acting director of libraries at the time of the FBI's visit, the woman who had personally kicked the two female agents off Columbia's campus. Turned out she was a principal antiwar activists at Columbia in the 1960s. Allies of the program would later criticize the FBI for not doing their homework and checking who the top dog at Columbia was. In my opinion, however, the woman's leftist leanings played into the Bureau's hands. And they undoubtedly knew who she was.

2 Chronicles of Higher Education, 7/20/88, p. A11

3 American Libraries, 11/87, p. 814

I remembered when Agent Mike Berns had asked me for a list of attendees at the LACUNY conference, that he had promised one of his buddies. And later for a list of my supervisors at Columbia. Were the two requests connected with the Library Awareness Program? Was his buddy part of the program? Did his buddy also want a list of my supervisors?

They got nothing from me, but that didn't mean they couldn't have gotten the intel from somewhere else. The ALA (American Library Association) publishes a directory of all libraries in the United States that gives the names of librarians and supervisors at a particular institution. So after the FBI pulled up her name, they went to their indices. They knew who she was, what she'd done, her political views, etc. They knew they had someone guaranteed to be the most hostile, most offended by the program. So they threw a lighted match on the gasoline and *Boom*! The fires of public outrage exploded in all the newspapers and did not abate until they had reached Ted Koppel's Nightline. I remember watching the night the program aired and being surprised at how little effort the Bureau's spokesman put into defending the program. Then I realized that he didn't really care. Let the opposition howl, that only furthered the government's ends, because the next time an intelligence officer from the Eastern Bloc went to a library hoping to make a contact, in the back of his mind a very real fear had been planted:

What if this person goes to the FBI?

One FBI agent connected with the program was quoted as saying, "We're still getting calls from people who (have been) approached or picked up by Soviets in libraries."4

When Michael had warned me not to have anything to do with

4 American Libraries, 10/88, p. 44

anyone while at Columbia, I thought he was afraid of another Val incident. Guess not. By then the Soviets must have already known about the program long before me and the rest of the American public.

Again, it never ceased to amaze me how much each side knew about the other.

Chapter 36
The Knocker and the Duster

"We want you to get to know the guy selling the airplane parts. You'll be a munitions broker working for a hostile foreign power."

***

Friday, October 2, 1987

I walked into this high toned eatery on Broadway & W. 60th expecting the smoky aromas of food in preparation to fill my nostrils. Instead, being here was like stepping into the valley of the Jolly Green Giant. A fresh scent of flowers overpowered grease and bacon. Every table in the spacious dining area sprouted a crystal vase of real flowers with soft white petals, yellow buds, and nonthreatening green stalks — no thorns allowed. The ambiance said that spring would always be in season here. Each vase centered a tablecloth of blinding whiteness more suited for Mt. Sinai than an omelet parlor that took itself far too seriously. What, like nobody ever spilled the ketchup here? The way I figured it, this place was way too dainty for one roofer and two U.S. Customs Special Agents. And I'd left behind many red stains on plenty of table cloths over the years.

Too late for breakfast, too early for lunch, there were only a handful of patrons in the dining area on Friday. A pretty waitress in pleated black slacks, white shirt, black vest and black bow tie, hovered nearby like a hummingbird ready to dart in and snatch our orders. No need for me to open the black imitation leather menu embossed with gold lettering and gold tassels. I knew exactly what I wanted. To the waitress, "I'll have a western omelet and a coffee, please." I glanced at Bob sitting directly across from me. "Think breakfast is gonna cost you guys plenty."

"Don't worry about it," Bob said.

I turned to his partner John, seated on my right, and shot him a grin. "I'm not."

Bob and John ordered eggs sunny side-up with bacon and sausage, and coffee. Then Bob began to rigorously rub his knife and fork with a napkin — talk about dainty. He glanced around and said, "This place is full of weirdoes."

I had no idea what he was talking about.

How did we end up in a high-class restaurant in the vicinity of Lincoln Center? Because last night on the phone I couldn't adequately verbalize to Bob how to get off the George Washington Bridge and onto Route 1-9 leading to the Red Oak Diner. "It's easy to get lost in Jersey," I told him. "I've known people who have gone there never to be heard from again."

Bob chuckled; then he suggested that we meet at the Gulf & Western Building at Columbus Circle. "We'll drive around and find a place."

I took the A Train down to 59th. No sooner did I come out of the subway and into the open air when Bob and his partner pulled up. I got into the back seat. Bob introduced me to John (mid 40s), who sat up front on the passenger-side. John's black hair and neatly trimmed beard was streaked with gray. A bit rotund, he had a kindly face. They made a good team. Bobby the Knocker could put a bad guy on his ass, and then John the Duster would pick the guy up, wipe him off and say, "Now let's talk."

Bob wore a blue corduroy suit, a cream colored shirt and blue knit tie. John had on an expensive looking dark, pin striped suit, white shirt and red tie. And me: jeans, a red sweatshirt, and my ratty green parka. That made us the odd triple.

Bob drove us north on Broadway in search of a coffee shop or diner. We went as far as W. 96th Street and found nothing but greasy, little dumps serving E. Coli on a roll. We turned around and ended up back where we started, the high rent district.

After the waitress served our food, John and Bob stared down at their egg drops: tiny yokes not much bigger than half-dollars.

"Don't eat too fast, Bobby," John said, "or you'll miss breakfast."

Bob snickered, "Wonder where they hide the pigeons?"

I began eating and looked across at Bob. He was once again dipping his napkin into a glass of water and scrubbing all traces of microbial life off his utensils. I could only imagine the sandblasting that would've occurred had we ended up in one of those bacteria infested cafeterias uptown.

I asked Bob, "Exactly what is it you guys want me to do?"

Without looking up: "We got this guy we want you to meet." He paused, holding up his fork for closer inspection. "Sells airplane parts." Then he did the same with his knife. "He's asshole buddies with an Israeli who sells eavesdropping equipment." Bob explained that it was illegal to sell or even advertise for sale eavesdropping equipment. "We want you to get to know the guy selling the airplane parts. You'll be a munitions broker working for a hostile foreign power."

That sounded like something out of a *Die Hard* movie — a role I was ready, willing and eager to parachute into — but was I as good of an actor as Bruce Willis? I shot Bob a *You Gotta Be Kidding!* look.

Bob read my face. "Don't worry. We'll tell you what to do and say. It won't be as hard as you think. Once you get in with the parts dealer, you mention that from time to time some of your clients are interested in eavesdropping equipment. Then he introduces you to his pal and we pop 'em both."

ASAT?

When Bob decided that it was finally safe to eat, John filled me in on these high tech smugglers. "We deal mostly with businessmen trying to ship embargoed goods out of the country. Rarely do we deal directly with foreign intelligence officers."

Bob added, "It's not like the people you've been dealing with. These other guys (the techno-bandits), they're just in it for the money. And that makes them careless."

"Their greed does 'em in every time," seconded John.

"At least the Russians are acting in their national interest," Bob said.

"Yeah, I know," I said. "That's why I respect the Soviets. These other guys, they're just a bunch of shits."

Bob winced. "Ye...ahh we...ll," his words came out like sausage through a grinder. "I suppose you can have a certain amount of respect for the Russians. But in my mind, they're scum bags too. If these people love their country so much, let 'em stay there instead of coming over here to steal what we have."

Guess I hit the wrong button; so much for philosophical discourse. Like Jim said, real cops. I changed the subject: "How come when you do catch these guys, they get such light sentences?"

"Sometimes we cut 'em deals," John said, "so they'll lead us to bigger fish. These people will think nothing of turning in a friend or competitor."

"Sounds like a nice bunch." Then more to the point: "Why me?"

"First of all," Bob began, "you don't look like a cop."

I grinned and aimed a thumb at John. "Neither does he. He looks like a professor." Sensing that I may have unintentionally hurt John's feelings, I quickly added, "I mean that as a compliment, John. You look like a scholar. Bet you're good undercover." I grinned and pointed across at Bob. "Now this guy over here, he's a guy you better not mess with."

Bob and John both grinned. Then Bob continued, "It's better to use somebody like you because you're new, you'll take a fresh approach. And you've had undercover experience. You've been fooling Soviet intelligence — one of the best in the business — for what, four or five years now?"

That lit me up like one of those sunshine, smiley faces. Any more compliments from these guys and I might go supernova.

"If this first operation is successful," Bob added, "which we think it will be, then we might set you up in a dummy corporation complete with assets totaling in the hundreds of thousands of dollars — which you can't touch of course."

Of course, but the way I figured it, the idea of having hundreds of thousands of dollars attached to my name would be a prelude to the millions of dollars I'd have in my bank accounts after my memoir was published.

"We'll have telephone lines coming right into our offices at the World Trade Center," said John. "We'll place all the advertising and handle any legitimate business that might come in. Your job will be to meet the bad guys."

Bank accounts stuffed with cash had to take a seat in the back of the bus, though. Die Hard Incorporated now rode up front, ready to jump off and do battle to save the free world from all enemies both foreign and domestic. A new career: John Daniel Pansini, by day a mild mannered hammerhead for the Billy Grame Roofing & Siding Co.; by night a secret operative for United States Customs. Could life *get* any better? And forget about that bus-metaphor-thing! Now I was like a rocket on a pad poised to launch. It was a brief flight of fancy, though; my lunar module returned to earth when Mission Control reminded me that there was a very noticeable difference between the way the FBI and U.S. Customs operated: a thing called *realism*. The FBI had always stressed real people with real histories, real situations, etc. And here Customs talked about a false company with false assets and a false identity.

I wondered out loud: "How carefully are these guys gonna check me out?"

Bob shrugged, "Not very."

"They have neither the resources nor expertise," added John. "While working with us you'll be paid the going informant's rate."

"Which will be a hell of a lot more than what the FeeBees are giving you," said Bob, jabbing a thoroughly sanitized fork in my direction.

"And in the event of an arrest," said John, "you'll be entitled to substantial reward money."

The thought of *substantial reward money* set all the lights on my console flashing. Ready to blastoff, I still had one last check to make:

"My current relationship with the Soviets, will it impact on the case you're proposing?"

"No," John said. "The Soviets are interested in high-tech; this case deals with munitions."

"But we'd still like to know if Katkov contacts you again," Bob said.

"Don't worry about it, Bob. Soon as I hear from him (Katkov), you'll hear from me."

My relationship with the Federal Bureau of Investigation had just ended in divorce, so naturally I had nothing nice to say about my ex. "There were opportunities to do some innovative things with this case, but they just weren't interested."

"You're a bright guy, John," John said, "but there are things you're not privy to. None of us are. They know what they're doing, believe me."

"Sometimes they'll let you think they're dumb," Bob added, "but don't ever underestimate those guys."

"But they lied to me so many times." I went on to whine about FARA and other indignities. Hypocrisy coming from me the betrayer, the one who had committed an adulterous act with Customs in the first place. But my marriage to the Bureau had been one of convenience, probably doomed from the start. Perhaps this new relationship with U.S. Customs would turn out better. Hopefully, I'd learn from my mistakes. One adventure had ended, but a new one was about to begin. And hopefully there would be many more to follow.

"This first case will be good practice," I said, eager to get going. "Can't wait 'til we get to the big guys, you know, the narco-nuclear-smuggler-terrorists."

"Uh, I think maybe you should calm down a little," Bob said, making pat-down motions with his hand. "Let's concentrate on these guys first. We'll save the world later."

I smiled. "OK. Whatever you say, you guys are the bosses." Love is so much more wonderful the second time around. My energy was boundless and enthusiastic — and loud.

That spooked Bob. "I think, uh, maybe you should talk a little quieter," he said, making nodding motions at something behind me. "A couple of weirdoes just sat down."

I turned my head slightly for a quick look. The weirdoes were an old guy in his 50s and a young actress. He wore a black beret; she was wearing long black garments that seemed to flow from her like a shadow — very sexy. They were two tables away to my left. I picked up snippets of conversation. (We spies have acute hearing.) He told her about a show he was producing.

"You were talking too loud, John, know what I mean?" Bob eyeballed the theater people again.

"Oh, sorry." Nodding my head ever so slightly in the direction of Grandpa, "Don't worry about him. Sounds like the old guy's just trying to get laid."

I asked for suggestions on reading material to familiarize myself with munitions.

"*Jane's*[1] is a good source," John replied, referring to a worldwide source of military weapons and systems. "There's a huge market out there for spare parts that certain countries are not able to gain access to."

---

1 Various serials published by Jane's Information Group about weapons and weapons systems.

I snickered. "Yeah, like Iran."

Bob offered an example: "Suppose you're looking for a gun barrel for a cannon, but you can't buy it because there's only one manufacturer, and he can only sell to the military. But you also know that certain other countries have stockpiles of these weapons. And there are certain people who have certain contacts with those governments. If you know the right people, you can get whatever you want."

John added, "These countries have want lists of weapons systems and these guys all know it. They know it like the back of their hands. If you named a system you were interested in, the guy would know immediately who you were brokering for."

Just then an old man in a dark suit and black fedora sat down at the table next to us. Bob started acting paranoid again. When the old man took out a newspaper, Bob's eyes signaled, *Meeting Over.*

Outside, Bob said to me, "I'll be calling you soon. Gotta work out a few details. And don't forget, if Katkov makes contact, we wanna know."

We shook hands. Bob and John both shook like wimps, especially Bob the macho cop. It was like he was afraid of catching something.

I got home from work early on Friday, October 9th and took a nap on the sofa. At 3:30 p.m. a series of rings snuck under the rim and crept into my twilight zone. It took several seconds for my dozing brain to connect those loose tendrils of sound to coherent thoughts: *The phone is ringing... not the one next to me the one in the back room... the spy phone... the one Michael calls on... KATKOV!*

I jumped up and ran into the back room, nearly trampling Stinky.

"Hello, John. Is Michael. And how are you?"

"Michael! So good to hear… Where are… How are… Thought you were in… What happened? In July? I thought—"

"Do you have anything to tell me?" A pause on his end.

A pause on my end, too, so I could unscramble my eggs. Then, "Nothing yet, but I've got something in the works."

"Good. I have been ill, and it will take me some time to get my strength back. I will see you again in early December."

"OK, but if something comes up before then," I said, about to lay groundwork for a Customs sting, "I'll run my ad in the *Times* again. I'll run it for two weeks."

"OK. And how is your health?"

"Michael, I feel great! Fan-tastic!"

My happy, cheery, smiley tone was not enough to allay Katkov's concerns. Not just one question, but a whole string of health related questions. Finally he asked me one more time, "Are you sure you've got nothing to tell me?"

"Nope."

"OK. Is so good to hear your voice. Bye."

Even better to hear his voice; I waited a decent interval before placing a call to Jim, and then to Bob. Neither was in so I left each the following messages:

To Jim: "Tell him Vito called. Our friend has made contact."

To Bob: "Tell him Julius called. Our friend has made contact."

In my excitement, I'd confused my own code names. Anyway, so who'd call first? Who wanted Katkov more?

Chapter 37
A Lurking Presence

"He's in a bind and doesn't even know it. For him, there's no way out."

Tuesday, October 13, 1987

And the winner: Bob! He called and sounded as excited as me. He said that although he had no intention of interfering in the FBI's case, "That would be very unprofessional, but I'll be honest with you. It will be a real feather in my cap if we nail Katkov, too. Next time you see him (Katkov), tell him you can get him computers."

"You bet I will. Already got an opening. I told him that if I need to get in touch with him before early December, I'll run my *Times* ad. You give me a good cover story, and I'll run the ad."

Two days later, on Thursday, October 15th, 1 p.m. at the Star Diner: "Give it to me, word for word, as close as you can," Jim said, his pen poised between the knuckles of his left hand. He had called this morning saying he had to meet me this afternoon. He said that he never got my message, that it was Bob who told him about Michael.

"But I called you," I insisted. "*First.*"

He said he believed me, but things around his office had been a "little screwy", and my message might have gotten lost. More likely it was because I messed up my code names.

I began repeating my telephone conversation with Michael. When I got to the part where Michael said that he'd been sick, without looking up, Jim absently remarked, "That's what he's been telling everyone."

Everyone in this case had to be a singularity: the FBI/CIA's other asset.

"This next meeting with Michael," I asked, "is it gonna happen or what?"

"That depends," said Jim. "We still intend to talk with him, and that talk has to take place soon. His family went home in June, and it doesn't look like they'll be back. Michael will probably go home for good in March or April (of 1988). He's being rotated; his tour is over so we have only one more shot at him. He has to be at point X at a certain time and date that only he can set — probably in mid-December. If he meets with you first to introduce you to your new case officer, that's great. If not—"

If not I was out of luck. No more Michael, no more nobody.

"You guys still intend to tell Michael about me?"

"It's been decided that since you've got something going with Customs, and we don't wanna jeopardize that, we're not gonna. We've got more than enough on Katkov." Jim said, referring to Michael by his real name instead of "our friend." Guess it didn't matter anymore if anyone overheard us talking or not.

"We can really burn his ass," he continued. "He's in a bind and doesn't even know it. For him, there's no way out."

His words laid in my mind like a heap of stinking garbage. For sure I'd trashed Michael's life the minute I put the FBI and CIA onto him. His future might be headed for a landfill, but what about me? Working with U.S. Customs looked better and better. I bulldozed through guilt feelings regarding "our friend". My mind headed for a whole new adventure: scooping up bad-asses for U.S. Customs.

Then Jim added that the FBI would prefer that Katkov met with me first so they could see who the new guy would be, "but this other thing takes precedent."

"Gotta give you guys credit," I said referring to the obstacle I had placed in their path, namely United States Customs. "I presented you with a problem, and you simply maneuvered around it."

He flashed a smile, "Yeah," which disappeared just as quickly. "Michael is very good, the best I've ever seen," Jim freely admitted. "Once we let on that we know all about him, his career goes down the tubes. Why should we allow one of their better guys to work his way up. Better to let one of their screw-ups do it."

"Like Val," I said.

"That guy." Jim dismissed Mr. Bolochine with a smirk and a flap of his left hand. "He was in way over his head from Day One. As for Michael, he's no Moscow Boy. He's off one of their collective farms, a real hardworking, bright guy. No way we're gonna let someone like him, the cream, rise to the top."

Made sense, at least I performed one small service for my country. I could take comfort in that, but not a whole lot, because guys who worked their way off the farm had to be admired, enemies of the state or not. We were the same age, but Michael had achieved far more in his life than I did in mine.

Jim said that the decision to move against Michael had been made at the highest levels of the State Department. "The timing is crucial. The government doesn't want to embarrass Gorbachev when he comes to Washington for arms control talks (in December, 1987)."

"I tell you this," I said with great conviction, "Michael will never go for your deal. So either he'll go quietly or the Russians will make a big stink. You guys better be real careful."

"I can assure you, it won't be handled like that Zacharov-Daniloff thing. If he tells us 'Thanks but no thanks,' he'll be quietly sent home so as not to ruin the spirit of the summit."

As things turned out, either Jim had dis-informed me again or even he wasn't privy to the machinations of certain administration hard-liners; more on that later.

"Bob mentioned the possibility that one day we might even bag another Russian," I said, "one not connected to this case at all."

"That would be fine with us. We've worked joint operations with those guys many times. But if the Soviet involved is a diplomat, then we have jurisdiction because it involves a lotta coordination with the State Department and things could get sticky."

"Yeah, Bob told me. Because of my experience, I'd like Customs to use me against Syrian or Iranian intelligence, the real bad-asses. I know they do a lotta munitions shopping in this country. I'm skeptical about one thing, though. Customs wants to provide me with a false company and a false identity. What worries me is how closely they'll check me out."

Jim agreed that what Customs proposed would never work against the Russians, "But some of these other outfits, they're not that sophisticated. I used to work in a section that followed the Libyans and Iranians. Those guys knew how to *dry clean* themselves — lose a tail in a car by going up a one way street in the wrong direction, driving through parking lots, drive-up windows in banks," he grinned before adding, "or even McDonalds. They'd do all that, we'd follow them right into all those places, and they still wouldn't know they were being followed."

"Pretty dumb fucks, huh?"

"I'll say. The Syrians are a lot smarter, but they're not in the same league as the Sovs."

"How do the Soviets check out people? Do they check birth and other public records?"

Jim laughed and shook his head no. "Their mind-set hinders them. In their country, the government controls everything, including public records. For that reason they don't trust them. For example, we can't go into New York City's files and insert false birth records because here that's illegal. But they can't see that."

According to Jim, the Soviets had another way of *vetting.* They ask the same questions, in different forms, about *legends* trying to trip someone up. "And they're very good at it too."

No shit. Guess all those times I chose caution over the money with Katkov kept me in the game for four years.

I asked when I might see him again. Jim said that Katkov would be going home in November for a national celebration — November 7, 1987 marked the 70th anniversary of the Russian Revolution — and he'd be back in early December. "I'll be on vacation for the next two weeks. If something important happens, though, you can beep me. I have Mike's old beeper. Or you can call the office. Mike will be there."

I nodded. Then, "That letter of commendation and a copy of the waiver I wanted, is that why you're not using me?"

"All I can say is that while I personally have no problem with it, going to Customs like you did, that really ticked some people off."

I assume he meant the People Down South. "Yeah, well, they can all go fuck themselves."

"Funny, they said the same thing about you."

We laughed.

"One more thing," Jim said, "that friend of yours, you still running into him on Fridays at McDonalds?"

"Yeah. Why do you ask?"

"Just curious."

I remembered that Comrade Bolochine had used the same two words in 1984 when I had pointed a probing question at him. I suspected there was a lot more drama going on behind the scenes, machinations that left me out in the cold.

On Tuesday, November 9th, at 7:30 in the morning, Bob called. He said he tried reaching me last night until eleven.

"Had a hockey game. Sorry."

"I can't see you this week, something's come up. I'll call you next Monday."

"What about the asshole buddies?" I asked referring to the Israelis Customs wanted me to sting.

"I'm still working on that."

True to his word, Bob called me a week later, on Monday morning, November 16th. He said that he wanted to meet me for lunch on Wednesday.

"Anything with the asshole buddies?" I asked eager to get a move on it saving the world.

"Nothing yet."

Bob sounded like a busy man: "There's a lot going on right now, what with the summit coming up and all."

Since we had nothing to discuss, I told him to call me on Wednesday instead and skip the lunch. He was appreciative.

Bob called back on Wednesday at 6:30 p.m. We briefly discussed Ronald McDonald and who he might be. He had no idea either. When I mentioned that I hadn't been to McDonalds for breakfast the last two Fridays, he said, "Go there this week."

On Friday, November 20th, I *did not* see Ronald in McDonalds, but around 11 a.m., two cop-types sauntered in. The first one looked to be in his late 30s. He had neatly combed black hair and wore a dark suit and topcoat. The other guy was older, in his 40s, balding with curly reddish hair and beard. He looked like a Viking, as in Norseman. He wore a suit too, but he was not nearly as fashionable as his younger partner.

The two guys were exceptionally loud and macho, not only drawing my attention but the attention of everyone else in the place. They took seats in a booth at the far wall, the wall with the full-length mirror. I sat across from them in a booth next to the window that faced 181st. They left before I did, walking right passed me and out the front door. They stopped momentarily at a newsstand. It looked like they were headed up the hill. At 181st and Ft. Washington Avenue there was a subway station, a stop on the A-Train. I got up to follow because I suspected these big mouths were FBI deliberately drawing attention to themselves. As I pushed open the front door, I got shoved aside from behind. A young black guy nearly bowled me over. A young white guy had chased him out of the restaurant. As soon as the black guy got outside, two more toughs, one white, the other Hispanic, grabbed him. The three of them had him up against the door frame with one pushing his forearm into the black guy's throat. This looked to me like a racial incident in the making. The two big mouths, still standing at the newsstand about twenty feet away, turned around. If they were FBI would they intervene and blow their cover? I stepped outside also. Just a couple of feet away, I was unsure of whether to intervene to help the black guy. I've been in only one fight in my life, when I was eight. While I wasn't looking forward to #2, I couldn't just watch a guy get pounded until I knew what for.

As it ended up the three toughs in this mini-street-drama were the good guys. Apparently the black guy had dipped into an old lady's carry bag and snatched her wallet. The good guys saw it happen and gave chase. The next person out the door was the old lady. They gave her back her wallet.

"Thank you. Thank you so much," she said.

"You're welcome, ma'am," one of the good guys replied.

The old lady dropped the wallet back into her carry bag and walked away.

"I didn't do nothing!" The snatcher's pleas fell on six deaf ears — eight counting mine.

New York sarcasm: "No asshole," said one of the toughs, "it just jumped into your hands all by itself, huh?"

It looked like the snatcher was about to get a heavy duty beating; after finally figuring out what this was all about, they could've killed the bastard for all I cared. Instead they just shoved the snatcher around before letting him go.

"If I ever see your fucking face in this fucking neighborhood again," one of the good guys said, "you and your partner, wherever the fuck he is—"

No need to finish, the snatcher got the message.

When I turned around again, the big mouths were gone.

I didn't go in to work on Tuesday, December 1st. I got a haircut instead. At 10:40 a.m., I stopped in at McDonalds for a late breakfast. Either my powers of observation had seriously eroded, or my mind had (a strong possibility). Or maybe Ronald had a close blood relative who also liked McDonalds' coffee with his *New York Times*, but on Tuesdays not Fridays. A man who looked a lot like Ronald sat in a booth against the far wall. He wore a dark ski jacket and his hair was noticeably darker and fuller in the back. Was that Ronald or not?

I'd entered from the side entrance, so he did not see me come in. Instead of stopping to order breakfast, I kept walking towards the front door, taking a good, long look at the guy's face. I left the restaurant certain: *Yeah, that's him.*

As the day progressed, certainty turned to uncertainty: *On a Tuesday? Maybe just someone who happens to look like him... Coffee? Times? Dyed his hair? Let it grow?*

And uncertainty turned to paranoia: *Are they fucking with my head again? Who they?* But even paranoia needs some degree of rationalization:

Suppose he's in disguise. Eats here every day. Maybe it doesn't matter if he sees me; maybe I'm supposed to see him. Why?

Seeds of self-doubt that had been planted finally bloomed. Something I had been told a long, long time ago: *"It's not uncommon for someone in your position to imagine all kinds of things."*

At 2 p.m., I called Jim and told him about the guy with dyed hair.

"Hey, this is New York," he replied. "People do all sorts of strange things here."

"Like dye their hair?"

"Sure," he replied casually. Then, "Julius, what possible reason could this guy have for following you around like this?"

"What if the GRU suspects I'm controlled?"

The only way the GRU could come to suspect me was if they were getting inside information. From whom? From a mole inside #26 Federal Plaza?

FBI agent Edwin Pitts — arrested on December 18, 1996, for spying for the Soviet Union from 1987 to 1992 — was stationed in New York and operational at the time of the Katkov Affair.

Or a mole inside COURTSHIP? CIA officer Aldrich Ames — the counterintelligence branch chief for Soviet operations was arrested on February 21st, 1994 for spying for the Soviet Union — was part of COURTSHIP from 1983 to 1987.

Of course I knew none of this at the time, an neither did anyone else. Jim said, "That's not even a remote possibility. Nobody knows about you, Julius,"

"You better hope so, Jim," I replied, still suspicious.

Jim mentioned that Michael had just returned from the Soviet Union. "You might hear from him anytime between now and the summit." (Gorbachev was scheduled to arrive in Washington in just six days, on December 7th.) "But after that, he won't be bothering you anymore."

The next morning I went to the Post Office to check my box. I crossed St. Nicholas at 180th, and I spotted two All-American, Midwestern cop-types (definitely not New York's finest) in a late model, light blue sedan with black wall tires and a long, whip antenna on the roof. They were stopped at the light. I deliberately crossed in front of their car for a good look. I saw a Police Identification sign on the dashboard. It looked an awful lot like one I'd once seen in Mike Berns's car. Unfortunately, I couldn't read the border to see which arm of the law — Customs? FBI? DEA? — the sign had been issued to. When I made eye contact with the driver, and he noticed me noticing him, his right hand reached across and removed the sign.

Jim's words were like loose nails in my apron: *"He'll never bother you again."* No shit! The two big mouths in McDonalds on Friday, cars with police stickers cruising the neighborhood? My guess: the FBI had thrown a net around Washington Heights, a net guaranteed to be spotted. Should Michael or any other Soviet be on the prowl they'd know: *Asset Pansini has been compromised. Better run for cover.* An obstacle (me) had been neutralized and an asset (also me) betrayed without the need for a signed waiver. I had to admire the FBI/CIA's resourcefulness.

Customs agent Bob Del Toro called me that night. We discussed the possibility that if I met with Katkov one last time, he might pass me off to a new GRU officer. According to him, CIA didn't exist. He might have been right. In four years, I'd never seen them, but I'd always felt their lurking presence.

(Audio 37.1) 4:57

Chapter 38
The Dispossessed

"He was scared, but he went down like a pro. He didn't cry or lose it. A lotta of 'em do.

Friday, December 18, 1987

***

At 7:33 a.m., my consciousness was parked horizontally in the Do Not Disturb Zone. Suddenly I felt tiny teeth dig into my big toe: "Ow!"

That had to be Stinky, the orange tabby, expressing certain needs that had to be satisfied — *his* — and certain obligations that had to be met — *mine.* The bite was his text message: *Get your ass the hell out of bed and feed me!*

I played hockey last night, getting in around two a.m. Today was a day off from my new job as reference librarian at Cooper Union. The school was a small art, architecture and engineering college downtown. That meant I'd get up when *I* wanted not when *he* wanted; noon sounded about right. I tucked my feet back in, rolled over onto my stomach, and pulled the covers over my head. Then I felt four tiny feet strolling up one of my legs, across my rump, and back. Bookie, the little gray princess, and about half Stinky's weight, nestled herself comfortably on top of my head. I shook her off. She jumped back on. I shook her off again. She jumped back on again. A cat for a hat, but not for long because she finally stepped off.

Then I awoke to the sounds of empty food bowls being batted across the kitchen floor. Guess the cats were playing their own hockey game. I knew what havoc those little beasts could cause in the kitchen. I got up.

Damn fur balls ruled my life!

Stinky, the over eager, vocal one, meowed and rubbed up against my leg. Bookie, befitting her royal heritage, was more patient. She sat on her haunches with her tail swishing back and forth across the floor — more sweeping that I'd done all month. She looked up at me, her big green eyes saying, *Hurry, please.*

As I reached into the cupboard for a can of cat food, the spy phone in the front room rang. "Hold on, guys," I said to the cats. "Be back in a minute." I headed out of the kitchen to pick up. My dramatic self said, *Gotta be Michael. This is gonna be big!*

I said, "Hello," expecting to be greeted by a Russian accent.

But this particular voice came straight out of Brooklyn not Moscow. "Did you see the papers this morning?" said Bob.

An unexpected call from U.S. Customs on a Saturday morning asking if I'd read the newspapers — that had to mean bad news. A wary: "No, I just got up."

"They popped him yesterday. It's all over the papers."

Guess I should've seen this coming. Last spring I'd caught a glimpse of THE END skulking around a corner. I'd thought that by calling in U.S. Customs I could slam the door on its ugly face. But yesterday, the fucker came back and finally kicked that door down. THE END barged in like an unwanted relative and threw me out of my own life. Angry and frustrated, I let loose:

"But they (the Bureau) told me that they were gonna keep this quiet because they didn't want to ruin the spirit of the summit."

The Reagan—Gorbachev Summit had ended one week ago, on December 11th. Then I remembered something Mike Berns had once bragged to me: that Mikhail Katkov would take his rightful place in history. Guess publicly expelling Michael had always been their plan, the spirit of the summit be damned.

Bob told me to go get the newspapers, that he'd call me tomorrow.

I hung up, shuffled back into the kitchen, and sat down. Then I slammed a fist against the table. Stinky and Bookie jumped and booked the hell out of the kitchen. "Sorry guys."

I closed my eyes, chanted a silent mantra: *Fuck! Fuck! Fuck!...*, took in a deep breath, held and released. Calmer now, I stood up and shoved the chair back under the table. When I looked down I saw that the cats were back at their food bowls staring up at me. For these creatures the sum total of their existence was to eat, sleep, shit, play, and wake me up in the morning. I envied them their simplicity.

"You guys are gonna have to wait 'til I get back."

Five minutes later, I was washed, dressed and out the door.

As for the cats, let them eat each other.

The local stores in the Heights only sold the *New York Post* and the *Daily News*. If I looked real hard I might also find a copy of *New York Newsday.* Of course I wanted them all, but I also wanted the *New York Times* and the *Washington Post.* I knew a bookstore on Broadway and West 96th where I could round up all the newsprint I wanted in one-stop shopping. I caught the #1 Local on 181st. I made good connections; the gods that ran the Transit Authority were with me that day. Back home in twenty minutes, I dumped the newspapers in a stack on the kitchen table. After feeding the cats, I began to shift through the news.

Every damn paper said the same damn thing: Soviet diplomat Mikhail Katkov had been caught "red-handed" on Thursday, December 17th, with "highly sensitive" documents relating to Star Wars. They also reported the arrest had taken place in the residence of an unnamed defense contractor; other than that, not much in the way of details. The *New York Times* even admitted, "Events surrounding the case remain murky."

Murky for everyone else, but not me. I knew the whole damn story.

I sat in the middle of the sofa with an orange fur ball sleeping on one side of me and a Russian blue ball on the other.

"Excuse me," I said to Bookie, picking her up and depositing her on the floor. I moved to the end of the couch and dialed the phone. Even I had a few "murky" details that needed to be cleared up. My first words to Jim Knapp:

"Been reading the papers."

(Audio 38.1) 0:09

"We did it," he said, and I bet his grin spread from ear-to-ear.

Wish I could share the joy. Instead, "What time did you pick him up?"

"It was about mid-day."

When I asked where, Jim replied, "In Manhattan, at a guy's residence. We caught him with the goods in hand and said, 'Time to go now.'"

"Think I'll be contacted again," I asked, "maybe from another Soviet?"

Jim was blunt: "Probably not. Although your name never came up — we didn't want to discuss you — they'll do a damage assessment. Anyone having anything to do with Mikhail will probably be cut off."

With that, *One Last Hope* laid down, folded its arms across its chest, closed its eyes, and died.

"What happened? Thought you guys were gonna keep this thing quiet so not to ruin the spirit of the summit."

"I was really shocked because we were supposed to keep it quiet," Jim said. "And we *did*. Then something got out."

I reminded Jim that the newspapers cited someone in the administration as the source.

"Yeah," he admitted. "The name came from Washington."

"I think someone's up to something" I said, convinced certain administration hard-liners were spreading mischief. "There's more here than meets the eye."

"It's probably someone too stupid to know that they weren't supposed to say anything."

Leaks spring in Washington when someone deliberately drills a hole in the pipes. As for ruining the spirit of the summit or the arms control treaty (that had yet to be ratified in the Senate), Jim assured me the Katkov Affair would have no affect on that whatsoever. "Both sides want it (the treaty) too much." In regards to the media coverage, he added, "If you read the papers, you can see, they just don't know that much."

Not surprising given that the press is so dependent on what the government tells them. Even Woodward and Bernstein needed a Deep Throat, who turned out to be FBI Associate Director Mark Felt.

(Aud 38.2) 2:45

"So how did he (Michael) react?"

"We brought him down to the office, and had him in one of our interview rooms. Made him nice 'n comfy."

Ironic if they had him in the same room where I first met FBI agents Dan Pierce and David Nelson, the room with the big sign that read, "All matters discussed in this room are secret."

"How was his demeanor?" I asked.

"He was shocked. We really blind-sided him; he never saw it coming."

Poor bastard.

"The guys on the street who took him out said he was as white as a sheet."

Despite its high dramatic content — what a scene that would've been to witness — a piece of me was glad the arrest had not taken place in my apartment. I didn't have to look Michael in the eyes and see hate coming at me like I was the guy on the spinning wheel and he was the one throwing knives.

"Once we had him in the office, though, he was Mr. Calm, Cool & Collected. At least he tried to give that impression. He was scared, but he went down like a pro. He didn't cry or lose it. A lotta of 'em do. Everyone who saw him said, 'That's a pro going down.' "

That eased my pain a little. "So I guess he didn't take your deal (to defect-in-place), huh?"

"We tried to talk to him but it was like —*forget it.* You were right on that point. You said he wouldn't, and he didn't."

"That's an awful lot to ask of somebody, to betray their country. Then what happened?"

"We just waited for his guys to come down and pick him up, and that was it." Jim added that Michael would be on a plane heading back to the U.S.S.R. on Sunday.

Set up, swept up, taken down, and gone in two days. Not even enough time for Michael to get a grip on what just happened to him.

"So if I hadn't caused you all that trouble with Customs, then this would've happened in my apartment?" That part of me, the grand palace where my ego resided, still craved high drama and wished I could've seen the whole damn thing.

"No it wouldn't, because he (Michael) had a source (the other guy) with access to secret information that he didn't have with you."

"This guy, was he Joe Public off the streets like me?"

"*Oh no.* If you think he was just some guy — no, no, no. There was something special about this person. Whether he was an asset or an undercover agent, I can't get into that."

No need to. No doubt their other source was the same hook they'd had in Michael all along, the person Mr. Berns had spoken of when he hinted that I should be more cooperative or I'd be out on my ass. The guy had to be the name the government inserted into the *Directory of Persons Interested in Technology Transfer* before I had handed it over to Michael. (The FBI had instructed me to delay giving Michael the book. "They're a few moves we'd like to make first," Mike had said.)

"The (*New York*) *Post* said something about him buying secret documents relating to Star Wars," I said.

"You can't arrest him for espionage unless he's doing it."

"But that's not the way it's done. What about milk cartons in Jersey (dead-drops) and borzois (less productive GRU officers who service dead-drops). Even Mike (Berns) had admitted that Michael would never let himself get caught with classified documents on his person.

"Well, he did it this time."

Yeah right. No GRU or KGB officer of Michael's stature (one with recruited agents) would be that stupid. The term "caught red-handed" is gov-speak. Translated, it means that he came in, was handed an envelope containing classified documents, opened it, shit his pants, and then the FBI charged in and arrested him before he could even wipe.

"By the way," I said to Jim, "I went to McDonalds this morning, didn't see my friend (Ronald McDonald)."

Jim laughed. "Maybe it's his day off." He still had his doubts as to Ronald's connection to this case, but he did admit, "If he was (with the Soviets), you won't be seeing him anymore, that's for sure."

(Audio 38.3) 3:04

For sure: I never did see Ronald again, which led my conspiratorial mind to speculate that he was connected to the FBI, maybe even with their Special Group. Ronald's job might have been to keep me occupied and out of the government's hair while they maneuvered an ending to the Katkov Affair.

"Guess I'm not gonna get my letter of commendation, huh?"

"I'm gonna be straight with you, Julius. I was putting in for it, but when you went to Customs like you did and talked about Michael, I got into a lotta trouble. Not a little trouble, a *lotta* trouble."

"Why you? I was the one who did it."

"Yeah, but I was the one handling the case. Frankly, that really put my ass in a crack."

I told Jim how sorry I was, and that trouble, like sewage, always dumps on the poor bastard living in the basement.

Then Jim took an unexpected turn onto a road marked, *Philosophical Discourse*: "Do you know one of the questions we wanted to ask Michael had he cooperated? Why did they send you to the West Coast?"

“Well, I have my theories.”

(Audio 38.4) 1:28

“We all have theories, but we just don’t know.”

(Audio 38.5) 1:07

“What do you think is gonna happen to Michael?”

“He’ll go home, get a desk job and a pat on the back for not defecting.”

“Do you think he would’ve shit if he knew that I was the reason for his demise?”

“Hell yeah!”

“Because I thought I did a pretty good job, handling Katkov, I mean.”

“Let’s face it Katkov was one of the sharpest people they’d ever sent over here.”

"You could've told him, you know," I said, referring to the fact that, after much stalling, I had finally given the FBI verbal permission to tell Michael about me.

Jim started off by saying that the FBI had decided not too because of my special relationship with Customs; then he admitted something that stunned me: "While we never mentioned your name, there were other discussions about the possibility of someone else;" i.e. that the Bureau had another controlled asset working against Katkov. "Anybody who examines what we said is gonna figure it out in about ten minutes."

"That it was me."

Bluntly, "Yeah."

(Audio 38.6) 2:14

With or without my signature on a release, the U.S. intelligence community had decided to blow my cover right out of their collective assholes. Later, when I told Customs agent Bob Del Toro that the Soviets now knew all about me that was the last I ever heard from him.

That meant no follow up book, *Roofman Helps Bring Down Ring of Narco-Nuclear-Terrorists!!!*

When I first took up residence in the Katkov Affair I knew that I merely rented and someone else owned the property. Most of the time I felt like I was living in one of those grand California homes built on stilts and shoved up against a hillside. Even though I managed to escape a few mud slides and earthquakes that had threatened to send me crashing into the sea, the federal government held the mortgage. Today they foreclosed.

Just like that, my secret life as a secret agent came to an abrupt end.

Later, I called my father. He said he had seen it on the news last night. It looked like I had come up a day late and a dollar short.

"I thought that was your guy," my father said.

An angry, "Then why the hell didn't you call me, Dad?"

I would have preferred to see it in real-time, not read about it in the papers the next day.

(Audio 38.7) 1:41

As for me, whenever I listen to the above tape, I take pride in Jim Knapp's last words spoken to me on that December morning in 1987:

"You did a good job, Julius. You were a pro with him. Most people wouldn't even have the guts to meet them (the Soviets) the first time."

Thanks, Jim, you made me feel like *we* did accomplish something worthwhile. And like Anne had told me all those years ago:

"You're living a middle-aged juvenile fantasy, John."

For sure.

Epilogue: The Prince & the Pauper

Right: Where Michael was arrested. Left: Where I lived. Guess who was the pauper.

November 12, 2022

I found out today that Special Agent Mike Berns had passed away of pancreatic cancer on March 19, 2014. He was only sixty-one-years-old; too young and much too soon. In March of 2014 I was sixty-six; so was the other Michael, the one with the surname Katkov.

The last time I saw Mike was August, 1987. He'd driven me down to #26 Fed Plaza. He was dressed so slick I asked him if he'd gotten a promotion.

He smiled and replied, "Something like that." The man had

always been modest.

Thirty years in the Bureau, he had a distinguished career. His success continued after retiring from the FBI. He worked as an instructor for a tactical operations group.

When he drove me back uptown to my library job at Columbia, I also remember giving him a hard time about the Wennerstrom Affair. I said that was proof that the GRU did carry out counterintelligence operations.

In fact, I remember giving him a hard time about a lot of things.

I feel like shit, as in piece of. I remember when he told me, "I'm not the enemy, John."

He was right, of course. Too bad I was too blind to see it. Right now, November, 2022, living in the Post-Trump era, I can see that the vast majority of the men and women who work for the FBI are dedicated public servants.

RIP, Mike.

***

I titled this chapter the Prince and the Pauper. Obviously, the pauper was me. As for the prince, his name was Milton E. Stanson, the FBI's other guy. At the time, he was in his mid-sixties. When I read his memoir (f), I thought:

Kind'a old to be playing the spy game.

Now that I am in my mid-seventies, I tell myself: *Wish I was sixty again.*

Anyway, I miss being a roofer, roofing defined me. Now, instead of banging nails, I bang words, sentences and paragraphs into a computer. I'm a writer of novels, screen and stage plays, and this memoir, I SPY. Oh, how I miss the glory days when I was up on a roof while spying on the side instead of sitting on my ass in front of a screen.

How did I *acquire* such positive intelligence on Mr. Stanson? Because of a phone call I got on March 30, 2013, from a guy named Anthony O'Dwyer. I figured he was calling in regards to my ebook, ROOFMAN: A True Story of Cold War Espionage. I self-published in 2011.

About time someone recognized what a great story this is!

Anyway, O'Dwyer said he was doing a movie about "someone" he would not name. His company was Plume Inc. I judged from his website that he was mostly a photographer.

BTW: In 2022, the domain name is for sale.

Mr. Stanson's building was located at 21 E. 10th Street. It's in the heart of the West Village, an extremely upscale neighborhood. It was in his apartment, 11D, where Michael was arrested by the FBI on 12/17/87. Mr. Stanson moved to California a few years later.

BTW: If anyone is looking for a luxury apartment in 2022, it's listed for 2,295,000; well beyond my ways and means.

So when Jim Knapp told me that Michael was "arrested right here in Manhattan," he was talking about Milton Stanson's luxury apartment. It's all in Mr. Stanson's memoir, CODENAME SHORTFALL: The True Story of a Madcap Spy for the FBI.

Kind of rhymes, huh?

The book is available from Amazon. It was published on November 20, 2013. Mr. Stanson was wrong about Michael's affiliation. Throughout the book he refers to Michael as a skilled "KGB agent." According to my FBI case officer Pat McKinney,

Michael was a skilled GRU *officer*. And according to Jim Knapp, "He was one of the best they've (the GRU) ever sent here."

It had served me well to press all my FBI case officers to ask questions and not take anything they said at face value. Also, being a *libraryman*, I kept all documents related to the Katkov affair.

O'Dwyer and I began to exchange a series of emails. I picked up some positive intelligence from his emails. He wrote: "I don't believe he (Stanson) knew about you" — Oh yes he did! — "but you sound like you had the same handlers."

By the way, O'Dwyer did buy a copy of my ebook, ROOFMAN, and that was where he learned my side of the story.

So how did I figure out that the "other guy" was Milton E. Stanson? A combination of my innate Sherlock Holmes, serendipidy and PhotoShop. God bless Adobe!

It seemed O'Dwyer was bit careless and left enough of Mr. Stanson's signature for me to PhotoShop for a first name: Milton. From that starting point, after a long hard road with many curves and dead ends, but eventually I was able to get his last name.

Closing out his section, sadly Mr. Stanson died from a fall down a flight of stairs circa 2020. O'Dwyer never did do a movie, and finally one very interesting detail: yes, Mr. Stanson *did* know about me but not my name: From p.223 as it appeared in his memoir:

"Then cryptically Mikhail blurted out -- obviously inspired by the progression of my relationship with him, 'I trust you, not other helpers.'

"When I mentioned it to Mel (Mike Berns, no doubt), he said the FBI knew all about how Mikhail had been dealing with a conniving flake, who the FBI from their own viewpoint and observations, had also learned not to trust as an informant... Apparently, neither Mikhail nor the FBI, each for their own reasons, had determined this contact, whomever, to be just an agent of trouble, neither significant nor pertinent enough for their individual objectives."

Reading the above, I felt like being a fly on the wall in another guys' book. Fascinating.

As for Michael, I often wonder what his life has been like back in the USSR (now Putin's Russia). I hope life has been good to him.

***

In answer to what trouble Michael was in the summer of 1987, I present the reader with this possibility: In June 2018, at the time of the Mueller investigation, I got into it with a Russian troll on Twitter. I will quote from the emails we exchanged. Fuck Elon.

Readers are left to come to their own conclusions.

John Pansini @JohnPansini

Mueller just requested 150 more blank subpoenas and news reports that Michael Cohen is about to flip on Trump. Witch hunt my ass! The orange clown is going down, people.

Sergey Kyznetsov @AricEndre

You've been saying this for 2+ years now.

John Pansini @JohnPansini

Mueller investigation has been going on for only a year. But thanks for keeping track of my tweets, Comrade. Here's a good book that Putin will enjoy:

Then I gave him a link to my ebook.

Sergey Kyznetsov @AricEndre

Replying to @JohnPansini

Also, I haven't been keeping track of your tweets. No sane, logical person would ever do that.

Have to admit, this troll's command of English is excellent.

John Pansini @JohnPansini

Replying to @AricEndre

Not keeping track of my tweets? Then how do you know what I said 2 years ago? Are you clairvoyant? Mr Kyznetsov, you are a GRU troll. Beware, I kicked ass on a GRU officer a lot smarter than you, Comrade.

Sergey Kyznetsov @AricEndre

Replying to @JohnPansini

Because I know weirdos like you. Are you seriously trying to get me to buy your shitty book? Wow, you must be struggling.

No shit, I was struggling! ROOFMAN's sales were worse than flat, they were abysmal. Next, a new Russian troll took over from Sergey. Maybe his shift at the GRU troll factory was over.

infiltrating the international meme community @IlyaBayona 1m1 minute ago

Replying to @JohnPansini

Finally? How long have you been trying? agent Panini. Yes, we hold dear Mr Katkov in GRU Troll section. We have portrait of him next to instant Kasha Machine. Legend says he was trying to find American partner to help him sneak in Betamax Porn into Russia. Operation Pornostroika.

Wonder if they kept Michael's Beta Max porn also next to the instand Kasha Machine? Bet there was plenty of jerking and pulling going on in that factory.

And in closing, this might have been the trouble Michael had gotten in August 1987. The reader's guess is as good as mine.

Overall, an enjoyable exercise, matching wits with the GRU once again. And the new guy did send me this great photo of a Russian troll in action at the factory.

Thanks, @IlyaBayona!

(Epilogue Fig. 1.1) @IlyaBayona's selfie.

After the Facts

Colorado Springs, October

2022

Sitting here in Colorado, after so many years have past and so many miles from New York City, I still think about Michael. What happened to him? I can only hope that somehow he has built a new life for himself and his family in the new Russia.

Mikhail Katkov is an ethnic Russian, but he was born on a cooperative farm in the Ukraine. I wonder what he thinks of Putin's war of aggression. It's good that Michael is too old for Putin's call up. But what about his son? And what about Vladimir Bolochine's son, whom he loves so much?

About the Author

All a reader needs to know about me is on my website:

JohnPansini.com

My favorite photo of me. It captures my essence.
(Photo by Carl Bruce, circa 2000)

Thanks for reading I SPY

www.ingramcontent.com/pod-product-compliance
Lightning Source LLC
Chambersburg PA
CBHW030634150426
42811CB00048B/95

* 9 7 8 1 7 3 5 1 8 7 3 9 6 *